Mexican Business Culture

Mexican Business Culture

Essays on Tradition, Ethics, Entrepreneurship and Commerce and the State

Edited by
CARLOS M. CORIA-SÁNCHEZ *and*
JOHN T. HYATT

McFarland & Company, Inc., Publishers
Jefferson, North Carolina

ACKNOWLEDGMENTS: Carlos M. Coria-Sánchez is grateful for his Fulbright Scholar Grant, 2008–2009, to research for this book.

Names: Coria-Sánchez, Carlos Mateo, 1959– editor. | Hyatt, John T., 1981– editor.
Title: Mexican business culture : essays on tradition, ethics, entrepreneurship and commerce and the state / edited by Carlos M. Coria-Sánchez and John T. Hyatt.
Description: Jefferson, North Carolina : McFarland & Company, Inc., Publishers, 2016 | Includes bibliographical references and index.
Identifiers: LCCN 2016012525 | ISBN 9781476663081 (softcover : acid free paper) ∞
Subjects: LCSH: Management—Mexico. | Corporate culture—Mexico. | Work ethic—Mexico. | Business enterprises—Mexico. | Entrepreneurship—Mexico.
Classification: LCC HD70.M6 M49 2016 | DDC 306.3/40972—dc23
LC record available at https://lccn.loc.gov/2016012525

BRITISH LIBRARY CATALOGUING DATA ARE AVAILABLE

ISBN (print) 978-1-4766-6308-1
ISBN (ebook) 978-1-4766-2313-9

© 2016 Carlos M. Coria-Sánchez and John T. Hyatt. All rights reserved

No part of this book may be reproduced or transmitted in any form or by any means, electronic or mechanical, including photocopying or recording, or by any information storage and retrieval system, without permission in writing from the publisher.

Cover images © 2016 Thinkstock

Printed in the United States of America

*McFarland & Company, Inc., Publishers
Box 611, Jefferson, North Carolina 28640*
www.mcfarlandpub.com

Table of Contents

Preface	1
Mexican Business Culture in Trade Books: Past and Present CARLOS M. CORIA-SÁNCHEZ	9
Tradition and Modern Aspects of Mexican Corporate Culture ANABELLA DÁVILA *and* ANDREAS M. HARTMANN	26
Entrepreneurship in Mexico Past and Present JORGE OLMOS-ARRAYALES	38
Reconfiguration of Major Companies and Entrepreneur Subjects in Mexico: Culture, Productive Strategies and Relationships with the State MARCELA HERNÁNDEZ-ROMO	52
Human Capital Development in Mexico PRAMILA RAO	74
Perceptions of Ethical Decision Making in Mexican Business: State of the Literature and an Exploratory Study MIGUEL R. OLIVAS-LUJÁN	92
Communication in Mexican Business JOHN T. HYATT	107
Looking at Time and Business with the Mexican Lens OLIVIA HERNÁNDEZ-POZAS *and* SERGIO MADERO-GÓMEZ	124
Mexican Government in Business: An Institutional Analysis JUAN ANTONIO ENCISO-GONZÁLEZ	134
Online Shopping in Mexico: Exploring the Promising and Challenging Panorama TERESA TREVIÑO *and* FLOR MORTON	166
Advancement of Mexican Women in the Workplace CARLOS M. CORIA-SÁNCHEZ *and* JOHN T. HYATT	183
About the Contributors	193
Index	195

Preface

Even before NAFTA was signed, American businessmen and businesswomen already had much interest in the way Mexicans carry out business in the international arena. After NAFTA went into effect in January of 1994, and due to the subsequent rapid growth in trade, services, investments and business between Canada, the United States and Mexico, this interest increased even more, attracting not only businessmen and women, but also students and professors in International Business, International Studies, Latin American Studies, and Business Spanish courses and departments at several institutions of higher education in the U.S. and abroad.

For this study we are as objective as possible, relying on history and its consequences; on personal experiences and on the contributors' research and observations of Mexican business culture, companies, organizations' structures, business and government relationships, and the way Mexican businessmen and women function within their society and how they perceive Mexican cultural behavior in this area. We undertook this project because we truthfully believe that the topic is crammed with interesting concepts and ideas about Mexican business culture and its society, especially when supported by serious research. This point of view considers the Mexican angle and depends on the research and experiences of the authors of each essay. We are convinced that the subject of Mexican business culture, society, and institutions must be explored within its own boundaries; that is, to allow Mexicans and scholars with deep research in Mexico the opportunity to explain themselves, their own culture, their behavior, and especially their own knowledge and thoughts about why Mexico is the way it is.

To decode Mexican business culture and its society is not just a matter of storytelling; it is not about someone's own personal short-lived experiences in a certain place or with a given issue. Many foreign business travelers, vacationers and students *think* that they understand Mexico and its society after spending a week or two "south of the border." However, it is absolutely impossible to have a profound understanding of a nation, its customs, culture and way of life after such a short time. A Mexican is not just a product of the vagaries of birthplace or DNA but is an individual who is the result of hundreds of years of turbulent history and culture. There are cultural, psychological, sociological, and historical components that have to be taken into account to get as close as possible to an interpretation of the Mexican businessman and woman in both the public and private sectors.

What is the reality surrounding Mexican companies, culture, and society? One of the purposes of this study is to problematize ideas expressed in popular print or web venues through a cultural and social research lens to provide a real picture of Mexican business culture and organizations by scholars whose findings on certain topics are supported by strong academic inquiry.

As a starting point Coria-Sánchez will analyze some of the most important aspects that several guides treat in their works about Mexican society and the best way to conduct business in Mexico. We decided to begin with a critical analysis of trade books and analyze the stereotypes and concepts mentioned in them about Mexicans and Mexico in general to offer the reader a better conceptualization of some cultural issues that are extremely important for those interested in doing business south of the border.

In subsequent essays as part of a more extensive approach, professors with associations in Mexican business schools, corporations and international business will analyze those subjects which we consider to be of import to people eager to learn about culture and business in Mexico; which, consequently, would have an immediate effect on their future commercial or professional relationships within the country.

This book is, then, an analysis that relies on extensive research through observations, theories on culture, international business culture and theory, business data, historical, psychological and anthropological analysis of Mexican behavior, Mexican history, and most important, inquiry carried out by Mexican scholars and others with strong roots in Mexico. Businesswomen, businessmen, people involved in different kinds of international business counseling, small- and medium-size company owners, and the common Mexican citizen who can tell us through their own voices about their country, their business practices and social culture, and why they conduct themselves the way they do. This study is not limited to a specific time and space; as mentioned before, we will hear the voices of people from several areas in the Mexican Republic. Based on the cultural and historical information provided throughout this analysis the readers will have the opportunity to judge for themselves what could be considered a stereotype, a generalization or a truth regarding some issues in Mexico and its business culture. While on the topic of history, it is imperative that the reader understand the nation's business and economic climate through the 20th century until today.

The 20th century in Mexico was rocked by turbulent changes coupled by economic growth and instability. From 1911 to 1917, the nation experienced a revolutionary war, which culminated with its current Constitution of 1917. This Constitution was and is highly nationalistic as it granted Mexico and the Mexicans a series of rights while prohibiting a great deal of foreign influence in the nation on political and economic fronts (i.e., the Mexican Constitution explicitly prohibits the existence of foreign troops on Mexican soil and for this reason the United States has not been able to send the U.S. military to Mexico to support the nation in its war against the drug cartels). The Constitution also ushered in the political rule of the Institutional Revolutionary Party (PRI), which was founded in 1929 and would go on to hold the Mexican presidency and complete control of the nation's political system until 2000. Aside from being corrupt and undemocratic, with rigged elections and ubiquitous bribery and theft, the PRI was the architect of a series of economic policies which attempted to further insulate the nation's economy from foreign influence. During the greater part of the 20th century, there were numerous nationalized industries in Mexico, which included telecommunications and utilities. In 1938, Mexican president Lázaro Cardenas nationalized the nation's oil industry, thus creating PEMEX, the state-run oil monopoly which still exists today. Even today PEMEX is responsible for one third of Mexican federal government revenues.

Aside from nationalization of key industries during much of the 20th century, the

PRI attempted to further protect the nation from foreign economic influence through the famed policy of Import Substitution Industrialization (ISI). Following a 20th century Latin American trend with ISI, Mexico erected massive trade barriers through tariffs in an effort to keep foreign-made products out of Mexico. In theory, this policy was intended to make importation of foreign goods next to impossible as a result of the tariffs. On the home front, the Mexican government attempted to prop up domestic manufacturing industries through subsidies in an effort to keep jobs at home and protect the nation from foreign economic influence. This policy was applied in Mexico and Latin America to a myriad of industries including electronics, home appliances, and automobiles, just to name a few. In the 1960s domestic industry supplied 95 percent of Mexico's consumer goods. Depending on whom one may choose to ask, ISI was either a godsend for the Mexican economy or a curse which led to economic crisis. Many economists have contended that ISI is a route to economic development and job creation in developing nations while others argue that the policy simply creates uncompetitive domestic industries that are destined to eventually fail once markets are forced to open up. Regardless of personal opinion, the Mexican economy, with its state-run oil monopoly and policies of ISI, grew at an average annual rate of 6 percent in 1940–1975 creating what become known as the "Mexican Miracle."

However, the early 1980s were times of turbulence for the Mexican economy as the nation suffered adversely from plummeting global oil prices, which greatly reduced the government's revenues. Many economists contend that Mexico's economic problems that began in the 1980s were a result of the failures of ISI while others blamed a mismanagement of Mexico's oil export industry in the 1970s when prices were high. (It is well documented that the Mexican government squandered the revenues from oil exported to the United States during the 1970s, thus leaving the nation with severe budget problems in the 1980s when prices plummeted.) By August of 1982 Mexico announced default on its foreign debt and was forced to apply for emergency rescue funds from the International Monetary Fund. With the restricting of its debt in the 1980s, Mexico was forced to implement a plethora of economic reforms, among those the opening of the economy to foreign investment in efforts to accumulate capital. Furthermore, the country was forced to drastically cut domestic spending on social programs and to devalue the peso, thus tossing millions of Mexicans into poverty. This policy of "Shock Therapy" (so nicknamed by political scientists and economists) created an extremely difficult climate for businesses, as Mexico, along with the rest of Latin America, saw economic stagnation for much of the 1980s creating what would become known as "The Lost Decade in Latin America." As mentioned, the 1980s was also the birth of a new economic policy of open trade and free markets in Mexico. Little by little in the 1980s and 90s, culminating with the implementation of NAFTA in 1994, the PRI opened up the nation to free trade and foreign direct investment. (In this text, when contributors refer to the "opening" or "liberalization" of the Mexican economy, they are referring to this migration toward free trade that began in the 1980s and continues today.)

In regard to free trade today, Mexico is one of the most, if not the most, open economy on the planet as it boasts free trade with more countries than any other nation on earth. Aside from NAFTA, the nation's most famous trade agreement, Mexico has free commerce with all of the Central American and several South American countries, the European Union as well as Japan, creating a total of 32 free-trading partners. As recently as 2014 Mexico agreed in principle with China on improved trade relations, though not free trade. Mexico's largest and most crucial trading partner is of course the United States. The two nations today are symbiotically linked through trade and commerce and cannot survive without one another. Even Mexicans today who detest free trade recognize that Mexico could in no way revoke NAFTA. When referring to the two nations' economies, Mexicans often opine, "When the United States has a cold we have the flu. When the United States has the flu, we have pneumonia." Across the border, the economic dependence on Mexico is nearly identical for the American economy. Apart from billions of dollars' worth of American goods being trucked across the border into Mexico, Americans enjoy fresh fruits and vegetables from Mexico's booming agricultural industry, along with car parts, electronics, tequila, jewelry and a myriad of other products. It also cannot go unmentioned that the American economy benefits from Mexican immigrant labor in its cities and countryside. While the United States is Mexico's largest trading partner, Mexico currently ranks third on America's list of commercial partners only behind China and Canada. Nevertheless, many analysts prognosticate that before 2020, Mexico will jump Canada and China to become America's most valued trading partner, thus making the U.S.–Mexican border the most important economic border on earth.

This irrevocable economic relationship with the United States is one of the reasons that we have chosen to embark upon the project of writing this text. We feel that it is imperative that the American or other foreign businessperson has a profound understanding of Mexico and its business practices before attempting to do business in the country. Our hope is that after reading this book that the reader will have a greater in-depth understanding of Mexican business from a historical and cultural perspective.

In "Mexican Business Culture in Trade Books: Past and Present," Carlos M. Coria-Sánchez states that what the trade books say about Mexican business culture and society is detrimental to a healthy relationship between American businesspeople and their Mexican counterparts. The essay will bring up some issues that the reader can examine and see how these trade books support prejudices and stereotypes while others contradict those assumptions. Coria-Sánchez will problematize several topics in trade books and contextualize them; the way he will do it is a very simple one: he will open the door for a continuous dialogue between the trade books' subjects and their contextualization and rebuttal through deep research. This analysis does not intend to justify any Mexican cultural business practices; on the contrary, Coria-Sánchez is being objective to find a reason for such conducts through literary works, anthropological, psychological, historical, and international business culture approaches, as well as interviews with several Mexican scholars, employees of large companies, business owners.

In "Traditional and Modern Aspects of Mexican Corporate Culture," Anabella Dávila and Andreas M. Hartmann ask and answer the following question: Which features characterize the corporate culture of Mexico's most successful companies? This question reflects a recent interest among local and international business academics and executives because the analysis of a company's culture can lead to an understanding of particular practices that correspond well to the dynamics of the field and help achieve organizational excellence and ultimately, superior performance. Some scholars have described the culture of Mexican companies as being in the middle of a transition process, where they constantly adopt theories, methods, practices and tools proposed by developed countries. The proposition is that imported management systems tend to fail during the implementation process and create an attitude of rejection. In this essay, Dávila and Hartmann paint a different picture: Mexican society has its own values developed through a particular economic, political, and social history. Successful companies adhere to these traditions while simultaneously taking part in an ongoing globalization process that requires structural and behavioral changes. Together, historical tradition and globalization processes shape unique organizational characteristics, defined as hybrid management style and business practice.

In "Entrepreneurship in Mexico Past and Present," Jorge Olmos-Arrayales establishes that Mexico is a country in which micro, small and medium companies represent 99.7 percent of existing companies and contribute 52 percent of GDP and 71.9 percent of employment. Hence, it is important to understand how these companies interact within their business environment but also look for creative ways to support themselves internally, since the majority of them have their origin in one single person: the entrepreneur. Since Mexican entrepreneurs are related to all kinds of economic activities and have a presence among all sectors, there is a need to elevate their initiatives into more formal and professional ways to create value for their ventures, their communities and ultimately to the country and region. In his essay, Olmos-Arrayales shows facts about micro, small and medium enterprises and their key players—the entrepreneurs—in order to know who they are and how they deal with their cultural business environment among other challenges. The essay will also analyze how these Mexican entrepreneurs interact and deal with other businessmen and -women as well as potential alternatives to better grow their startups.

In "Reconfiguration of Major Companies and Entrepreneur Subjects in Mexico: Culture, Productive Strategies and Relationships with the State," Marcela Hernández-Romo says that from 2000 until 2013, Mexico has suffered two important economic crises. One of them occurred at the beginning of the century, and the later one in 2008. At the same time, the neoliberal model has been deepening in the country. This essay analyzes the strategies used by both big companies and entrepreneurs in order to get through these crises of the 21st century and achieve internationalization. For this analysis, the two most important key economic centers were chosen (Mexico City and Monterrey) along with the most influential companies in those cities. A study is made of the reconfiguration in their business and productive strategies as well as their labor relations and their corporate culture with these developments. What is the new corporate culture in Mexico within the big companies? What ideas of the past remain in the collective subjectivity of their entrepreneurs and which have been transformed? This essay explains two entrepreneurial configuration settings, as a result of the combination of the culture, subjectivity and power in relation with the State, reflected in the entrepreneurs' decisions in their business strategies and within each corporation. The analysis goes with the configurationist perspective in which the focus of analysis is the relationship between structures / subjectivities / interaction-actions, based on their business and productive strategies, on their relation with the state, and their regional culture.

In "Human Capital Development in Mexico," Pramila Rao explains that, traditionally, training and development initiatives in Mexican companies were largely informal. Small- and medium-sized Mexican organizations did not adopt formal training and development practices. Rao states that this could also be due to the predominant existence of family-owned organizations that followed informal management styles. However, this informal approach to professional development slowly began to change as Mexico began to move from its insular trade policy to a dynamic global strategy. As the country began aggressively opening its doors to international trade and enhancing foreign direct investment in the 1970s, the government realized that training initiatives needed to be mandated to enhance the quality of its human capital. Mexican employees now were competing and interacting with multinationals, making employee development an important agenda for organizations. Thus, in 1978, the Mexican government introduced the "Training Law" to ensure organizations provided sufficient professional development to their employees. In this essay Rao provides historical and chronological perspectives to show how training and development has developed in the Mexican workplace, ensuring that organizations have proficient work forces to compete in the international arena. The essay also offers a perspective that goes against the stereotype of Mexicans not being trained or offered courses to increase their performance in the workplace and offer quality products to the world.

In "Perceptions of Ethical Decision Making in Mexican Business: State of the Literature and an Exploratory Study," Miguel R. Olivas-Luján states that scarcity of research on ethical business perspectives in Mexico contributes to stereotyped and superficial interactions between businesspersons dealing with Mexican individuals or organizations; this in turn becomes a major obstacle to the country's trade in an increasingly globalized world. According to Treviño in "Ethical Decision Making in Organizations," ethical decision-making is composed of individual and organizational influences. Using an evidence-based management perspective (Rousseau, "Is There Such a Thing as Evidence-Based Management?"), in this essay Olivas-Luján reviews published studies about business ethics in Mexico. He then presents results of an empirical organizational-level study in this nation, using the ethical environment construct developed by Treviño, Butterfield, and McCabe ("The Ethical Context in Organizations"), as well as questions on codes of ethics, ethics-related HR functions, and corporate philanthropy. Human resource managers from Mexican companies provided answers to this survey-based study. Results emphasize the importance of the top manager in generating an ethical environment. Surprisingly, no significant correlations were found between company size or ownership type and the variables under study.

In "Communication in Mexican Business," John T. Hyatt explores a sensitive part of Mexican culture while conceding that there is scant academic research that exits on the topic. Many foreign businesspeople often mistake Mexican warmth and kindness as an immediate willingness to move forward with a business deal. In Mexico, yes may not always mean yes, no doesn't always mean no, "mañana" might mean another day and the promise of a follow-up appointment may not be as certain as in a Western country. Hyatt continues by stating that the overall indirectness of Mexican communication is fascinating to many researchers but often frustrating to those involved in business. In this essay Hyatt seeks to explore and explain Mexican forms of communication as well as its distinctions based upon socioeconomic status, education and hierarchy through historical and cultural perspectives while providing strategies and recommendations for the foreign businessperson to be better equipped for Mexican cultural differences in communication.

In "Looking at Time and Business with the Mexican Lens," Olivia Hernández-Pozas and Sergio Madero-Gómez argue that Mexico has the great potential to experience a prosperous future. Mexico, they say, is a country open to international trade, characterized by economic and political stability, abundant with natural resources and an internal market of more than 112 million people. In the last decade, Mexico has notably reduced poverty and experienced an expansion of its middle class. In addition, Hernández-Pozas and Madero-Gómez continue, Mexico's talented engineering workforce is the largest in the Americas. However, a failure to understand how Mexicans look at time and business would become a missed economic opportunity for many, they say. Disappointment and frustration can appear if foreign businesspeople do not interpret Mexican culture correctly. In their essay, then, the concept of time and the rationale behind differences in behavior is discussed from the Mexican cultural standpoint. Mexican business practices of management, leadership and employee engagement are also examined though a historical and cultural perspective. The purpose is not only to highlight what is important for Mexicans when doing business, but also, why it is so vital, and how international business people can better adjust to the cultural differences.

Juan Antonio Enciso-González in "Mexican Government in Business: An Institutional Analysis" states that Mexico has become one of the main participants in global trade and investment. It is therefore important to understand the country's business cultural environment, both from economic and political perspectives. In this essay, Enciso-González presents an institutional analysis model to evaluate the impact of "government" in Mexican business activities. This model assesses the formal and informal "institutional" rules that impact business activity, for domestic and international companies. The proposed model can be used to evaluate different sectors, Enciso-González says. It also presents a comparison of the institutional quality of Mexico versus different countries, both partners and competitors. Enciso-González brings his argument to a close with conclusions and recommendations for a better understanding of the cultural business environment in Mexico.

Teresa Treviño and Flor Morton in "Online Shopping in Mexico: Exploring the Promising and Challenging Panorama" state that in recent years, the Internet has revolutionized how people communicate, make decisions and make purchases. As a result, e-commerce has emerged as a new way for companies to reach consumers and expand their business. In developing countries, the acceptance of online transactions has been slow, but an increasing number of people and companies have acknowledged the advantages of an online economy. Many studies have addressed issues related to e-commerce; however, there is scant research concerning this phenomenon in the Mexican context. Therefore, the essay offers an overview of the overall Internet shopping environment in Mexico, important cultural trends in groups of consumers as well as their attitudes and behaviors toward buying online, new shopping channels such as social networking sites, and the barriers that e-commerce has overcome. Additionally, the essay addresses the favorable panorama for online purchases in Mexico in the years to come. This research aims to provide important insights for international students, professors, managers and entrepreneurs interested in the Mexican culture with respect to online shopping.

In "Advancement of Mexican Women in the Workplace," Coria-Sánchez and Hyatt establish that Latin American societies are known for being male-dominated in nearly all aspects. However, they argue, contemporary Mexico boasts more educated women than ever as well as a rapidly changing professional sector that is seeing more women hold high-level positions in government, business and education. Despite these advancements, the role of Mexican women in business is far diminished when compared to western societies and even other Latin American countries (i.e., Argentina, Chile, and Uruguay). Mexican businesses, explain Coria-Sánchez and Hyatt, tend to be controlled by men at ownership and management levels, as a conspicuous glass ceiling still exists in the country today. Pay discrepancy between men and women is still alarmingly egregious throughout the private sector from small, privately owned firms to multinationals and many careers and positions are still considered essentially off limits to women as a result of culturally defined gender roles that can change at an alarmingly slow pace. However, women in Mexico (especially in major cities) have made tremendous strides in workplace advancement over the last 40 years. More American businesswomen and -men as well as educators and students of international business must be aware that many Mexican women are heads or CEOs of large corporations. In this essay Coria-Sánchez and Hyatt analyze, on a small scale, the history of Mexican women from the Conquest to the present and their struggles to have the same opportunities as men. It also evaluates the current status of women in Mexican business by taking an in-depth look at decades of advancement as well as contemporary challenges for the female Mexican worker. Coria-Sánchez and Hyatt will explore industries and careers that offer more opportunities to women while highlighting those which tend to discriminate more.

Mexican Business Culture in Trade Books
Past and Present

CARLOS M. CORIA-SÁNCHEZ

For the last quarter of the 20th century something "atypical" has been taking place in American colleges and universities disrupting the tranquility and traditions of foreign language departments, particularly disconcerting to the literature sections: business Spanish courses. As a reaction to the demands of students taking Spanish for business courses, several language as well as international business departments across the country accepted programs or courses that combined both foreign languages and business into their curriculums. Mexican business culture became an important element in these programs and classes, not only for students and their professors, but also for those Westerners doing business in Mexico.

To fill the vacuum, several text books emerged. The following textbooks on Spanish for business present concepts and cultural aspects of doing business in Spanish-speaking societies; none of them, however, focus entirely on Mexican business culture: *Éxito comercial* (2014), *Entre socios: Espanol para el mundo profesional* (2010), *Spanish for Business* (2001), *Saldo a favor* (2000), and *Vistas comerciales y culturales* (2000). These textbooks range from beginning to advanced levels of Spanish for business; they present cultural information about the best way to do business in the Spanish-speaking world and convey the importance of business culture in the modern world, as Geert and Get Jan Hofstede state: "The theme of cultural differences is, of course, not only nor even primarily of interest to social scientists or international business students. It pertains to anyone who meets people from outside his or her own narrow circle, and in the modern world this means virtually everyone" (x).

Also during the last ten years of the same century there has been an influx of trade books aimed at offering cultural advice to American businesspeople on how to conduct commercial relationships with their Mexican counterparts. In spite of lacking deep research basis, these guides became the only source for many people involved in business in Mexico and in American higher education to teach Mexican business culture. Unlike textbooks, which treat Latin American business culture in general, there are a large number of trade books or guides on the market, most published after NAFTA went into effect, which specifically address Mexican business culture. My research for this area of study began with trade books or self-help guides dealing solely with Mexico. The list is extensive: Jay M. Jessup and Maggie Jessup's *Doing Business in Mexico* (1993), Paula Heusinkveld's *Inside Mexico: Living and Doing Business in a Changing Society* (1994), Peggy Kenna and Sondra Lacy's *Business Mexico* (1994), Anita Wilson's *The Complete Guide to Doing Business in Mexico* (1994), Eva Kras' *Management in Two Cultures: Bridging the Gap Between U.S. and Mexican Managers* (1995), Boye Lafayette De Mente's *Why Mexicans Think and Behave the Way They Do!* (1996), Glenn Reed and Roger Gray's *How to Do Business in Mexico* (1997), Christopher Engholm and Scott Grimes's *Doing Business in Mexico* (1997), Mark Cramer's *Mexico Culture Shock: A Guide to Customs and Etiquette* (1998), and Randy Malat's *Passport Mexico: Your Pocket Guide to Mexican Business, Customs and Etiquette* (2003).

Unfortunately, most of these trade books can produce general preconceptions, contradictions or negative stereotypes, and they should not be used as a model to generate social and cultural awareness without a deep and well-rounded understanding based on solid research. Indeed, those trade books published mainly in the U.S. that do offer some insight into business culture in Mexico reinforce North American stereotypes about Mexicans instead of trying to create bridges of communication and a better understanding of both Mexican and American societies and cultures. These guides make generalizations about Mexicans without first having analyzed an important amount of data to sustain their assumptions about something as significant as another culture.

The vast majority of these kinds of guides endeavor to educate their readers with a few pages of information on pre– and post–Columbian history, current customs, dress, political parties, machismo, and other issues, many not directly related to cultural business practices in the country. The rest of the information is mostly devoted to giving advice on trade, imports and exports, tariffs, logistics, and other topics. However, they persistently repeat the material provided between each other and do not offer insight or profound research on Mexican business culture. Geert and Gert Jan Hofstede comment: "In the booming market for cross-cultural training, there are courses and books that show only the sunny side: cultural synergy, no cultural conflict. Maybe that is the message some business-minded people like to hear, but it is false. Studying culture without culture shock is like listening to only the foreigners who are from here" (xi).

Most of the trade books are written with unabashed prejudice, emphasizing negative stereotypes and centuries-old generalizations. These overviews reveal what Nancy Alder mentions about American companies: "immediately following World War II most firms operated primarily from a domestic ethnocentric perspective. Firms produced unique products and services that they offered almost exclusively to the domestic market. The uniqueness of the product or service and the lack of international competition negated the firm's need to demonstrate sensitivity to rational cultural differences" (7).

It seems that these longstanding ideas still prevail in the authors of these books. These works portray ideas rooted in the middle of last century; they do not take into account the need to create bridges of communication between countries with commercial ties, Mexico and the United States in this case, which should understand and respect one another's cultural differences.

These trade books do not offer data on which to base their statements or theoretical cultural sources of business relations or historical backgrounds to sustain the information they offer. Neither do the authors of these guides allow for Mexicans to represent themselves, to have a voice. These guides present Mexicans from an outside Western perspective, one of intellectual superiority. The U.S.–Mexico relationship has always been one of hate and love and power. ("Poor Mexico, so far away from God and so close to the U.S.," said Mexican president Porfirio Diaz.) These writers demonstrate that idea of American power by depicting Mexicans according to their own North American terms and concepts of what a business culture and society "should" be like. It is unwise to advise American business people and students on unfounded topics; after all, these businessmen and women interested in Mexico will at some point have to understand what Earley and And talk about in regard to cultural intelligence that "refers to a person's capability to adapt effectively to new cultural contexts" (59).

This study takes into consideration the voices of Mexican businessmen and businesswomen, professors, and people involved in the daily commercial life of Mexico through personal interviews and research on the culture of international business as well as present historical and psychological data.

Mexican business culture is not only about individual experiences concerning a certain theme. This topic is much bigger than simple observations of one small Mexican community. The subject invites more than just a couple of interviews to understand, in all its magnitude, Mexican business culture and the best manner to conduct business in the country. In their excellent study on cultures and organizations, Geert and Gert Jan Hofsted quote Claude Levi-Strauss who stated: "One culture has no absolute criteria for judging the activities of another culture as 'low' or 'noble.' However, every culture can and should apply such judgment to its own activities, because its members are actors as well as observers" (11). From this standpoint, it would be only fair to allow Mexicans to also take part in this discussion and hear them talk about the topics that relate directly to their own culture and experiences.

The interviews presented here were not chosen arbitrarily. A voice is given to a wide spectrum of Mexican mid- and high-level employees, executives, university professors, and small and mid-size business owners among several more interviews carried out in different parts of the country. The subjects for this study came from the common workforce, from important universities, companies, and business centers in Mexico. The interviews were meant to be casual conversations that took place within their work place or at meeting places outside their work. Several important issues in Mexican business culture were covered such as Mexican work ethics, bribery and corruption, and nepotism, among others.

Alejandra Anaya is a mid-level executive at PEMEX, where she works in information technology; her office is based in Mexico City. Ana Chio works for IBM as a consultant and her office is situated in Mexico City. Susana Salazar is an employee at JP Morgan also in Mexico City. Dr. Javier Beltran is an organizational psychologist at the Universidad Veracruzana where he holds a teaching and research position. Dr. Javier Jimenez is a corporate psychologist also at the Universidad Veracruzana where he teaches and researches. Ms. Paredo is the owner of her mid-size company, Corporacion Paredo, in Veracruz. Her company imports and sells motorcycles throughout its own stores in the southwest region of Mexico. Ms. Margarita Acosta in an entrepreneur in Guadalajara; she has several small and mid-size businesses. Dr. Isabel Soberano is part owner and president of the Universidad de Xalapa where I was based during my Fulbright Grant to conduct this research. Dr. Soberano oversees the academic and administrative operations of this small private liberal arts university in the heart of the city of Xalapa. Ms. Consuelo Reyes is an accountant; she teaches and offers her services as a consultant to several small and mid-size businesses in the Veracruz area. Ms. Nora Elia Cantú is based in Monterrey where she is an executive working for Banorte, one of the largest banks in Mexico.

Moreover, this study will shine a light on certain topics that might negatively impact those individuals planning on conducting commerce south of the border, and on those who merely wish to learn the business culture in Mexico. The destructive influence of the Western trade book on students and businessmen and women could be detrimental in their future business relationships with companies in Mexico. It is imperative to have a deep knowledge of a certain culture to understand how and why people behave in both business and society in general and Mexican business culture is no exception.

But trade books will not deepen the learner's knowledge of Mexican business culture; rather, they merely deepen one's knowledge of Western business culture while re-affirming subconscious assumptions of Western superiority. Geert and Gert Jan Hofstede say in *Layers of Culture*: "Every group or category of people carries a set of common mental programs that constitutes its culture. As almost everyone belongs to a number of different groups and categories at the same time, people unavoidably correspond to different levels of culture" (10–11). Trade book authors do not grasp that these various layers of culture and cultural interferences thwart their analyses and influence what they see in the "other." What we can see in their analyses is a Eurocentric viewpoint.

Mexican psychologist Dr. Santiago Ramírez takes into account cultural, psychological, sociological, and historical components to illustrate this about Mexicans: "*Desde hace tiempo, con muy diferentes criterios, con diversos enfoques y desde ángulos variados, el mexicano y su manera de ser se han transformado en una preocupación substancial del propio mexicano*. For a long time now, under different criteria, diverse approaches, and various angles, Mexicans and their behavior have turned into a main concern that worries Mexicans themselves" (15). It would be reasonable to think that if Mexicans show despair in their attempts to understand and express their own identity and conduct, those from "outside" who recount their particular experiences about Mexican commerce should be cautious when talking about cultural issues and not impose their own cultural values and views.

For example, it is important to "turn the mirror on ourselves," as Ned Crouch mentions: "As we examine Mexicans through the lens of culture, we also turn the mirror on ourselves, asking why we work the way we do. A fuller appreciation of the differences between Mexicans and Americans, and the reasons behind these differences is key to exploring effective approaches to resolving conflicts and building relationships" (xix).

In general, it appears that many trade books and their authors are trapped in what Monaghan and Just perceive as "frozen in time, outside any historical context, and without reference to neighboring societies" (25). Coria-Sánchez says that one of these trade books, *Inside Mexico* (1994), "focuses entirely on the culture of the Mexican society, placing herself [the author] within the social, political, cultural, and economic life of Xalapa, Mexico" (52). Indeed, Dr. Heusinkveld only highlights the people of Xalapa; she does not offer any information about visiting other places to expand her study. Other authors state that their experience is based in Mexico City or Guadalajara; others don't mention any places in particular. It is essential to note that the aforementioned city close to the Gulf of Mexico is not a major industrial center. Xalapa's economy revolves mostly around small and mid-size businesses, the services and agricultural aspects of commerce and is home to one of the most well-known universities in Mexico and Latin America, the Universidad Veracruzana. Heusinkveld examines Mexican business culture in general from the city of Xalapa.

Nevertheless, her study, and others, fall short because they reinforce negative stereotypes about Mexico. Certainly these harmful stereotypes as well as those from other trade books augment the prejudices that already exist in the American culture concerning Mexican society. At the same time, these stereotypes hinder the understanding of traditions, customs, and attitudes about Mexican culture. This study includes research conducted in many metropolitan areas such as Mexico City, Veracruz, Oaxaca, Guadalajara, Puebla, Tabasco, Monterrey, and Merida.

Heusinkveld is the only author who highlights the same stereotypes that she had growing up: "It [Mexico] was the land of sombreros and mustachioed guitarists, of mysterious temples and sun-drenched beaches. This alluring land seemed to bear no relation to the more sobering image presented in the United States newspaper headlines –the Mexico of poverty, overpopulation, illegal immigrants, and political unrest" (ix). Evidently, approval of such negative images would create a deeper sense of unease among American businessmen and women interested in a commercial relationship with Mexico. Heusinkveld's childhood depiction clearly resembles the old image of a Mexican napping under a tree, a big sombrero covering half his face. An image, says John Charles Chastain, "refuted by the hard-working reality of the Mexican farmworkers who migrated into the southwestern United States as *braceros* ('hired hands') after World War II" (21).

Ned Crouch makes a compelling statement: "In the case of Mexicans, we understand that they are not lazy or incompetent. We know how and why they get to work and travel as they do" (23). Heusinkveld on the other hand, sustains that "the puritan work ethic is only part of the motivation that drives Anglo-Americans to work so hard.... In Mexico, by contrast historical experience has not demonstrated that hard work is any guarantee of success.... The Mexican is more likely to say that things happen to people—a reflection of the basic fatalism inherent in the Mexican character" (52–53).

One more trade book emphasizes this Mexican attitude towards life. Kenna and Lacy say, "Many Mexicans believe in fate and take what comes to them with resignation to the inevitable. Those who take this fatalistic attitude don't feel they have control of their destinies" (13).

Randy Malat assures his readers that "the sense of fatalism and powerlessness so characteristic of Mexican culture can play a role in the workplace. Workers who feel that their skills and initiative are not appreciated may conclude that the enterprise at hand is unimportant" (38). Although Malat advises that foreign executives should "be careful not to label such an attitude as laziness" (38); the damage has been done.

These assertions could make anyone conclude that, indeed, Mexicans are lazy and unappreciated workers because they leave everything to God. John Charles Chasteen writes, on the contrary, about what trade books say is the point of view in regards to Latin Americans, not just Mexicans: the lack of the "Protestant work ethic ... and their tropical climates further discouraged economic activity with debilitating heat and too many sensuous satisfactions—mangoes, papayas, and passion fruit—literally, as well as figuratively, growing on trees. In this version, Latin America [and Mexico of course] historically was racially, culturally, or environmentally determined and more or less inescapably so" (21).

The authors of these trade books lack a cultural and psychological perspective on Mexican fatalism which is not inherent to all Mexican people. It is true that low income workers and employees suffer, to a degree, of fatalism, or determinism, which is part of the environment in which they are born and raised. Most of these people in the lower status of the Mexican social hierarchy have a sense of resignation and silence in front of the economic, political, and social injustices that they have endured for many years. Ross, Mirowsky, and Cockerham say that "since fatalism has been identified as a characteristic of Mexican culture, fatalistic perspectives may promote psychological distress" (383). Although this study is quite biased by making generalizations such as "It is because Mexicans and Mexican Americans tend to be poor and not well educated that they are fatalistic," the analysis shows that "when social class is controlled, Mexicans are not more fatalistic than Anglos." Hence, fatalism, or determinism, can also be observed within Anglos living at the poverty level. Fatalism is not inherent to Mexican culture but to social class. From this study we must consider that it was carried out in two places: El Paso, Texas, and Ciudad Juarez, Mexico. In the specific case of Mexicans, Ciudad Juarez cannot be used as a sample to "prove" that all Mexicans are fatalistic. The big difference between Mexican people living on the border close to one of the most industrialized and economically developed countries in the world differs from those Mexicans in Chiapas and Oaxaca, for instance, living close to one of the poorest areas in the world, Central America. Contrary to what Ross, Mirowsky, and Cockerham say, not all Mexicans are poor and lack education; not all of them belong to a low social class; and not everyone has a sense of fatalism. This study, along with the trade book authors, makes a generalization about Mexican culture in its entirety and creates a big gap of misunderstanding about Mexican culture instead of building bridges of communication and understanding between both societies. American and foreign businessmen and women must be aware that high-level managers and entrepreneurs in Mexico will in most cases show no traces of fatalism at all. The United States and its citizens must be provided with well-researched information about the country they want to do business with; they cannot be isolated in their own beliefs as the best in the world. Adler very well establishes that "no nation can afford to act as if it is alone in the world (parochialism) or as if it is superior to other nations (ethnocentrism).... Like many business people the world over, Americans must now compete and contribute based on world-class standards and on a global scale" (13). American citizens, indeed, need to be offered cultural information, not stereotypes, that will actually help them to be world citizens in the business environment.

This analysis of the Mexican attitudes towards work is based on the Western established notion that Catholic beliefs disregard the "better" work ethics of Protestant North America. It seems that the goal of this Eurocentric point of view is to try and create a homogeneous culture according to their own cultural backgrounds; everything different is not acceptable. These writers who "study" Mexican business culture and society do it departing from their own reality. If this fatalistic characteristic were part of Mexican culture in previous generations, it would be unfair to generalize and apply the same measure of fatalism to the new younger Mexicans influenced by new technology, modern, up-to-date learning materials, and especially a globalization that keeps these different groups in touch with fresh trends and business attitudes around the world.

In his classic work *Orientalism*, Edward Said says: "Sir Alfred Lyall once said to me: 'Accuracy is abhorrent to the Oriental mind. Every Anglo-Indian should always remember that maxim.' The European is a close reasoner; his statements of fact are devoid of any ambiguity; he is a natural logician, albeit he may not have studied logic; he is by nature skeptical and requires proof before he can accept the truth of any proposition; his trained intelligence works like a piece of mechanism.... Orientals or Arabs are thereafter shown to be gullible, 'devoid of energy and initiative,' ... Orientals are inveterate liars, they are 'lethargic and suspicious,' and in everything oppose the clarity, directness, and nobility of the Anglo-Saxon race" (38). We can very well apply these same premises to the present thoughts and writings of these trade books and their beliefs about Mexican fatalism, lack of reasoning, lack of energy and initiative that clearly contradicts that of the more advanced logical, developed mind of the Anglo American citizen.

The authors of these trade books are clearly conditioned and limited by their own society and cultural traditions; they do not take into account what is written about Mexico by Mexicans. By basing their assumptions on their own narrow experiences and on what has been written before them, they are also conditioning and limiting Mexican business culture and society to their ethnocentric point of view. Instead, what is needed during these times of globalization and exchange of products and services, is a cross-cultural approach to stop prejudices and stereotypes about Mexicans and their society. Anyone dealing with people from other countries (Mexico in this particular case) should be aware of the benefits of cross-cultural training. About this Earley and Ang say, "Cross-cultural competence can be viewed as a set of congruent behaviors, attitudes, and policies that come together in a system or agency or more professionals and enable the system, agency, or professionals to work effectively in cross-cultural situations" (263).

What these trade books do not offer is a background to support their claims. Dr. Santiago Ramírez proposes a psychological foundation based on a historical context: "*El trauma que la conquista le imprimió al indígena fue de tal magnitud, que sus posibilidades de lucha en la nueva cultura se anularon, su mecanismo de defensa y su fuerza es aceptar lo que tiene, desconfiar de todo aquello que el español, el criollo o el mestizo ladino le pueden ofrecer. Al través de varios siglos de historia sabe que nada bueno le pueden dar, ya que si realmente fuera bueno los otros grupos culturales lo tomarían para sí.* The trauma that the conquest imprinted on the indigenous people was of such magnitude that their chances to overcome the new culture were almost nonexistent; the indigenous' defense mechanism and their strength come from accepting what they have, not to trust anything from the Spanish, the Criollo or the Mestizo. Throughout several centuries of history, the indigenous people have learned that the aforementioned groups cannot give them anything of value because if it were good, other cultural peoples would take it for themselves'" (73).

This explanation from Santiago Ramirez does offer a better-informed and well documented perspective: however, if fatalism was a trend in Mexican culture several decades ago, it is less acute in today's globalized Mexico. The new generations of Mexican employees and businessmen and women take control of their lives and are facing more and more positive and negative rewards and consequences for their job performance and decisions that they make throughout society.

Present-day Mexican generations do not show fatalism as much as despair at the fact that many American companies, for instance, have practices in Mexico that would be grounds for civil suits in the U.S. For example, some of these companies, when hiring women, want to know if the woman being interview is married, if she has children, if she will get married soon, if she is pregnant or if she will get pregnant shortly. Alejandra Anaya (2009, personal interview) brings up another example that "employees conform to what they have because some companies don't encourage employees to go back to school and do graduate studies." Dr. Javier Beltran (2009, personal interview) maintains that "many foreign companies create a corporate ceiling that local employees cannot surpass. These companies create a comfort zone where the most important goal to reach is to meet the employees' basic needs. After that nothing else is so imperative." For decades, many foreign companies who didn't trust the administrative capacities of local managers, brought executives from their home offices in the United States or Europe to occupy high level positions in Latin America thus creating this glass ceiling for Mexican employees. This is beginning to change some as more companies hire Mexican managers and executives as they feel they can trust them more and also depend on their labor.

On a different topic, Heusinkveld does not offer any kind of inquiry to validate her statements and assures her readers that "relatives drive for hundreds of miles to attend a quinceaños." Rosa, a Mexican-American woman, does not go to work because she has to attend a party and this is common practice among Mexicans. Continuing with her descriptions on parties, the author states: "A Mexican businessman might postpone an important meeting to attend the birthday party of a niece or nephew" (4).

However, new research through the psychological study by David Myers shines light on the issue stating that "children in these cultures [Mexican and non–Western societies] grow up with a stronger sense of *family-self* a feeling that what shames the child shames the family, and what brings honor to the family brings honor to the self." Thus, we can understand that the need for members of some cultures to attend family events is an important part of their lives because of the family's strong ties among all its members. The case of Rosa, the Mexican-American woman and the quinceañera party amid Mexicans and Mexican-Americans should not be generalized. If Heusinkveld carried out her research in Xalapa, it is strange that she mentions the case of a Mexican-American woman living in the U.S. Cultural changes have taken place and there are significant differences between Mexicans and Mexican-Americans.

About family and priorities, Geert and Gert Jan Hofstede propose an excellent contextualization on the topic of collective and individualistic societies: "One owes lifelong loyalty to one's in-group, and breaking this loyalty is one of the worst things a person can do. Between the person and the in-group a mutual dependence relationship develops that is both practical and psychological"; on the contrary, in individualistic societies, "the purpose of education is to enable children to stand on their own feet ... neither practically nor psychologically is the healthy person in this type of society supposed to be dependent on a group" (75).

Heusinkveld lacks a cultural and family structural approach like the one presented by Geert and Gert Jan Hofstede to support this discussion about Mexican families and their behavior toward business. Indeed, we can say that Mexicans have close-knit families that could fit in both individualist and collectivist structures; since individualism is associated with a nuclear family structure and collectivism with an extended family organization such as grandparents, aunts, uncles, cousins, etc. In this regard, the author of this trade book fails to mention that Mexican families are so supportive of each other that most sons and daughters do not leave the paternal home until they get married or have to move to another city due to job responsibilities. We must convey to our American and foreign businessmen and women that families hold Mexican society together during good and bad times. Nothing is more important to Mexicans than their families; their lives are built upon them. However, to blindly assert that a Mexican business person would cancel an important meeting to attend a birthday party is unrealistic in these times of globalized commerce and competitiveness. Close friends, as family members, are extremely important in Mexico. Mexican business culture emphasizes the customary trend of creating a friendly relationship prior to engaging in business with someone they do not know. Many American and Western businessmen and women should be aware of this custom before they initiate a business relationship in Mexico. Trompenaars and Hampden-Turner are very clear on this issue: "One serious pitfall for universalist cultures [rules are more important] in doing business with more particularist [relationships come first] ones is that the importance of friendship is often ignored" (40).

Heusinkveld, Kras, Engholm and Grimers, and Malat, join forces when it comes to reinforcing stereotypes about Mexico, in this case, bribery and corruption. Heusinkveld says: "most Mexicans view bribes as a necessary part of life" (57). Kras states: "various forms of corruption exist and are very widespread. One of the most common forms involves some kind of bribery" (40). Engholm and Grimes mention "a tradition of bribery has arisen from public officials neither qualified nor sufficiently educated to serve.... A civil servant culture does not yet exist in Mexico" (6). Randy Malat establishes that "nothing gets done in Mexico without bribes and payoffs. Corruption is rife in many aspects of Mexican life, from electoral fraud to diversion of funds by government officials, from payoffs for commercial concessions and contracts to *mordidas* ('bites') slipped to the police" (24, my emphasis).

Consequently, Mexican people, it seems, cannot live without bribes and corruption. We could hardly agree that these comments benefit American businessmen and women in their attempts in reaching a better understanding of Mexican business culture. These statements will not help close the gap between both the American and Mexican societies in terms of understanding each other. In fact, one other trade book contradicts the above-mentioned authors. Jay and Maggie Jessup say: "Overall, integrity is the order of the day. In the course of doing business with Mexico, we are constantly impressed by the honesty and integrity of the government officials" (10).

If bribery and corruption were the order of the day in Mexico, many American companies wouldn't invest in the country. Mexico is, after all, the number eight auto maker in the world and number one in all of Latin America. Labor costs in China are rising, and more difficulties are emerging for American manufacturers—such as lack of quality control in China and traveling back and forth. Once the Chinese low labor cost dream comes to an end, being just across the border will be a plus for many American companies willing to go back to Mexico. Many companies see Mexico as a land of product manufacturing heaven. Damian Cave reports: "American manufacturers of all sizes are looking south to Mexico with what economists describe as an eagerness not seen since the early years of the North American Free Trade Agreement in the 1990s. American trade with Mexico has grown by nearly 30 percent since 2010, to $507 billion annually, and foreign direct investment in Mexico last year hit a record $35 billion. Over the past few years, manufactured goods from Mexico have claimed a larger share of the American import market, reaching a high of about 14 percent" (1–2).

American and international companies would not manufacture, sell, or buy products to and from Mexico under these conjectures of bribery, corruption, and lack of civil servant culture. The trade books testimonials, from an "outside" perspective, enclosed in a small space and time do not do justice to what should be a well-researched cultural report. They are beset with negative insensitivity. What we need is to contextualize these arguments under solid research. Geert and Gert Jan Hofstede emphasize, "What is called *corruption* is partly a matter of definition. We speak of corruption when people use the power or their position to illegally enrich themselves or when citizens buy the collaboration of authorities for their private purposes. But what does one say about excessive levels of chief executive compensation in some companies and a large amount spent in some countries on lobbying...? In Japan, China, and many other cultures, the giving of gifts is an important ritual, and the borderline between gift giving and bribing is diffuse ... under conditions of poverty, acquiring money in unofficial ways is not just a matter of greed; it may be a matter of survival" (62).

It is true that some degree of bribery and corruption does exist in Mexico but only in a dissimilar way to that in the United States where lobbying from financial, gun, and pharmaceutical companies, and political campaign donations can also be considered a way of corruption. The only difference between a campaign donation and a bribe is that they have different names.

Let's not forget the way directors and CEOs of non-profit organizations enrich themselves while maintaining a tax exempt status. From a small soccer club in Charlotte, North Carolina, where an executive director makes almost $50,000 for 20 hours of work a week compared to a full time teacher who makes much less than that, to a national organization, directors get extremely handsome monetary rewards. A case in point is Goodwill which "paid more than $1.1 million in total compensation to its then–CEO, making him the highest paid Goodwill executive in the country. The highest-paid employees of 101 Goodwill organizations received, on average, a total compensation package worth nearly a quarter-million dollars per year, or $24.7 million in total compensation. Seventeen Goodwill entities reported executive compensation in excess of $1 million per year with 30 CEOs receiving more than $293,000 per year in total compensation. A husband-wife Goodwill executive team in North Carolina collected a combined $795,372 in total compensation. Goodwill entities spent more than $39.1 million in travel-related expenses, of which 14 entities spent more than $1 million in travel-related expenses. Thirteen organizations spent more than $100,000 in annual conference expenses," says watchdog.org (1).

Individual cases differ from the widespread practice of corruption and bribery; American society could see these problems as non-common habits. There is, however, a long list of examples of recent bribery and corruption in the United States, according to the FBI: "Two commissioners in Lackawanna County, Pennsylvania were convicted of racketeering and other charges in connection with accepting and demanding payments and other benefits from people doing business with the county; A Nashville, Tennessee, police officer was indicted for accepting cash while delivering drugs and drug money to several locations for local drug dealers—all while wearing his uniform and driving his police car; A special agent with the U.S. Immigration and Customs Enforcement's Homeland Security Investigations was arrested in Arizona on charges that she illegally accessed, stole, and transferred sensitive government documents to family members and associates with strong ties to drug trafficking organizations; A county judge in Cleveland was convicted of accepting bribes, including campaign contributions, in return for fixing cases. So far, this particular investigation has implicated dozens of elected officials, public employees, and contractors within the county; A former mayor and a magistrate from South Daytona, Florida were both charged with accepting bribes from purported investors in exchange for lowering city code liens on a large investment property" (p. 1); and more recently in 2014, "former New Orleans Mayor Ray Nagin was sentenced to 10 years in prison for bribery, money laundering and other corruption that spanned his two terms as mayor—including the chaotic years after Hurricane Katrina hit in 2005" (p. 1). Following with disasters, this one took place recently in 2015: "The New York Attorney General's Office executed a search warrant at the offices of GEB HiRise Engineering in

Uniondale, New York in a criminal probe over allegations of fraudulently changed engineering reports for Superstorm Sandy flood claims."

So do Americans see bribery as part of life as Mexicans do according to the authors of these trade books? Would it be fair to turn the tables around and say that bribery and corruption are an intrinsic part of American life and business culture? It is a fact that thanks to the low levels of corruption in Mexican business that the country has experienced more worldwide investment in the last years, especially after NAFTA as Damian Cave said in his *New York Times* report. Again, Charles Mitchell, with respect to corruption in business, says: "Today, countries agree that the economic costs are real: Recent studies have shown a direct correlation between the level of corruption and the amount of direct foreign investment a country receives; the higher the corruption level, the lower the investment amount" (158).

To assert that most Mexicans view bribes as a necessary part of life, as the authors of these trade books have stated, they must categorically place these assertions within their historical, political, and economic context. Richard Lewis helps us understand this attitude about bribes [la mordida] in Mexico: "While the Mexican gives freely to his guest, conducting business and obtaining many social services incur a cost which is normally obviated in the U.S. ... Mexican civil servants, officials and police are paid very little and usually seek to augment their meager salaries by accepting what Americans call *bribes*" (534). Contrary to what we read from the trade books, corruption and bribes are not inherent to Mexican life. Bribes do exist but at a lower level than before, and gifts are used as business practice and should not be wrongly judged without proper research on the topic. Dr. Javier Beltran (2009, personal interview) says that Mexican companies sometimes elect to go unnoticed or clandestine to avoid bribes as they are something they don't agree with. Dr. Javier Martines (2009, personal interview), on his part, explains that the new generations are changing Mexican society; they are eliminating corruption, bribery, and dishonesty.

The authors of these guides do not take into consideration what Geert and Gert Jan Hofstede advise: "It does call for suspending judgment when dealing with groups or societies different from one's own. One should think twice before applying the norms of one person, or group, or society to another.... In these postcolonial days foreigners who want to change something in another society will have to negotiate their interventions" (6). It must be noticed that in many cases bribery and corruption are better dealt with in the American judicial system; in Mexico few cases are prosecuted. However, when we read so many of these cultural generalizations about bribery and corruption in Mexico, we notice that they start taking the shape of social well-informed research, which it is not. Those who teach cultural awareness should provide up to date material in terms of significant research, not only observations based on a couple of particular experiences written in a trade book. That would be the best way to diminish the pernicious effects that these guides have on our students and business people and to build a better understanding of Mexican society and business culture. These guides should not emphasize their ethnocentric perspective because, according to Earley and Ang, "an emphasis on Western psyche detracts attention from the importance of cultural and national differences in people's values and beliefs, and how these differences may affect work behavior" (11).

One other noteworthy topic treated in these trade books has to do with nepotism. Five of these trade books reference it. Peggy Kenna and Sandra Lacy state that: "In Mexico, family and friends are often favored as employees because they are seen as being trustworthy. Promotions are often based on loyalty to a superior, rather than performance within an organization" (25). Eva Kraus mentions: "in all Mexican businesses, from the largest to the smallest, hiring practices strongly favor relatives and friends of employees and avoid, as far as possible, unknown or un-recommended persons" (50). Boye Lafayette De Mente notes: "Nepotism is alive and flourishing in Mexico.... Nepotism among the professions and government is another matter, however. It remains one of the most corrupting influences in Mexican society impacting on all the domestic and international affairs of the country." Randy Malat explains: "Family members are likely to work together as well.... Most of these entities are family businesses—ventures ranging from shops, restaurants, and small factories to taco stands and other forms of street vending" (14).

None of these authors support their comments with either well-informed research or through field investigation on the topic. These assertions about all large and small companies' practices of nepotism go from preposterous to ridiculous. Can one imagine a Ford Motor Company assembly plant in Mexico with hundreds of workers and employees being run only by family members, from the production lines to the high level executives? Can we think of a Walmart Supercenter also in Mexico with hundreds of employees all of them being related to each other so the company can function? Those remarks by authors like Kraus and the others' claims are built like a castle of cards.

How different would be Mexican and American practices of nepotism? Let us ask a few questions. How about small and medium size family-owned businesses in the U.S. where family members share all the responsibilities because they trust each other in a way they could not trust someone from outside? What about companies such as Hobby Lobby and Chick-Fil-A where only family members are at the top of the corporate pyramid? Walmart was founded by the Walton family and it has been run by them for many years. What can we say about Ivy League universities that give first consideration in admissions to children of politicians and other people of power and influence, and whose parents, brothers or sisters have studied there too? Why do advisers at many colleges and universities tell students to join a fraternity or sorority to start creating a network of new friends whose parents can help them later on to land jobs?

What is needed is a voice from within from small and medium size family-owned businesses in Mexico. We need to research and ask those involved in these practices of nepotism to explain from their own perspective why Mexican businesses still rely on family members and friends to run their companies. According to Alejandra Anaya (2009, personal interview), "nepotism is part of the Mexican culture at all levels. Especially, small and medium size family-owned businesses that hire their own relatives and close friends to administrate all aspects of the company." Dr. Javier Jimenez (2009, personal interview) says that "there is a reason behind hiring a relative or a close friend: We [Mexicans] don't work as a team, we work as family, with our family in the company. We don't incorporate someone we don't know because we don't trust them. Family ties are stronger than business' ties. We need someone to watch our backs, not because of their productivity but because of their faithfulness to us."

Dr. Isabel Soberano (2009, personal interview) says: "Nepotism is a grave problem in Mexican family-owned businesses because few of them demand that their employees/relatives get more education for the job they have to perform, especially small businesses. However, she says, it is a family issue. Feelings get in the way and don't allow for someone to fire a family member so the family ties are not broken; there is no pragmatism." I have to add that by the time I interviewed Dr. Soberano, her son was the vice president of the university and her stepson was director of research. Also other high level posts were secured by some of her best close friends across campus. Thus, family and friends are trustworthy and can take better care of the business at mid and high levels than someone from outside, an unknown person to the family.

Ms. Paredo (2009, personal interview) states that "paternalism and nepotism go hand in hand, it is a way to maintain the business within the family so every member is in charge of taking care of it. The company will grow as long as all members of the family depend on and watch each other's backs to succeed, no one outside the family will care about the company as much as a family associate would. Employees are not given an executive post that easily, it has to be someone with good education and skills."

Ms. Margarita Acosta (2009, personal interview) explains that "nepotism is not a bad thing since it is to protect the company. It is better to hire someone within the family who one can trust than hiring an unknown person."

These interviews and comments are not to be considered as a general sentiment of the Mexican people, but they can be used as a sample of what is and why nepotism works for many small and medium size family-owned businesses in the country. In Mexico these kinds of companies, as we have seen, depend on their families to succeed; it is a fact that many of these establishments have and will keep trusting a family member before they hire someone from outside for a high level position. This is not to say that these businesses do not do it and never will, but even if they hired someone external to the family circle, that person will have to come recommended by someone within the family or a close friend. When these companies start growing they do indeed hire employees with good education and skills to perform their duties. It would be illogical to think that a medium size company would not need external help from well-educated MBAs, engineers and accountants.

The assumptions by the writers of these trade books are permeated by a Eurocentric standpoint that we can compare to that of Said's *Orientalism* where he mentions the article by Harold W. Glidden on the Arab people, "which from our point of view [European] is 'aberrant' but for Arabs is 'normal.' Arabs stress conformity ... that Arabs can function only in conflict situations; that prestige is based solely on the ability to dominate others" (48). The Anglo perspective on these guides is one of superiority over the inferior Mexican business culture full of nepotism that arises on an aberrant, conformist society where the owners dominate their employees and everything that surrounds the business.

It makes perfect cultural sense that companies rely on the practice of nepotism since these are family businesses and as we have seen before, family is the base of society and nothing will change this aspect of Mexican business culture. To try to do it would be futile. However, to say that this practice applies to both large and small companies is preposterous. Large national and international Mexican corporations, like in the U.S., see some degree of nepotism but not to the extent as some of the trade books intend us to believe. Bimbo, CEMEX, Grupo Modelo and other international Mexican companies started out as small family businesses. It was the family that allowed for these businesses to expand to other continents and afterwards hire hundreds of low-, medium-, and high-level employees to run these organizations. American businessmen and women must learn about this cultural Mexican phenomenon before starting a commercial relationship with their Mexican counterparts, as Gerry Darlington says: "Once this awareness has been raised [other's values and beliefs], they can choose to make behavioral adjustments to enhance their capability to work successfully with people from other cultures" (35).

In conclusion, the most important topics treated in these trade books on Mexican business culture and society are a distortion of reality. To say that Mexicans are lazy because they are fatalistic and do not follow the protestant work ethic; that Mexicans' irresponsibly prioritize a family party over a business meeting or work; to spread the biased cultural aspect of a Mexican who cancels an important business meeting at the last minute; to propagate the illogical idea that bribes and corruption are an intrinsic part of Mexican life; and to promulgate the preposterous notion that nepotism is a practice in Mexican business that prevents the country from advancing in the national and international commerce arena, are indeed, all unsubstantiated accounts that lack a historical or theoretical background or context of any kind. Remarks like these stem from a fundamentally ethnocentric outlook. The cultural background of the trade book authors is one that tries to impose on and transform the Mexican business culture and society. These writers do not welcome Mexican business culture as it is; they attempt to modify it for their own benefit and that of other readers in their own culture. These authors do not appreciate and put into practice what Trompenaars and Hampden-Turner explain: "Cultural awareness then, is understanding states of mind, your own and those of the people you meet" (201).

In the 16th century Juan Ginés de Sepulveda and Bartolome de Las Casas debated about the humanity of the American Indians. Sepulveda argued from a complete Western perspective, founding his arguments in philosophical ideas from Aristotle, that Indians were fit for slavery and that the Spaniards had the right to punish the Indian's savagery and convert them to Christianity. On his part, Las Casas contentions were based on his living experience among the Indians, arguing that Aristotle's concepts did not apply to the Indians who were reasoning human beings, had a soul, and should not be brought to Christianity through the use of force. In what would be considered a perpetuation of thoughts from the European standpoint, the authors of these trade books would like to punish Mexican business society for being different and force this society to bow to Western values. Their view is that Western culture is superior merely because that of the Mexicans does not comply with their notion of traditional Western civilization.

It is indecorous that the authors of these guides do not employ their business expertise to write a multifaceted study of Mexican business culture; none of these trade books explore the complexity of their own culture, much less others. Richard Lewis contextualizes business culture this way: "We can achieve a good understanding of our foreign counterparts only if we realize that 'our spectacles' are coloring our view of them. What is the route to better understanding? To begin with, we need to examine the special features of our own culture" (21).

Said mentions that Lord Cromer, an English diplomat, said: "As I am only a diplomatist and an administrator, whose proper study is also man; but from the point of view of governing him. I content myself with noting the fact that somehow or other the Oriental generally acts, speaks, and thinks in a manner exactly opposite to the European" (39).

In our specific case, the writers of these guide books hold a Western point of view in discordance with Mexican business culture which acts, speaks, and thinks in a dissimilar way. Instead of comprehending these cultural differences and closing the gap between the West (U.S.) and Mexico, they magnify this hole of misconstruction between both societies. These writers who at some point may have traveled and visited Mexico and possibly lived there for either a short or long period of time, exercise some intellectual power through their works on Mexican business culture and society in general; such intellectual power I shall call "Mexicanism" in the manner Said christened the term "Orientalism" to describe the same category of experience on the Arab world.

The Mexicanism of these trade books seems to depict the same images as did American and English writers of the 18th century when traveling to Latin America for business reasons hoping to expand trade. One of them wrote, according to John Charles Chasteen, "corrupt, stupid, beggarly and dishonest set of beings, chained in ignorance and swayed by superstition and the most gloomy bigotry." "Superstition" and "gloomy bigotry" were Protestant code words for Catholicism, and denunciation of Latin American "vileness were plainly racist" (115), finishes Chasteen.

"Mexican business culture and society" have been the point of "study" of several trade books that have created an image of Mexicanism during the last 25 years of the 20th century and into the 21st century up to the present day. These authors are clearly influenced by early writings on the same topic augmented by their own points of view. Mexico has been conjured up from a Western idea in order to fit what some people would like to hear. The consumers of these works are Westerners as well, and the writers conform to the idea that there is a dialogue between the same perspectives and cultural values. Mexico and its business culture and society are the objects of study without Mexican input, or Mexican participation. Mexicans do not play a part in this global conversation which is about *them*, and they are less than observers, they are the "other."

This kind of Mexicanism has become a profitable career for those who rely on their own limited experiences and possibly on short recounts of other self-help texts written in the past. Mexico and Mexicans are what the authors want them to be, not what they actually are. Mexicans and their business culture and society have been dehumanized and, once again, they have to prove their humanity, and demonstrate that they have souls and are reasoning human beings to those who hold different values and codes. To describe a modern Mexican business culture would conflict with the image of the Mexico of bribery and corruption, illegal immigration, and poverty.

Mexican business culture is described through Western lenses, codes, regulations, systems, and values of the writers of these trade books who create a falsified global interpretation of the Mexican in what can only be described as Mexicanism.

With the growing number of serious research being conducted and the number of well-informed works published to teach social and business culture competency in Mexico, professors and businesspeople must be less inclined to use trade books for academic and business purposes. In fact, professors and businesspeople should be more proactive and ought to avoid trade books as pedagogical tools to teach and further understand social, historical, and cultural awareness in Mexican business.

Discussion Questions

1. Why is it important to learn "business culture" in the modern world?
2. Is there a difference between "culture" and "cross-culture"?
3. How would you define the concepts of "preconceptions" and "stereotypes"?
4. What are some of the most common stereotypes about Mexicans and their society?
5. What is the difference between "parochialism" and "ethnocentrism"?

6. How similar is the comparison between Arab and Mexican cultures?
7. How can we define cross-cultural competence and why is it so important?
8. Describe the various business culture and cross-culture theories explained in the essay.
9. Discuss the difference between universalist culture and particularist culture.

Key Learning Terms

Stereotype: Characteristics given to groups of people in regards to race, nationality and sexual orientation.

Cultural awareness: The capacity to communicate that involves becoming aware of our own cultural values and beliefs.

Cross-cultural awareness: Observing and contrasting two or more cultures or groups.

Cultural intelligence: A person's capability to adapt effectively to new cultural contexts.

Fatalism: A philosophical doctrine that establishes that all events are subject to fate; people who leave everything to God.

Ethnocentrism: The belief in the superiority of one's own culture over another one.

Nepotism: Favoritism to hire, give job positions, or give contracts on the basis of family relationship or friendships in business or politics.

References

Acosta, Margarita. Personal interview, 2009.
Adler, J. Nancy. *International Dimensions of Organizational Behavior.* Mason, OH: Thomson/South-Western, 1997. Print.
Anaya, Alejandra. Personal interview, 2009.
Beltran, Javier. Personal interview, 2009.
Cahill, Danielle, and Sandra de los Ríos. *Vistas comerciales y culturales.* Victoria, Australia: Thomson-Heinle, 2002. Print.
Cantu, Nora. Personal interview, 2009.
Carney, Carmen, and Carlos Coria-Sánchez. *Entre socios: Español para el mundo profesional.* New York: W.W. Norton, 2010. Print.
Cave, Damian. "As Ties with China Unravel, U.S. Companies Head to Mexico." *New York Times*, May 31, 2014. Print.
Chasteen, John Charles. *Born in Blood and Fire: A Concise History of Latin America.* New York: W. W. Norton, 2001. Print.
Chio, Ana. Personal interview, 2009.
Cramer, Mark. *Culture Shock: A Guide to Customs and Etiquette, Mexico.* Portland, OR: Graphic Arts Center Publishing Company, 1998. Print.
Crouch, Ned. *Mexicans and Americans: Cracking the Culture Code.* London: Nicholas Brealey International, 2004. Print.
Darlington, Gary. "Culture: A Theoretical View." *Managing Across Cultures.* Ed. Pat Joynt and Malcom Warner. London: International Thomson Business Press, 1996. Print.
De Mente, Boje Lafayette. *Why Mexicans Think and Behave the Way They Do!* Phoenix Books Publishers, 1996. Print.
Doyle, S. Michael, and T. Bruce Fryer. *Exito comercial.* Boston: Thomson Heinle, 2014. Print.
Earley, Christopher, and Soon Ang. *Cultural Intelligence: Individual Interactions Across Cultures.* Stanford: Stanford University Press, 2003. Print.
Engholm, Christopher, and Scott Grimes. *Doing Business in Mexico.* Englewood Cliffs, NJ: Prentice Hall, 1997. Print.
Galloway, Victoria, and Elmer A. Rodríguez. *Saldo a favor.* New York: John Wiley and Sons, 2000. Print.

Heusinkveld, Paula. *Inside Mexico: Living, Traveling, and Doing Business in a Changing Society.* New York: John Wiley and Sons, 1994. Print.
Hofstede, Geert, and Gert Jan Hofstede. *Cultures and Organizations: Software of the Mind.* Boston: McGraw-Hill, 2005. Print.
Jessup, M. Jay, and Maggie Jessup. *Doing Business in Mexico.* Rocklin, CA: Prima Publishing, 1993. Print.
Jimenez, Javier. Personal interview, 2009.
Kenna, Peggy, and Sondra Lacy. *Business Mexico.* Lincolnwood, IL: Passport Books, 1994. Print.
Kras, Eva. *Management in Two Cultures: Bridging the Gap Between U.S. and Mexican Managers.* Boston: Intercultural Press, 1995. Print.
Lewis, Richard D. *When Cultures Collide: Leading Across Cultures.* Boston: Nicholas Brealey Publishing, 2006. Print.
Malat, Randy. *Passport to Mexico: Your Pocket Guide to Mexican Business, Customs, and Etiquette.* Petaluma, CA: World Trade Press, 2003. Print.
Mitchell, Charles. *A Short Course in International Business Culture.* Petaluma, CA: World Trade Press, 2000. Print.
Monaghan, John, and Peter Just. *Social and Cultural Anthropology: A Very Short Introduction.* New York: Oxford University Press, 2000. Print.
Myers, David G. *Psychology.* New York: Worth Publishers, 2007. Print.
Noble, Judith, and Jaime Lacasa. *The Hispanic Way.* Lincolnwood, IL: Passport Books, 1995. Print.
Paredo. Personal interview, 2009.
Ramirez, Santiago. *El mexicano: Psicología de sus motivaciones.* México: Ed. Grijalbo, 1997. Print.
Reed, Glenn, and Roger Gray. *How to Do Business in Mexico.* Austin: University of Texas Press, 1997. Print.
Reyes, Consuelo. Personal interview, 2009.
Rush, Patricia, and Patricia Houston. *Spanish for Business.* New Jersey: Prentice Hall, 2003. Print.
Salazar, Susana. Personal interview, 2009.
Soberano, Isabel. Personal interview, 2009.
Trompenaars, Fons, and Charles Hampden-Turner. *Riding the Waves of Culture: Understanding Cultural Diversity in Global Business.* Boston: McGraw-Hill, 1998. Print.
Wilson, Anita. *The Complete Guide to Doing Business in Mexico.* New York: AMACOM, 1994. Print.

Tradition and Modern Aspects of Mexican Corporate Culture

ANABELLA DÁVILA *and* ANDREAS M. HARTMANN

Mexico's industrial development has produced unique characteristics in terms of business corporate cultures (Sobrino 252). The country has improved its industrial (UNIDO) and educational standards in engineering (Rascón et al.) and other fields, which constitute important elements of its particular business culture. From the cultural perspective, industry and education are the main drivers that have instilled in Mexican society traits of a work culture oriented towards productivity and competitiveness. The economic history of the country shows that in the early decades of the 20th century, which represented the beginning of the Mexican industrial era, the industrial worker was portrayed as responsible, accountable, honest, and having a great sense of duty (Reygadas 135).

In the Mexican northeast, a group of Spanish immigrants imbued with an entrepreneurial spirit became builders of industry and the main promoters of basic and higher education (Alba 1). It was the closed and cohesive social structure of this group of immigrants that laid the foundations for a homogeneous and singular work culture (Flores, Olvera and Gonzalez 95). This social structure facilitated the transfer of cultural patterns among generations, although it developed into slightly diverse work culture patterns across the country.

A Culture with Traditional Characteristics

There are two main traits of the corporate culture of Mexican companies that can be characterized as traditional: family businesses and paternalistic-benevolent leadership.

Family Businesses

Most of the large and small and medium enterprises (SMEs) in Mexico have been created and managed by members of the nuclear or extended family (Sargent and Ghaddar 99). Given this structural characteristic, we currently find that the corporate governance of large and old companies is exercised by members of the third and fourth generations of the founding families. Some researchers have identified successful large companies with professional family members as top managers who have been educated in the most renowned domestic and foreign universities (Sargent 20). One of the main concerns of family-run companies is the succession plan. Since the opening of the economy in the early 1980s, most large companies in Mexico have designed succession plans as part of their corporate governance practices. Take the example of CEMEX (cement and building materials) that in May 2014 lost its prominent President of the Board and CEO, Lorenzo Zambrano, a Stanford MBA graduate and grandson of the company's founder. Zambrano had become CEO of the company 28 years earlier and rebuilt the company through a series of national and international acquisitions. He had turned the company around, making it one of the most-admired Latin American companies because of its advanced technological and financial systems. Soon after Lorenzo Zambrano's death, the company announced that its Board of Directors, by unanimous decision, had appointed his cousin Rogelio Zambrano as Chairman of the Board of Directors and Fernando A. Gonzalez as Chief Executive Officer. Rogelio Zambrano had previously served as a member of the Board of Directors, and Fernando A. Gonzalez had previously held the position of Executive Vice President of Finance and Administration. In this way, it was made clear to all stakeholders that the Zambrano family would keep control and that CEMEX was a serious company with a highly formalized governance system. According to the financial press, one could question the appointment of these executives in particular, but everyone would agree that the succession plan was executed according to the company's plan and at the right time. The purpose of the succession plan was to continue the operation of the company without leaving any space for financial speculation (De la Torre). Other major companies—particularly those that are listed in the Mexican Exchange Stock Market—report their corporate governance practices in their annual reports and on their websites.

Paternalistic-Benevolent Leadership

Management scholars argue that, under the family governance structure of Mexican firms, the predominant leadership style is paternalistic-benevolent (Martinez 76). This style of leadership is generally related to positive behavior by organizational members. In a review of academic studies published worldwide, Pellegrini and Scandura found that companies in emerging markets highly value such loyalty, commitment, and engagement (573). However, we found no studies showing whether Mexico-based multinationals modify their paternalistic leadership style when operating in the United States or in other parts of the world. The paternalistic-benevolent leadership style fits well with the idiosyncrasy of the Mexican worker, who behaves as a subordinate expecting employment protection from the owner of the company or immediate superior in exchange for loyalty and compliance with instructions.

There are multiple explanations for this intricate relationship of reciprocal job-related expectations. From the psychological perspective, it can be argued that typical Mexican workers exhibit a high degree of dependency on authority figures because of their need for moral support to provide individual development. In addition, Mexican workers respond better to collectivity-based management practices that enhance the sense of community within the work group (Dávila and Elvira 551). Such practices include internal promotions, time for socialization at work, investment in employee training, and a non-confrontational approach in performance appraisals, as well as rewards directed at work groups rather than individuals (Gomez and Sanchez 2197).

From the sociological perspective, it can be argued that Mexican workers face a relatively small labor market with few opportunities for career development or job mobility. Therefore, workers respond to the opportunity of being given a job by exhibiting compliant behavior (Dávila and Elvira 549). Moreover, many business owners feel responsible for the jobs they have created and see their companies not only as a means for their personal income but also as social institutions that significantly contribute to the well-being of their workers (Elvira and Dávila 2266). In fact, Mexican companies started the practice of offering diverse economic benefits to employees and their families at the beginning of the 20th century; these benefits include: housing mortgages, private health services, food and grocery vouchers, scholarships and sports clubs memberships, among others. One can argue that these benefits should be provided by the government because they are the foundations of human development in any given society. However, scholars argue that due to the lack of proper institutions or the inability of the government to provide for the well-being of its citizens, companies have taken over a part of these responsibilities, if only for their own employees (Dávila and Elvira 549; Elvira and Dávila 2267; Logsdon, Thomas and Van Buren III 53). In this sense, the inability of official institutions to protect work relationships and enforce labor rights (Bensusan 562) has reinforced the paternalistic culture. In fact, strikes are rare in Mexico, and formally established firms try to avoid firing workers because the law mandates large severance payments. As in many countries, it is unwise for an employee to publicly confront his or her superior, though abuses do exist and many companies pay low salaries, especially in marginally productive industries and in the vast informal sector.

From the historical perspective, it can be argued that the paternalistic-benevolent leadership style has been preserved from the colonial days. On the haciendas that constituted the main form of economic organization in mostly rural Mexico, landlords operated a patronage system (Hartmann and Dávila 24) in which the worker and his or her family received welfare benefits that contributed to the establishment of a protectionist-dependency relationship (Howell, De la Cerda, Martínez, et al. 460).

Two common themes emerge among the three perspectives that seek to explain the paternalistic-benevolent culture in Mexican organizations: one is the close and personal relationships that founders, top managers, or superiors have with their workers; and the second one is the compliant behavior that workers exhibit towards their employers or supervisors to reciprocate protection. These two themes can be considered the foundations of an idiosyncrasy that has contributed to good employment relationships and labor stability in the country, at least in the private industrial sector.

The values behind the paternalistic-benevolent culture in Mexico are related to the well-being of the employees. The value of family in one's life is central to the Mexican culture, and companies enact this value through several activities. For example, once a year most of the companies offer an open-house activity inviting the workers' families to the factory facilities. Many companies celebrate popular holidays such as Mother's Day or Children's Day and popular religious holidays such as Our Lady of Guadalupe and Christmas. Moreover, companies offer training courses for the workers' spouses in home economics or personal relationships aiming to involve them in their partners' personal development. For working mothers, many companies operate daycare facilities in an alliance with the Social Security Institute—e.g., the Day Care Center for working mothers at Telmex (telecommunications).

The local community also benefits from the paternalistic-benevolent culture of the

Mexican companies. Many companies support art and history museums as well as educational and research centers through private foundations. For example, the Soumaya Museum, the most visited art museum in Mexico, was created and sponsored by the Carlos Slim Foundation, and the Carso Center for the Study of Mexican History was created and sponsored by Condumex (cable and electric components), a member of the Carso business group. In addition, other companies sponsor amateur and professional sports teams and tournaments. The most popular sport in the country is soccer, and several business groups such as Bimbo (bakery), CEMEX (cement and building materials), and Banamex (financial services) sponsor professional soccer teams. However, other sports such as golf, cycling or baseball are also promoted by private companies. These social activities by Mexican companies go back many decades. Moreover, in the last few years, U.S.-style corporate social responsibility (CSR), with its main focus on environmental issues, has become a major concern for large companies in Mexico, a trend that is supported by nationwide industry associations. In 2013, more than 50 percent of the publicly traded companies in the country had CSR systems in place (Garza), although the thorough documentation and implementation lag behind the United States.

In addition to cultural and sports activities, family values are also embedded in the daily operations of the companies. Many companies prefer to hire family members or close relatives. The main assumption behind this practice is that the trust, loyalty and responsibility that keep families together will be present in the employment relationship and thus benefit the company. However, some companies restrict this policy and only admit employees' relatives when they work in different organizational units (Dávila and Elvira 12).

Women's career development is highly encouraged by professional associations and the Mexican Secretary of Labor. However, women's participation in top management positions in big business is rarely observed. A quick review of major Mexican companies' annual reports shows this lack of participation. This might be due to the heritage of a traditional family company culture where only male family members occupy top management positions, which is common to many emerging economies. In turn, this practice causes a lack of experience in hiring executive women, which reduces the breadth of experiences and perspectives that could be available to boards and top management teams (Ibeh, Carter, Poff, et al. 66). Female members of prominent families tend to be in charge of cultural or educational initiatives sponsored by the companies. For example, Nina Zambrano, younger sister of the late Lorenzo Zambrano, is the CEO and President of the Board of the Museum of Contemporary Art Museum in Monterrey. As a result, women have found other working spaces for professional development, such as working for foreign multinationals. This sidestepping is evident in the 2014 ranking of the Most Powerful Businesswomen in Mexico, where 40 of the top 50 female managers hold positions in foreign-based companies (CNNExpansión). Women have also found spaces for professional development by becoming entrepreneurs; being in charge of governmental agencies, educational services or non-governmental organizations; and acting as promoters of cultural and political initiatives. Additionally, it is common to find Mexican women as owners of small businesses in the service and retail sectors.

Religious practices play an important part in work centers. On the one hand, it is common to observe popular religious representations in work organizations. For example, older organizations such as Vitro (glass conglomerate) have portraits and even chapels of Our Lady of Guadalupe on their company grounds. Ernesto Martens, a former Vitro CEO, stated in an interview: "our workers use the most advanced German machinery under the watchful eye of Our Lady of Guadalupe" (Nichols 164). In this vein, Christmas parties and pilgrimages organized by the workers are also examples of popular religious events. On the other hand, some business persons that are not used to observe religious practices in the work place might feel surprised by these representations. However, the Mexican worker currently expects freedom to practice his or her faith openly at the workplace. Although Catholicism is the primary religion in the country, there are workers that practice different faiths or none at all.

In conclusion, features such as family management and the paternalistic-benevolent leadership style maintain the traditional corporate culture dimension within Mexican companies. It may be perplexing to observe how this set of cultural characteristics coexists with a different set of practices associated with modern management methods. In this regard, multinational and domestic Mexican companies are portrayed in management textbooks or teaching cases as successful companies. Alfa (diversified conglomerate), Bimbo, and CEMEX are frequently mentioned in MBA strategy courses because they represent the evolution from a traditional to a modern management corporate culture. In contrast to the prevailing view, we propose that both dimensions are present in the same company and coexist by means of unique management practices. Next, we discuss the analysis of the modern dimension of Mexican corporate culture.

Modern Characteristics of the Mexican Corporate Culture

Most of Mexico's modern corporations operate in the form of business groups. Economic historians and management researchers have analyzed Mexican business groups from their early creation at the beginning of the 20th century to the period of economic opening in the 1990s (Flores and Dávila 94; Hoshino 302; Sargent 16). In general, most of the business groups maintain the same characteristics: They are diversified in non-related fields of economic activity; they have developed international strategic alliances or other forms of international collaboration; they have financed their national and international expansion through internal resources; they have internationalized their operations after the economic opening of the country; and they continue to be managed by the third or fourth generation of the family founders. Examples of modern management practices in these Mexican organizations are participatory management, advanced manufacturing systems, professional talent development, innovation in technological and production processes, as well as CSR initiatives.

Participatory Management

Several empirical studies on Mexican companies report the use of committees for different purposes. For example, a case study of an international joint venture between a Mexican conglomerate and a U.S. company in the auto-parts industry identified inter-hierarchical and inter-functional committees as central elements to the management style of the company (Dávila and Garcia 379). This company obtained the Ibero-American Quality Award for its management and manufacturing processes. Inter-hierarchical and inter-functional committees are an effective mechanism for reducing the effects of steep hierarchies and leveraging managerial efficiency. In another case study of a Mexican multinational, the inter-hierarchical committees were central for introducing managerial changes in the company headquarters and its international subsidiaries (Molina 110).

Thus, a common characteristic of today's Mexican manufacturing firms that break away from traditional practices is that there are fewer hierarchical levels than were reported in the literature before the opening of the economy (see De la Cerda and Núñez 90). Moreover, the use of diverse types of organizational committees increases the cooperation and commitment that companies need from their employees. This mechanism fits well with the collectivistic-oriented practices preferred by Mexican workers (Dávila and Elvira 9). In our view, organizational committees were the underpinnings that prepared Mexican companies for successfully managing the abrupt changes in the economic, social and political business environment.

Competitiveness in Manufacturing

The first steps toward competitiveness in manufacturing started with the export-oriented Maquiladora Program (labor intensive in-bond manufacturing) in 1965 (Gómez 59). The program allowed foreign assembly plants to be located on the Mexican side of the northern border to manufacture diverse goods such as electronic parts or textiles, using tax-free foreign machinery and components. The output of the assembly processes was to be returned to the U.S. for final assembly or packing. Having the highest support from government during the economic opening in 1986, the program underwent several modifications aimed at keeping the manufacturing process in the country and attaining independence from the original U.S. investments. Due to these efforts, the program had both positive effects and limitations. Among the positive effects, scholars identified an increment in employment and exports as well as the modernization and diversification of companies' production networks. Limitations include an increased dependency on the U.S. economy, limited contributions to the overall value added to products, and a lack of integration with local production networks (Gómez 57). Today, some maquiladoras and other foreign-owned facilities in Mexico are totally automated and can be classified as fourth-generation companies. The reason is that information systems allow these facilities to perform coordination activities of the value chain similar to those of the company's central office, including innovation, knowledge transfer and participation in regional innovation systems (Carrillo and Lara 23). Although the academic debate on generalized spillovers of technologies to local firms remains inconclusive (Görg and Greenaway 171), the Mexican auto-parts and aerospace components sectors have benefited from these technological advances, for which the country is globally recognized as a competitive location.

The competitiveness of the manufacturing sector has also been driven by the adoption of information systems, which today are a requirement for participating in international production networks. Therefore, only small firms operating at a local level still function without these tools. In contrast, major Mexican companies manage their manufacturing through the most advanced information systems in the world, allowing them to base operational decisions on real-time information. For example, CEMEX began by automating plant operations and then moved on to sales and accounting operations. At the end of the 1980s, it had set up a satellite network that could transmit all internal data to its headquarters in Monterrey, Mexico's northern business capital. International business scholars attribute the success of CEMEX in its early national and international expansion to this feature:

A few established companies have leveraged emerging information-infrastructure capabilities to become more efficient and innovative—and are leading change in their industries. For example, Mexico's global cement-manufacturing company, CEMEX, caused a stir in an industry not known for its dynamism—the cement industry. Its model features small batches of cement mix sold as needed over the Web and delivered promptly [Prahalad and Krishnan].

Successful companies develop internal group norms that are part of a culture of pride, which generally accepts and adopts modern management models. In the 1980s, the quality movement arrived in Mexico, leading to a quality-oriented culture in major companies, their suppliers and clients. Examples of modern manufacturing practices adopted are as follows: total quality management, lean manufacturing, just-in-time inventories, *kanban* internal manufacturing system, Six Sigma, automated controlled supply chains, and robotics (e.g., NEMAK—the world's leading aluminum cylinder head manufacturer—has over 100 robots operating in its plants). Moreover, many Mexican companies have been certified by the International Organization for Standardization (ISO 9000). Due to this competitive manufacturing culture, Mexican companies are now taking part in global supply chains. For example, in the auto parts industry, Saint-Gobain, the world's leading glass manufacturer for several applications, established a plant in Morelos (near Mexico City) in 1996 because of the region's competitiveness in auto parts.

Several societal actors have participated in the development of a highly competitive manufacturing culture. The Secretary of Economy established the National Quality Award in 1986 and later introduced the National Competitiveness Model that can be transferred to any company that wants to participate. Higher education institutions and research centers have also contributed to the development and adoption of modern manufacturing systems. Major universities and engineering schools work closely with the industry and jointly develop patents and other innovations. Important consulting firms also operate in the region and specialized publications such as *Manufactura*, a major national magazine, provide the latest news on best practices as well as philosophies and options for modern industry equipment, supporting the development of such a culture. Other important actors are the industry associations that offer diverse services for their members and organize conferences and meetings for knowledge transfer and networking.

A manufacturing culture oriented towards competitiveness would not be possible without competitive managerial talent. Human capital is highly valuable to international multinationals such as Schneider Electric, a company that arrived in Mexico 60 years ago as a traditional manufacturer but is currently developing engineering and innovation at its Monterrey Innovation and Development Center that operates with 125 engineers working on different innovation projects, with plans to expand its R&D function to a total of 300 engineers (Coronado). Of course, one might wonder how representative these examples are of the whole country. In a large study on the application of advanced management practices across twenty countries, Mexican firms came out at rank 11, behind the U.S., Japan, and several Western European countries but ahead of Chile, Argentina, and Brazil, as well as China and India (Bloom, Genakos, Sadun, and Van Reenen 19).

Managerial Capability

Corporate modern business culture in Mexico is based on the distinctive managerial capability of its executives. Despite having a family-oriented corporate culture, top management teams—family members, close relatives or other prominent members of the society—have been trained in prestigious business schools around the world; most of them are bilingual (Spanish-English) and have had international work experience (Sargent 18). Moreover, the number of Mexican executives on international assignments is increasing steadily.

Tortilla maker Gruma received an in-company MBA program for its executives in development from the University of Texas at Austin. Other major universities' representatives and business school deans from such prestigious schools as Harvard and MIT visit Mexican cities quite frequently to keep in touch with their graduates. CEMEX implemented a conspicuous leadership development program with the help of Tecnologico de Monterrey (Mexico), Stanford University (U.S.), and INSEAD (France).

Personal relationships are an important element of any corporate culture. Accounts of traditional work culture portray Mexican employees as being afraid of conflict and confrontations because of the personal relationships that operate at the workplace (Dávila and Elvira 7). However, Mexico's modern executives behave quite assertively. In an indepth case study, it was found that executives spoke up in meetings without being afraid of negotiations and confrontations. In fact, assertiveness increased with the person's level of education. The sense of business was stronger than any personal relationships or commitments (Dávila and Garcia 382). Furthermore, participatory management, competitive manufacturing practices, and the development of managerial capabilities are the appropriate foundations for moving towards a culture of innovation.

Innovation

Although Mexican companies should have all the elements to develop significant innovations, by international standards, this is a pending assignment for most corporations, even though a significant number of companies has started to create strategies for driving innovation. Among the most recent strategies, Mexican companies have developed bridges among different socioeconomic actors. For small and medium size firms, support for innovations is being offered by several government-sponsored institutions.

The Secretariat of Economy and the National Council of Science and Technology (CONACYT) have developed a joint fund for micro, small and medium enterprises that develop technological innovation projects and compete in niche markets with high added value in areas such as biotechnology, agribusiness, advanced manufacturing, and clean technologies, among others.

The Multilateral Investment Fund, a member of the Inter-American Development Bank Group, has approved an investment in the Venture Innovation Fund II, a Mexican early-stage venture capital fund that will provide long-term financing and value-added guidance on business development for up to 14 start-ups in Mexico (MIF).

According to the 2012 Survey on Technological Research and Development, conducted by the National Institute for Statistics and Geography in collaboration with CONACYT, only 5 percent of the companies surveyed performed any type of technological research and development (TR&D) (Lino). The study also revealed that 70 percent of all TR&D investments were made in just three federal entities: Nuevo León (northern Mexico), Mexico State (near Mexico City) and Mexico City itself, while other areas of the country show little or no investment in innovation. Regarding the type of innovation, the same study showed that among the 11.7 percent of the companies that reported some type of innovation (whether technology-based or not), 8.2 percent introduced a new product or implemented a new process, and 10.3 percent developed at least one innovation project. The projects mentioned were related to products (goods or services), industrial processes (including production methods), organizational processes, and marketing innovations (Lino).

Mexican companies are also implementing some bolder strategies for acquiring innovation capabilities, such as strategic alliances with international technological partners built around knowledge transfer initiatives. Although the management of international collaboration agreements is typically quite complex, Mexican executives have been able to meet those challenges because of their highly developed managerial capabilities. Vitro (glass conglomerate) and Alfa (diversified conglomerate) have successfully managed international collaboration agreements and joint ventures for more than 20 years. A case study in the steel industry shows that innovative knowledge comes from international suppliers, increasing the Mexican company's technological learning capabilities in investment, production and support functions, which resulted in higher levels of productivity (Jasso and Ortega 81).

Increased investment in innovation by Mexican companies translates into more highly skilled jobs. This tendency will directly impact the development of the country and the quality of people's lives. A culture of innovation emerges in organizations that promote a sense of community inside and outside the company. Thus, innovation has also been identified in CSR initiatives by Mexican organizations.

Social Responsibility

CSR is quite present in major Mexican companies (see Table 1). There are diverse examples of a serious concern of the companies for their employees' well-being and for the local community. Common examples include social assistance, support for education, public health, the arts, and environmental protection. CEMEX, for example, has launched a microcredit program to help poor people build their own houses. Legislation also supports companies in their efforts to develop green technologies. It is common to find companies that invest in water recycling programs, gas emissions and pollution control. Many companies have staff in charge of all of these programs and usually transfer their best practices to their suppliers and clients. For example, the Cuauhtémoc Moctezuma brewery operates under the corporate policy of restoring natural resources towards their sustainability and moving all the supply chain towards a green economy. Another Mexican company that operates under the same corporate policy is Herdez (processed food) (Jimenez). On the other hand, according to the business magazine Forbes Mexico, in 2013, only 28 Mexican companies had invested 19 percent (USD$400.3) more than in 2012 in programs and technologies to minimize their carbon footprint (Jimenez).

Table 1. *Forbes Mexico*'s List of the 36 Companies with Highest Social Commitment

Bio-Pappel	Grupo Herdez	Ford Motor Company México	Schneider Electric
Grupo Bimbo	Cuauhtémoc Moctezuma	Tenaris Tamsa	Empresas ICA
Nestlé			3M México
Continental Automotive	Procter and Gamble (P&G) México	British American Tobacco México	Arcos Dorados México (McDonald's)
Ternium México	Novartis Farmacéutica	Pfizer México	Dow Chemical
CEMEX México	Walmart de México	Daimler	Xerox

Rassini Piedras
 Negras
Coca-Cola
 FEMSA (KOF)
Kellogg Company
 México
General Motors
 de México

Hoteles City Express
Nissan Mexicana
 Automotriz
Iberostar
Alfa Holding
Grupo Posadas

Grupo Elektra
Hard Rock
Grupo Salinas
The Home Depot
 México
PepsiCo México

Source: Adapted from Jimenez.

Due to the variety of initiatives in CSR, one can say that Mexican companies seek a sustainable development approach in their social actions.

Toward a Mexican Corporate Culture for the 21st Century

The corporate cultures of Mexican companies share many common traits. On the one hand, we observe traditional cultural characteristics, and on the other, in the same companies we find a culture that supports modern management practices. This mix of cultural characteristics tends to be effective for emerging economies, such as Mexico. Culture functions as a glue that assures that the required economic, social and political elements are available for the implementation of managerial practices, balancing traditional and modern elements.

The 20th century finds Mexico to be in the midst of technological developments and foreign investments. However, local culture will continue to preserve traditional elements that bring social stability, labor peace, and modern management. Where these elements are present, Mexican companies look well prepared for their future development.

Discussion Questions

1. Identify the main competitiveness achievements of Mexican companies. What cultural elements support such achievements?

2. Review the corporate governance practices of CEMEX as reported on its website; what cultural elements can you identify that support such practices?

3. What are the underpinnings of the paternalistic-benevolent leadership style in Mexican organizations?

4. In the U.S. business culture, nepotism is usually frowned upon. What is the Mexican attitude towards such practices?

5. What is the role in Mexican society that businesses are expected to perform in terms of economic development?

6. Name the major obstacles for women's career advancement in Mexican companies.

7. How would you involve the human resource area in a Mexican company to develop workers' positive behaviors and attitudes towards organizational committees?

8. What is the agenda pending for Mexican companies to reach a higher level of global competitiveness?

Key Learning Terms

Contemporary management practices: Management practices aimed at increasing the efficiency and quality of work and implemented by professional managers.

Hybrid business cultures: Co-existence of traditional and contemporary elements within the business culture of one company.

Paternalism: Employee-worker relationship where protection and caring is exchanged for loyalty and compliance.

Succession management: Strategic planning within family firms to pass on the leadership position in an orderly way from one generation to another.

Traditional work culture: Values and behaviors of people in organizations that have been preserved from pre-industrial times.

REFERENCES

Alba, Carlos. *Historia y desarrollo industrial de México*. Mexico: Confederación de Cámaras Industriales y Colegio de Jalisco, 1988. Print

Bensusan, Graciela. "Las reformas laborales en América Latina." *Teorías sociales y estudios de trabajo: Nuevos enfoques*. Ed. Enrique De la Garza Toledo. México: Cuadernos A. Temas de Innovación Social Anthropos, UAM-I, 2006. 367–84. Print.

Bloom, Nicholas, et al. "Management Practices Across Firms and Countries." *Academy of Management Perspectives* 26.1 (2012): 12–33.

Carrillo, Jorge, and Arturo Lara. "Nuevas capacidades de coordinación centralizada." *Industria, trabajo y migración internacional en la frontera norte de México*. México: El Colegio de la Frontera Norte, 2010. 17–45. Print

CNNExpansión. "Las 50 Mujeres más Poderosas de Expansión: Ranking 2014." *CNNExpansión*. Cable News Network, 2014. Web. 30 Oct. 2014.

Colonado, Sonia. "Schneider resalta talento humano de NL." *El financiero*. Grupo Multimedia Lauman, 22 Oct. 2014. Web. 31 Oct. 2014.

Dávila, Anabella, and Marta M. Elvira. "Culture and Human Resource Management in Latin America." *Managing Human Resources in Latin America: An Agenda for International Leaders*. Ed. Anabella Dávila and Marta M. Elvira. Oxford: Routledge, 2005. 3–24. Print.

Dávila, Anabella, and Marta M. Elvira. "Humanistic Leadership: Lessons from Latin America." *Journal of World Business* 47 (2012): 548–554.

Dávila, Anabella, and Edmundo García. "Cultural Symbols as Change Agents: International Joint Ventures in the Mexican Context." *Transformative Organizations: A Global Perspective*. Ed. Vipin Gupta. New Dehli: Sage, 2004. 373–86.

De la Cerda, José, and Francisco Núñez. *La administración en desarrollo: Problemas y avances de la administración en México*. Mexico City: Instituto Internacional de Capacitación y Estudios Empresariales, 1993. Print.

De la Torre, Gerardo. "Sucesión planeada." *El financiero*. Grupo Multimedia Lauman, 21 July 2014. Web. 29 Oct. 2014.

Elvira, Marta M., and Anabella Dávila. "Emergent Directions for Human Resource Management Research in Latin America." *International Journal of Human Resources Management* 16, no. 12 (2005): 2265–82.

Flores, Óscar, and Antonio Olvera. "La industrialización en el noreste de México." *Historia y desarrollo industrial de México*. Ed. Carlos Alba. Mexico: Confederación de Cámaras Industriales and Colegio de Jalisco, 1988.

Flores, Óscar, and Anabella Dávila. "Reestructuración de las empresas siderúrgicas en Monterrey ante la apertura comercial, 1970–1998." *Integración regional de América Latina: Procesos y actores*. Ed. Jaime Behar, Rita Giacalone and Noemí B. Mellado. Stockholm: Instituto de Estudios Latinoamericanos de la Universidad de Estocolmo, 2001. 87–112.

Garza, Cristina. "State of CSR in Mexico: Humble Beginnings, Promising Future." *Triple Pundit: People, Planet, Profit*. Triple Pundit, 13 July 2013. Web. 25 Jan. 2015.

Gómez, Carolina, and Juan I. Sánchez. "HR's Strategic Role within MNCs: Helping Build Social Capital

in Latin America." *International Journal of Human Resource Management* 16, no. 12 (2005): 2189–200.
Gómez, María del Carmen. "El desarrollo de la industria de la maquila en México." *Problemas del desarrollo. Revista Latinoamericana de economía* 35, no. 138 (2004): 57–83.
Görg, Holger, David Greenaway. "Much Ado About Nothing? Do Domestic Firms Really Benefit from Foreign Direct Investment?" *World Bank Research Observer* 19, no. 2 (2004): 171–79.
Hartmann, Andreas M., and Anabella Dávila. "Ideologies and Practices of Management in Latin America." *Economic Growth and Technological Change in Latin America*. Ed. Bryan Christiansen. Hershey: IGI Global, 2014. 19–43. Print.
Hoshino, Taeko. "Indigenous Corporate Groups in Mexico—High Growth and Qualitative Change in the 1970s to the Early 1980s." *The Developing Economies* 28, no. 3 (1990): 302–28.
Howell, Jon P., et al. "Leadership and Culture in Mexico." *Journal of World Business* 42 (2007): 449–62.
Ibeh, Kevin, et al. "How Focused Are the World's Top-Rated, Business Schools on Educating Women for Global Management?" *Journal of Business Ethics* 83 (2008): 65–83.
Jasso, Javier, and Rodrigo Ortega. "Acumulación de capacidades tecnológicas locales en un grupo industrial siderúrgico en México." *Contaduría y administración* 223 (2007): 69–89.
Jimenez, Ismael. "36 empresas con un alto compromiso ambiental." *Forbes Mexico*, 11 Nov. 2014. Web. 25 Jan. 2015.
Lino, Manuel. "Empresas mexicanas, sólo 5% hace investigación." *El economista*. Periódico El Economista, 14 Nov. 2013. Web. 31 Oct. 2014.
Logsdon, Jeanne, et al. "Corporate Social Responsibility in Large Mexican Firms." *Journal of Corporate Citizenship* 21 (2006): 51–60.
Martinez, Patricia G. "Paternalism as a Positive Form of Leadership in the Latin American Context: Leader Benevolence, Decision-Making Control and Human Resource Management Practices." *Human Resources in Latin America: An Agenda for International Leaders*. Ed. Marta M. Elvira and Anabella Dávila. Oxford: Routledge, 2005. 75–93. Print.
Molina, Christiane. *The Influence of Institutional Logics and Identification of Practice Transfer Processes*. Dissertation, Tecnologico de Monterrey. Monterrey, 2014. Print.
Multilateral Investment Fund (MIF). "MIF Invests in Mexican Venture Fund for Services Innovation." Multilateral Investment Fund, 3 June 2014. Web. 30 Mar. 2015.
Nichols, Nancy A. "From Complacency to Competitiveness: An Interview with Vitro's Ernesto Martens." *Harvard Business Review* 71, no. 5 (1993): 162–71.
Pellegrini, Ekin K., and Terri A. Scandura. "Paternalistic Leadership: A Review and Agenda for Future Research." *Journal of Management* 34, no. 3 (2008): 566–93.
Prahalad, Coimbatore K., Krishnan, M. S. "The Dynamic Synchronization of Strategy and Information Technology." *MIT Sloan Management Review*, 15 July 2002. Web. 31 Oct. 2014.
Rascón, Octavio, et al. *La Educación en Ingeniería en México y el Mundo*. Mexico: Academia de Ingeniería de Mexico & CONACYT, 2013. Academia de Ingeniería A.C. Web. 1 Nov. 2014.
Reygadas, Luis. "Estereotipos rotos. El debate sobre la cultura laboral mexicana." *Cultura y Trabajo en México. Estereotipos, Prácticas y Representaciones*. Ed. Rocío Guadarrama. Mexico: UAM, Juan Pablos Editor & Fundación Friedrich Ebert, 1998. Print.
Sargent, John. "Getting to know the neighbors: Grupos in Mexico." *Business Horizons*, 44 6. (2001): 16–24.
Sargent, John, and Suad Ghaddar. "International Success of Business Groups as an Indicator of National Competitiveness: The Mexican Example." *Latin American Business Review* 2 no. 3/4 (2001): 97–121.
Sobrino, Jaime. "Desempeño industrial en las principales ciudades de México, 1980–2003." *Estudios demográficos y urbanos* 22, no. 2 (2007): 243–90.
UNIDO. Competitive Industrial Performance Index, 2010. Web. 1 Nov. 2014.

Entrepreneurship in Mexico
Past and Present

Jorge Olmos-Arrayales

It is common to hear Mexicans ask themselves, "If we are so creative, why can't we do things better?" Sometimes they will say that they have invented so much that there is nothing left to invent. These phrases create amazement and a popular awareness about the inventive capabilities of Mexicans which, based on an environment with few opportunities for growth, allows them to look for alternative forms of subsistence even if they are not always part of the formal market.

Since Mexico's birth as a nation, a pro-activeness to create self-employment alternatives has pervaded a great part of the population, something that has not always translated into the generation of more and better companies and jobs but rather into initiatives of little added value that condemn people to remain on the outside of not only national but also international competitiveness.

In areas of a different nature, Carlos Slim—honorary chairman of America Móvil and number two on Forbes' 2015 billionaires list—is recognized and distinguished because of his strategic vision and great ability to make the decisions that have taken him to the top of the aforementioned list, but there are also a dozen Mexican businessmen whose business conglomerates are able to distinguish themselves and are on the vanguard, a situation that contrasts with the current national scenario and that demonstrates a very different reality about the Mexicans that decide to start a business or open a non-profit organization. Finally, there are people in both situations who identify a problem or need and look for resources and decide to confront such a situation by offering a product or service. In other words, there are entrepreneurs who decide to take risks and venture into starting their initiatives.

This essay will consider micro, small and medium businesses—MYPIMES—and the entrepreneurs who start them.

Current Situation

Table 1.1 takes a look at the business panorama in Mexico and it is possible to notice the specific importance that micro, small and medium businesses have in the country.

Table 1.1 Statistics of the Total Economic Units in Mexico (Millions)

México	2004	2009
Total number of businesses (in millions)	4.29	5.14

Source: INEGI Census, 2004 and 2009, www.inegi.gob.mx.

Despite having official data from 2009, it is possible to observe an increase in the number of economic units present in the country. Here our attention should be on the specific importance that each category holds in regards to its contribution to the Gross Domestic Product (GDP). In Table 1.2 we can arrive at an approximation of that.

Table 1.2 Contribution to GDP by Type of Economic Unit

Type of Economic Unit	2004	2009	% Contribution to GDP	% Change in Economic Units
Micro	4,075,602	4,888,854	8.3	19.9
Small	167,314	205,762	9.0	22.9
Medium	38,610	41,152	17.4	6.6
Large	8,580	10,288	65.3	19.9
Total	4,290,106	5,144,056	100.0	19.9

Sources: INEGI Census, 2004 and 2009; IMEF, Análisis Estratégico para el desarrollo de la Mipyme en México, 2010, p. 8.

The previous table shows us that despite both the micro and small businesses in Mexico representing the majority of the economic units, their real contribution to the country's economy remains low when compared to the contribution and influence that the large economic units have; it is also possible to highlight that the medium businesses do not show a growth dynamic like the previous ones, which allows us to presume that they do not have the natural evolution of growth and consolidation like that of a micro to small and small to medium business. This allows us to take a look at the situations that Mexican entrepreneurs assuredly face not only to start but also to operate their organization and make it grow.

An important fact that allows us to see what happens with MIPYMES from another perspective is related to a direct consequence that entrepreneurs provoke the moment they decide to begin operations (under either formal or informal circumstances) and refers to the capacity to generate jobs. According to the National Institute for Statistics and Geography (INEGI), 95 percent of the total economic units had ten people working in a microbusiness, generating a large quantity of jobs that the government and large businesses are unable to absorb (2010). This does not mean that they are value-added or well-paid jobs, a situation that contrasts with some positions that are available in large companies.

In 2015, the INEGI published the interactive website Directorio Estadístico Nacional de Unidades Económicas (DENUE). It is a report in which the data of 4,926,061 businesses in the country were concentrated so that the reader can access the most relevant data. But it is important to note that all fixed establishments are included without regard to their authorized registration, so some of the referenced businesses are in the informal sector. This provides a pattern to begin analyzing the existing cultural aspects that have to do with the motivation and desire to start a business but not necessarily with the preparation or planning, and much less within the formal market. That is to say, "We'll see how we do" and "If it works out ... we will wait as long as we can before registering with Hacienda" (the Mexican IRS). Because of this, it is important to indicate that the government has made important strides to incorporate more people into the formal economy in order to eliminate the informal culture. It is also important to mention that the government does not seem to show itself as transparent or accountable in regards to reporting what it does with the taxes of those who are in the formal economy. That is why it is common to hear people say that "they want to charge First World taxes in exchange for Third of Fifth World services."

Table 1.3 Classification of Mexican Companies (Based on Number of Employees)

Size	Sector	Range in Number of Workers	Range in Annual Sales (Millions of Pesos)
Micro	All	Up to 10	Up to $4
Small	Commerce	From 11 to 30	From $4.01 to $100
	Industry and Services	From 11 to 50	From $4.01 to $100
Medium	Commerce	From 31 to 100	From $100.1 to $250
	Services	From 51 to 100	From $100.1 to $250
	Industry	From 51 to 250	From $100.1 to $250

Source: NAFIN, www.nafin.gob.mx, 2009.

In Table 1.3 we can recognize that a large percentage of entrepreneurial initiatives in Mexico greatly influence employment in diverse economic sectors. However, this does not necessarily signify that they possess high value within the market; they maintain aspects of a traditional character.

To demonstrate this, in Table 1.4 it is possible to identify that a large percentage of typical or traditional products remain within a range of low added value contrasting with the production of high value goods whose origin is principally large businesses.

Table 1.4 Classification of the Industry by Technological Intensity

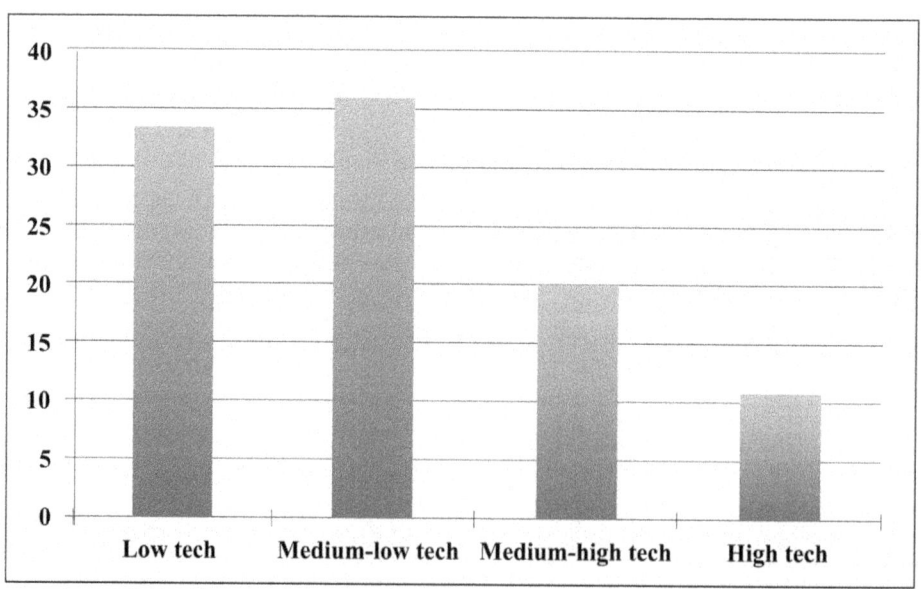

Source: Taken from Clemente Ruiz Durán, Nueva política industrial. Opción para un desarrollo sustentable e inclusivo en México, Political Analysis Foundation Series of Friedrich Ebert Stiftung, *2013, p. 23. Elaborated by the author based on information from INEGI, the 2009 economic census and the OECD, classification of the industry by technological intensity.*

Vertical Axis = Added Value Manufacturing

33.4 percent = Food, beverage, tobacco, textile, leather, wood, paper and printing; sources of innovation: principally from the following chain providers: machinery, chemical, etc., and from quality norms and regulations.

35.9 percent = Petroleum and its derivatives, plastics and rubber, basic metals, non-metallic mineral based products; sources of innovation: innovation centered on input-output processes with an increase in design orientation.

20 percent = Machinery and equipment, electronic apparatuses, transportation equipment; sources of innovation: design, processes, complex production systems, value chain, business-level research and development.

10.8 percent = Computer equipment, communications, measuring and electronic components and accessories, aerospace and pharmaceutical industries; sources of innovation: high degree of research and firm development, with interaction of research centers and universities. Just as there are entrepreneurial proposals with diverse levels of added value, there are a series of alternatives in scenarios that can impact the performance of the initiative. In other words, practices and very timely actions are mixed by the company for its growth and the formality that it may or may not have. This is done in such a way that within the structure of the organizations, low production persists in regards to their stake in traditional initiatives, representing a great challenge for the country, in other words, many micro and/or small business initiatives but of low value and impact for the economy as a whole and for the entrepreneurs and their families specifically.

Table 1.5 shows a categorization that tries to clear up the conditions in which businesses in Mexico can be found.

Table 1.5 Definition of Terms: Modern, Traditional, Formal and Informal

Category	Characteristics
Modern	—Makes use of business standards practices such as formal controls, resource distribution and administration systems. —Contracts qualified personnel, uses machinery and information technology to increase productivity —Has growth-oriented strategies and goals —Can be a micro-business
Traditional	—Does not use business tools or methods —Employees may or may not be formally contracted —Does not invest in equipment or technology to improve productivity
Formal	—Registered businesses —Pay taxes —Employees have rights
Informal	—Are not controlled by regulations —Are not officially registered —Principally exposed to and vulnerable to bribery

Source: E. Bolio, et al., *A Tale of Two Mexicos: Growth and Prosperity in a Two Speed Economy*, 2014, p. 5.

What is certain is that there are plenty of reasons to exist and stay in the informal market, but such a situation does not contribute to the formal economy and impacts the level of growth and productivity of the country as a whole.

When you listen to the entrepreneurs directly, you hear that they did not always have the resolve to turn their backs on the idea of formality because that was their original plan; a structural framework pervades that many times discourages to a greater or lesser degree access to formality.

To be able to achieve an increase in formality and boost productivity, multiple actions that foment a framework of certainty and fair play are required even though it is not always perceived in this way. Just trying to aspire to have greater dynamism and growth through the use of opportunities, it is necessary to create situations that encourage the generation of modern and formal businesses, but to find such a scenario there are high regulatory costs to pay. This implies the need to remove a series of barriers that impede such ends. Table 1.6 shows a series of measures that could support entrepreneurial efforts.

Table 1.6 Barriers That Impede Productivity and Growth

1) Reorient regulatory obstacles and remove deterrents to growth:
It is necessary to change the current conditions that do not encourage the economic entity to act in a homogenous manner and generate a gap between organizations.
  —**Reduce regulatory complexity:** Starting costs (and the time it takes for red tape) as well as resources demand for an expanding business increase.
  —**Increase the effective application of what should be (the law):** Enrollment in social security, adherence to environmental regulations, etc., do not necessarily take place, generating inequality during competition in the market.
  —**Remove the incentives to stay small and unproductive:** It is easy to establish that the stand owners in open air markets have fewer costs than established businesses.
  —**Generate greater labor flexibility:** Following regulations complicates life for the micro and small business, so many entrepreneurs prefer dealing with internal agreements.

2) Improve access to capital: The lack of capital drowns and/or frustrates not only the beginning but the expansion of many businesses.

3) Improve and increase the access to energy and infrastructure.
  —**Increase energy productivity:** In México, commercial use of energy costs 73 percent more than in the U.S.
  —**Drop in the infrastructure gap:** An estimated investment of $71 billion per year through 2025 to support the desired growth.
  —**Development of the abilities required for the job:** On average, Mexicans have few years of formal education. Generating scenarios with better preparation is necessary.
  —**Improve security:** It is one of the greater concerns of society as a whole.

Source: E. Bolio, et al., A Tale of Two Mexicos: Growth and Prosperity in a Two Speed Economy, 2014, pp. 12–15.

Due to situations like the ones previously mentioned, the spirit of the people who decide to start and then try to grow a business is not necessarily the best, but the way in which Mexicans face this situation is still palpable and admirable. It is just that the easiest alternative for starting and growing a business in many cases continues being informality. It is very common and lamentable to see informal street stands selling movies, electronics, clothes, fake brand-name apparel and food and to see temporary markets that steal electricity from street poles without paying taxes—stands that even surround the federal Supreme Court. Vendors already know that they need to pay their leader who represents them before the authorities in order to avoid any legal headaches. It is not difficult to describe the ease with which the informal market presents itself every day before the authorities, but in the end a social attitude of tolerance has developed among citizens and institutions. On one hand the citizen says, "If you the government doesn't provide opportunities for me, I will generate them myself, but don't bother me," or what ends up being the same, "If you won't help me … don't take anything away from me!"

If certain barriers that limit the creation of businesses have already been mentioned, it is equally important to keep in mind that the negative impact on productivity influences competition on a local, state and national level. Sadly, seeking specialized training in a natural and almost instinctive way does not form part of the cultural mindset unless it is required by an employer or is necessary within the framework of the formal economy. The government has generated initiatives like CONOCER (www.conocer.gob.mx), an initiative that established competitive standards so that any person can obtain certifications based not only on their knowledge, but also on their experience, ability and attitudes.

Another key initiative that the government also started is the Instituto Nacional del Emprendedor (The National Entrepreneur Institute, www.inadem.gob.mx) in order to support as many entrepreneurs as possible. Individuals able to see the an entrepreneurial ecosystem, apply for an on-line skills diagnosis related to entrepreneurship and are also able to look for potential support from the government no matter the stage of their initiatives.

What Happens to the Start-Ups?

It is possible to find information about the kind of companies that open in Mexico (INEGI) and it is also possible to identify that the majority are going to focus on commercialization or service features. Consequently, opening a new company with a certain technological ingredient is not a constant. On the other hand, Mexican entrepreneurs lack a greater vision that includes strategy and planning, according to what is presented in the bibliographic material "El libro del fracaso" (Fuck Up Nights y el Instituto de Emprendimiento Eugenio Garza Lagüera), which shows in its study that the lack of assessment and lack of ability to reach the break-even point and a lack of clear communication with the family in regards to new challenges (no vacation, different lifestyle than the previous one, etc.) provokes failures that keep entrepreneurs out of continuing with their initiatives (Almada). It is common to hear that a new business was started with great verve and an expectation that things would go well, putting aside the possibilities of growth and consolidation because that is what should be inherent from the beginning in the people and/or in the group of people in charge of stated initiative. That is why it is necessary to question oneself about the entrepreneurs' level of introspection and/or self-awareness to clearly identify their strengths as well as their areas of opportunity in order to reach a positive balance between administrative preparation and the planning that has been insufficient up to now. A cultural trait among Mexicans has to do with the famous phrase that is applied when the national soccer team has finished a match: "We won" or "They lost." Mexicans look to take ownership in the success of something that they cannot even control or intervene in directly, but there is an immediate rejection of the "other person" who fails. Could this be a clear symptom of the fear of failure?

In his book *Esquezofrenia*, Dr. Jacobo Neuman clearly shows how Mexicans speak with many excuses about why it is not possible to do certain things because everything becomes an excuse: "It's because I didn't know," "It's because I thought," "*Es que…*" (http://www.wikipyme.org/esquezofrenia/).

What Are Entrepreneurs Like?

We know that there are multiple factors that can make a person decide to create an initiative of economic character. Sometimes being unemployed is a great impulse. In others, certain elements exist that converge to give way to the formalization of the activity. The important detail here is that in Mexico there is a significant amount of people that culturally had been driven by external factors instead of internal factors. Here we are speaking of the romantic facet of being able to obtain great profits in the first months of the operation, even the fact that "I should continue the family business" whether it be a taco stand, a banquet hall or a law firm, businesses that most assuredly were funded by a grandparent and were passed down to the son but without the necessary scrutiny and oversight from the elder, thus jeopardizing the future impact the youngster will have on the business and creating a certain level of vulnerability for the source of family income. In other words, the cultural position that the Mexican family has on the value scale precedes the adequate management of the resources involved in the family-run organization. This is a situation that can differ greatly in North American businesses, ones that have placed an important emphasis on family succession to try to carry on the initiative begun by a predecessor, having a consequent intergenerational benefit (with or without the leadership of a family member) and a blunt philosophy of professionalism in the interior of the organization, looking to maintain a lifestyle aligned with the organization's values coming before personal values.

Additionally it is also commonplace in Mexican family entrepreneurial ventures that an individual or family will look to grow the business any way possible without a concrete plan for growth. Many of these businesses also lack contingency plans to assist family members who will run the business at a later time (especially should their time to take over the business come sooner than expected after an unexpected death).

In the same vein of "any way possible," there is another feature that prevails in diverse social strata which is related to machismo, since here the entrepreneur manifests that "I don't have to tell her how the business is going." That is to say that another aspect is shown that is rooted in regions of the country where the man is the one in charge and makes decisions, leaving the woman with the alternative of having to bear it because "it has always been this way" or simply taking a different path, generally with the children. Previously the point was made about paying more attention to the exterior than the interior; from the expression "That's life" to "This is how I want to live" there is a gap which later, and many times, generates a difficult load to carry.

In his book *Esquezofrenia*, Dr. Neuman shows in a very direct manner what corresponds to this particular way of viewing the world through situations or common responses that people have when the situation does not turn out how they were expecting ("expecting" isn't necessarily "working"; in Mexican Spanish all of the following phrases of excuse would begin with "es que," thus the title of the book *Esquezofrenia* – the term "es que" is also highlighted by Hyatt in his essay on communication).

Dr. Neuman also shared some other examples of how excuses are heavily rooted at the Mexican culture:

> "I didn't have enough time!"
> "Nobody told me!"
> "They don't pay me well!"
> "It can't be done!"
> "It doesn't work!"
> "We've always done it this way and it has worked fine!"
> "I don't know how to do it!"
> "It's too modern for me!"
> "You are going too fast!"

Dr. Neuman also makes an excellent contribution to cure this evil, and we can summarize it with the following:

> Think.
> Plan.
> Where am I?
> Where do I want to be?
> Define objectives and challenging goals.
> Evaluate available resources.
> Develop action plans.
> Measure your progress.
> Make decisions.
> Have initiative.
> Be creative, innovative, improve, do not copy.
> Forget about fear.
> Take risks.
> Act.
> Remember: Always with quality! [http://www.wikipyme.org/esquezofrenia/].

On the other hand, it is also possible to have contact with entrepreneurs that will do anything that comes their way in order to solidify their business but who, not being able to say no, many times over-schedule their activities, delivery times and obligations, and this makes them disappoint others. In other words, in general a Mexican will not tell someone "No" even if it is going to set him back. It is a very particular situation where one always wants to please the other, in the short term, even though it will not have a positive result for either party in the mid and long term (this is also further addressed in Hyatt). It was previously indicated that entrepreneurs need greater self-awareness and self-critical ability since, not being present in Mexican entrepreneurs, important aspects of time management and priorities are omitted. This awareness is more present in Anglo-Saxon culture where entrepreneurs evaluate their abilities and their situation in order to provide a response about the possibility of accepting the obligation and fulfilling it or not.

What Are the Challenges for Entrepreneurs?

The magazine *Expansión* has been carrying out a survey on Mexican entrepreneurs since 2004. The magazine published a special edition entitled "*Los Emprendedores del Año*" and in the 2013 edition *Queremos Conocerte* one can see that those surveyed stated that the principal problems that exist in the entrepreneurial ecosystem have to do with the following:

Training and consulting	38%
Lack of government support	38%
Lack of access to entrepreneurial capital	68%
Lack of access to bank finance	68%

From the previous information we can comment that in effect, from the need to update certain areas of knowledge and the unfavorable perception of the government, the idea of starting a business often paints an adverse and unfavorable picture. You can find government websites that have information about support for entrepreneurs, but usually one must know in precise detail all of the information published in order to obtain support, and if the entrepreneur is always busy trying to nurture his initiative, searching for institutionalized support becomes a titanic and almost impossible task which places the initiative in a state of operative and strategic precariousness. However, despite such a panorama there are companies that are able to excel and have been the motivation behind an analysis that had the goal of understanding the relevant internal and external factors. For example, after a study that was done the book *Análisis estratégico para el desarrollo del Mipymes en México* highlighted the success factors of MIPYMES:

- Being a medium sized company
- Having a manager with university education
- Having a formal, strategic plan
- Applying in a meaningful way and above all others the processes related to human resources
- Emphasizing the prevention of labor risks, administration of personnel, recruiting, selection
- Conducting performance evaluations [124].

An example of an organization that has gathered several of the previously mentioned elements and achieved success is Ingenia Muebles, www.ingeniamuebles.com.mx, a furniture company that has shown a tendency towards low cost furniture design and manufacture and whose business model has taken into consideration a close relationship with and attention towards customers. Just as Ernesto Vidal has noted, "We didn't invent a new style by ourselves. It was the customers who told us how they wanted their furniture. We just listened and reacted" (Suárez and Aguilar 118).

Therefore, it is imperative for Mexican entrepreneurs to look for spaces or forums for informational exchange and contact networks as well as platforms that include both training and the development of entrepreneurial skills. If that suggests a need, it also denotes another prevailing characteristic and that has to do with the idea "Why am I going to say what I have or what I know" since "another person can steal my idea and/or take advantage of my experience." In this vein, investing in human talents is valued little since one often asks, "What happens if I train them and they leave?" But here is another question that I heard some time ago and that I like to share with company decision makers: "If I don't train them and … they stay?" Such questioning should be more prevalent among everyone, with a desire to look for support and look for help instead of looking for the way not to be supported, in a desire of looking to collaborate rather than only compete.

Perspectives

But then what? What happens next? Surely there is a history of Mexican entrepreneurs in many areas and aspects of the country. Many times people—just as Scott Shickler and Jeff Waller argue in their book *The 7 Mindsets to Live Your Ultimate Life*—do not stop to consider all of the positive variables they have in their favor, and they pay more attention many times to all of the external and negative aspects. That is why when thinking about the future we should stop to consider other business alternatives in current sectors and, above all, sectors that have been identified as strategic. Entrepreneurs should keep looking to move their ideas and organizations and ideas forward, exploring new alternatives in order to offer, deliver and capture value among the market, for that reason the following table shares the current and future strategic sectors for all of the entrepreneurs who might be interested in consulting it.

Table 1.7 is a list of sectors that generate economic momentum. Strategic state sectors currently have an advantage, with opportunities for development and consolidation and by maintaining long-term, sustainable growth potential by maintaining.

Table 1.7 Current and Key State Sectors (Clusters)

State	Key Sectors (Clusters)	Future Sectors
Aguascalientes	Construction Products Agro-industrial Automotive Machinery and Equipment	Robotics Electronics Medical Services Textiles Information Technology
Baja California	Automotive Appliances Agro-industrial Metals and Machinery Construction Products Machinery and Equipment	
Baja California Sur	Tourism Agro-industrial Business Support Logistics	Energy Biotechnology
Campeche	Business Support Logistics Agro-industrial Tourism	Textiles and Clothing Research Services
Chiapas	Agro-industrial Tourism	Construction Products Textiles and Clothing Renewable Energy
Chihuahua	Automotive Construction Products Metals and Machinery Agro-industrial Electronics Machinery and Equipment	Appliances Information Services Tourism Aerospace Services and Equipment Wood Products
Coahuila	Automotive Agro-industrial Metals and Machinery Machinery and Equipment	Logistics Information Technology Aerospace Services and Equipment
Colima	Agro-industrial Logistics Tourism	Health Services Alternative Energy
Durango	Metals and Machinery Agro-industrial Business Support Wood Products	Research Services Tourism Renewable Energy Information Technology Logistics
Estado de México	Agro-industrial Chemical Products Automotive Mining Textiles	Tourism Logistics Aerospace Services and Equipment Research Services

State	Key Sectors (Clusters)	Future Sectors
Guanajuato	Agro-industrial Chemical Products Automotive Leather Footwear	Research Services Pharmaceuticals and Cosmetics Medical Equipment Tourism
Guerrero	Agricultural Products Tourism	Metals and Machinery
Hidalgo	Metals and Machinery Tourism Agro-industrial Construction Products	Renewable Energy Textiles and Clothing Logistics Information Technology Professional Services, Research and Innovation
Jalisco	Fashion Gourmet Medical Tourism Automotive and Autoparts Electronics Industry	Creative Industry Logistics Furniture and Decoration Information Technology Green and Alternative Energies Cultural Industry Aerospace Services and Equipment
Nayarit	Agro-industrial Tourism	Logistics Medical Services Pharmaceuticals and Cosmetics Information Services
Nuevo León	Construction Products Automotive Machinery and Equipment Appliances and Electronic Equipment	Medical Equipment Medical Services Information Technology Logistics Research Services Aerospace Services and Equipment
Michoacán	Information Services Agro-industrial Logistics Tourism	Textiles Metals and Machinery Construction Products
Oaxaca	Agro-industrial Tourism	Wood Products Textiles Construction Products Renewable Energy Metals and Machinery
Puebla	Automotive Textiles Metals and Machinery	Agro-industrial Tourism Metals and Machinery Medical Services Information Technology
Querétaro	Biotechnology and Food Automotive Appliances Business Support	Aerospace Service and Equipment Research Services Tourism Wood Products Information Technology
Quintana Roo	Business Support Tourism	Information Technology Renewable Energy Biomass Wood Products Agricultural and Farming Products Logistics

State	Key Sectors (Clusters)	Future Sectors
San Luis Potosí	Machinery and Equipment Logistics Automotive Metals and Machinery Agro-industrial Medical Tourism Construction Products	
Sinaloa	Agro-industrial Shipbuilding Industry Tourism	Biomass Wood Products Agricultural and Aqua-cultural Products Information Technology Aerospace Services and Equipment
Sonora	Automotive Agro-industrial Appliances Mining	Equipment and Services Information Technology Tourism Medical Equipment Renewable Energy
Tabasco	Agro-industrial Apoyos a negocios	Renewable Energy Metals and Machinery Tourism
Tamaulipas	Automotive Electronics Machinery and Equipment Chemicals and Petrochemicals	Agro-industrial Tourism Logistics Medical Equipment Research Services Renewable Energy Aerospace Services and Equipment
Tlaxcala	Tourism Agro-industrial Automotive Textiles	Chemicals and Petrochemicals Construction Products Plastic Products Metals and Machinery
Veracruz	Agro-industrial Chemical Products Metals and Machinery	Medical Products Renewable Energy Ports Construction Products
Yucatán	Logistics Tourism	Innovation Agro-industrial Renewable Energy
Zacatecas	Metals and Machinery Tourism Agro-industrial	Information Technology Mining and Non-metallic Products Automotive

Source: https://www.inadem.gob.mx/sectores_estrategicos.html. Elaborated by the author.

Recommendations for Entrepreneurs in the U.S. with Interest in Interacting with Mexicans

If you are exploring a possible commercial relationship with a Mexican entrepreneur, here are a few actions that could be useful:

From a personal perspective
　　Talk first about your family and not just about business (share photos, anecdotes, etc.)

Listen with care about the personal life of the Mexican entrepreneur (how he started, the relationships that are of greater influence in his business, etc.)

Show a genuine interest in the speaker (if that person notices your interest, you will have more opportunities to establish a comfortable and trusting environment in other phases of the relationship)

Develop patience (you will not necessarily get all of the details about your possible business in the first meeting)

Ask him how he sees himself in five or ten years (this way you will be able to see a certain level of planning or not)

From a business perspective

Establish commonalities (a favorable business climate will be useful)

Clearly identify the differences of opinion (remember that it is hard for them to say no; it is better to know this from the start)

Ask about the business structure (be clear about what infrastructure is available to you)

Ask for a business plan (which clearly indicates the actions to be followed in time and in form)

Use patience (there will always be personal/family aspects that will influence the company's performance)

Ask him how he sees his business in five or ten years (this way you will be able to see a certain level of planning or not)

Conclusion

In Mexico, creative attitudes toward a specific economic environment have been pushing people to develop alternatives in order to solve their problems from a day-to-day perspective. Due to a lack of a better environment that should encourage large companies to invest and generate more employees, and a plethora of governmental legal requirements that simply do not stimulate employment, people's option is to start up "something," but not necessarily based on a deep, professional and methodical market analysis, neither on a rigorous behavior for defining specific objectives in order to reduce or delete subjective perceptions about the organization. For those who finally "start-up," an alternative—and popular—way to do it will be through the informal economy in order to avoid legal requirements and associated costs related to start-up. Also, these types of new initiatives do not necessarily bring innovative proposals into the market and are limited to low value added proposal. Even though there is a level of entrepreneurship among Mexicans, there are some cultural aspects that influence entrepreneurs' behaviors—and their performance—on a lower or higher level such as locus of control (many consider that "external" elements determine their situation rather than internal ones), lack of training (it is about daily operating tasks that take them into routine rather than a self-actualization, constant training issue), family over performance aspects (due to he/she is from my "blood," I prefer to keep a certain type of stability no matter if this "respect" could have a negative impact in the organization), fear to rejection (due to I don't want people to reject me, I prefer not to say "No"), a potential of lack of strategic vision (since I am so involved at the operative level, and full of "emergencies," I have no time to look at the big picture) and so on.

If you are looking forward to setting up a professional relationship with a Mexican entrepreneur, you need to first of all understand that values could be different while doing business, this not necessarily negative or positive, simply different from other realities and it is important to know them in order to be prepared and come up with a relationship that could generate value for both parties.

Discussion Questions

1. How well do you know Mexicans—non-residents in the U.S.? Have you had the opportunity to interact with them?
2. Have you had the opportunity to speak with Mexican residents in the U.S.? What did you talk about?
3. Do you know any other Mexican entrepreneur besides Carlos Slim? Give a name, company and its business model.
4. What are the differences between entrepreneurship in Mexico and the U.S.?
5. What is the level of added value for the majority of ventures in Mexico?
6. Give suggestions for improving/increasing the quality of ventures in Mexico.
7. Discuss the main government support in the U.S. for entrepreneurs.
8. Discuss the main government support in Mexico for entrepreneurs.
9. How would you describe an informal business in Mexico?
10. Why do many entrepreneurs prefer to stay informal?

Key Learning Terms

Added value: The difference between the finished product/service and the incorporated costs referring to the production factors added to the same.

Informality: A situation which refers to the distancing from regulations and being outside of the regulations.

MIPYMES: Micro, small and medium-sized businesses (SME in English).

REFERENCES

Almada, A., et al. *El Libro del Fracaso*. México: FEMSA, el Gobierno de Guanajuato, Posible Promotora Social, 2014. Print.
Bolio, E., et al. *A Tale of Two Mexicos: Growth and Prosperity in a Two Speed Economy*. Mckinsey Global Institute, 2014. Print.
Consejo Nacional de Normalización y Certificación de Competencias Laborales (CONOCER). www.conocer.gob.mx.
Instituto Nacional del Emprendedor (INADEM). www.inadem.gob.mx.
IMEF. *Análisis Estratégico para el desarrollo de la Mipyme en México*. México, 2010. Print.
Instituto Nacional de Estadística Geografía e Información, México. www.inegi.gob.mx.
Nacional Financiera (NAFIN). www.nacionalfinanciera.gob.mx.
Neuman, Jacobo. *Esquezofrenia*. http://www.wikipyme.org/esquezofrenia/.
Núñez, Marco. "Un nuevo enfoque." *Expansión* 13 Sept. 2013: 162. Print.
Schickler, S., & J. Waller *The 7 Mindsets to Live Your Ultimate Life*. Roswell: Ultimate Life Media, 2011. Print.
Suárez, L., and P. Aguilar. *Emprendedores Endeavor. La nueva cara de México*. Mexico: V.V. Travesías Editores, 2013. Print.

Reconfiguration of Major Companies and Entrepreneur Subjects in Mexico
Culture, Productive Strategies and Relationships with the State

Marcela Hernández-Romo

In my book *Business Culture in Mexico* I showed that beginning in the 1980s Mexico began a restructuring of its production and business sectors focused on large companies, that took on different forms according to the region, sector, size of the company, and the traditions and cultures of those who held the capital (Hernández 60). Finally, I proposed that these changes granted a new role to business leaders, making them the hub of strategic decisions in the country, as well as responsible for restructuring their companies if they wanted to remain competitive.

These industrial profiles had differentiated depending on the regions (in the north—specifically in Monterrey—and in the center—in Mexico City). These regions represented the country's most dynamic economies, in terms of concentrating the largest number of major companies, the largest number of jobs, and the contribution to GDP. These two poles of development emerged at the end of the 19th century and remain at the forefront today. Meanwhile, the regions have business cultures of their own, with their specific circumstances, which lead to different entrepreneurial outlooks in terms of the relation with the state and for how they conceive the labor relations (company patrimonialism or state corporatism), and the productive strategies they implemented. I defined four entrepreneurial configurations based on their business and productive strategies, on their relation with the State, and their regional culture. The configurations are: the state patrimonial family configuration (CFPE), the subordination to the state configuration (CSE), the forgotten by the state configuration (COE), and the new volatile generation configuration (CNGV) (assembly off shoring plants). A very important code that applies to all these configurations and produces a different sense is the meaning of the relationship with the State. All of them redefined their business activities on the basis of their relationship with the State, changes in the political economy, and with political or economic crises.

In the period between 2000 and 2014 Mexico has passed through different processes, including two major economic recessions, one at the start of the new century and one in 2008. Another significant process is the entrenchment of the neoliberal model, which has increased polarization in society in terms of the disparity of income levels, and between the different industrial profiles described above, together with the growing significance of the services sector. Currently a major export sector has become consolidated, principally owned by foreign companies as well as a segment of Mexican businesses that have internationalized their companies. Most of what they produce comes from outside of Mexico, and they export a significant portion of what they do produce in Mexico, as well as encompassing markets in different countries and continents. One of the objectives of this essay is to analyze the strategies put in place by this group of large business owners to emerge from the most recent, 21st century crises, and to internationalize their companies.

In political terms, meanwhile, there have been significant changes with the alternation of the political party in government for the first time in 70 years, when the National Action Party (PAN)—led at the time by a former business executive—toppled the Institutional Revolutionary Party (PRI) in 2000 in the presidential elections with Fox. The latter was returned to government in 2012. Our particular focus in this essay is the impact on the business sector, and how the power of business leaders grows and acquires new forms of representation, participation, and political action, some of them in essence becoming a part of the State.

The second objective is to analyze the reconfiguration processes[1] undergone by companies belonging to the "State patrimonial family configuration" and the "subordination to the state configuration" as described above, in terms of their relationship with the State, with their different culture(s) (regional, family, national, entrepreneurial), and the resulting business and production strategies implemented. The changes in business practice also relate to generational changes. Fifteen years after first having analyzed these processes, we ask whether the large Mexican business owner and the business culture have undergone reconfiguration. Which business cultures can we actually talk about in Mexico in these cases? Which meanings from the past remain in their collective subjectivity, and which have been transformed to make way for new ways of seeing the company, the work, and the state?

In this sense the action of companies is partly configured in relation to the subjective fields of culture and power (Hernández, "Estrátegias de Subcontratación" 31). Thus, business practices acquire meaning in specific geographical spaces (country, region, community, company) defined at determinate historic moments, within specific socio-cultural and political contexts and within differentiated cycles of economic development and state policies (Hernández 59).

The period to be analyzed runs from 2005 to 2013, which allows us on the one hand to carry on where we left off in *Business Culture in Mexico*, which encompassed the period up to the turn of the millennium. On the other hand, this period enables us to take stock of how the neoliberal model in Mexico impacted on the actions taken by business leaders in relation to their companies, at a stage of its maturity and of great difficulties. Finally, it allows us to determine whether the Mexican business class came to understand itself as neoliberal, without the intervention of the State, and whether the latter in fact complied with the ideology of minimal intervention in the economic process, or if instead new relationships were established between the State and one or other of the most powerful business groups. Part of the information on the companies in question was obtained from their own websites, from the Mexican stock exchange, and from

Expansión review. It is also based on interviews with directors of major corporations, and visits made to some of the firms studied.

The Configuration of the State Patrimonial Family in the 21st Century

This configuration, which has existed since the dictatorship of Porfirio Díaz, and is partly connected to this past of accumulated inheritance, may be summarized—at risk of over-simplification—in terms of its cultural codes:

1. A pioneering, heroic, spirit of adventure that disregards laws that are not established by its own morality, that finds new meaning in business by setting capital in motion, reinvesting, and seeking new opportunities (strategic alliances, technology change, transforming the organization of work, training the family in business activities, sending the sons to study engineering in the United States (Hernández, "Productive Restructuring").

2. An exacerbated weight given to regional culture, which encounters a mythological reference point in the history of the forefathers, in the ethnic space constructed in time that acquires meaning in a particular vision of the world and of business, in daily life, and business practices, that confers an identity (Hernández, " La Cultura empresarial" 88). This constitutes a business culture comprising an *ethos* that is symbolically manifested in a professional work ethic, including codes such as vocation for work, family, regionalism, patrimonial relationships with workers, and the free enterprise ideology. The pleasure in work, for practical utility, for profit, austerity, and hard work (professional work ethic) are acquired values, partly due to the proximity of the United States, and the influence of that culture which leads to engagement with certain practices and values forged in the past and which combine with knowledge, ability, efficiency and specialization (Hernández, "La Cultura empresarial " 72).

3. The family as an institution that maintains unity within patrimonial families. The unification of capital between families, as a value understood between equals, between the same business class (trust, loyalty, shared risk), transferred to the idea of refusing to be subject to foreign capital (family control of administrative boards) (Hernández, "La Cultura empresarial" 88).

4. Ideologically they advocated for free enterprise, and sought for the entrepreneur to be seen as the new legitimate State, as the alternative and solution to the conflicts waged by and with the government, which they opposed. They sought by all means to weaken the State. They should control and redefine the country's economic, political, social and cultural relations in accordance with their own ideology. They claimed to seek new arrangements with society, with the church, and the government. The State they wanted was nothing other than a coalition of business families built around the ownership of their companies, related by patrimonial loyalties and blood, which came to comprise a coherent political force, creating a network of centralized and culturally integrated negotiations (Adams 112) (for example, the confrontation with the state in the seventies of the last century, and the call to collective action to unite all the business families in Monterrey or through chambers of commerce).

5. Labor relations based on a type of "white union" (a Mexican-style company

union that is subordinate to the management and not to the State) with subordinated relationship between boss and worker (De la Garza 24).

Reconfiguration of the State Patrimonial Family Configuration

At the end of the 19th century a group of businessmen from Monterrey began the process of industrialization of the north of Mexico, specifically the area around Monterrey. During the period of import substitution (1940–1980) this was consolidated and became a central pillar of industrialization known as the Monterrey Group. The two companies we analyze as part of the state patrimonial family configuration belonged to this group.

One of the founding companies of this group was Hylsamex, an icon of the family and of industrial development in Monterrey (Hoshino 47). One of its emblematic firms is Alfa. Currently, 45 percent of shares in Alfa belong to the family, and concentrate in four interrelated families: the Bernardo Garza Sada family (which holds the large number of shares), the Fernández Garza family, the Garza Medina family and the Calderón family. The current CEO and president represent two of the three branches of the founding family that remains part of Alfa: Armando Garza Sada and Alvaro Fernández Garza (CEO) as well as the former president and CEO Dionisio Garza (1994–2010). All three are grandchildren of Roberto Garza Sada, founder of the group and brother of Eugenio Garza Sada. The three cousins represent the branches of the founding family. Currently, Álvaro Fernández, CEO of Alfa, is president of the CAINTRA (Chamber of Transformation Industry), and his brother has been municipal president on two occasions for the PAN party in San Pedro Garza García, a wealthy suburb of Monterrey (Graglia, Diego and Flores 255).

Alfa has passed through three major crises. The first was in the 1980s, from which it was rescued by a huge loan from the State. The second was in 2002, when faced with the possible bankruptcy of the parent company Hylsamex plans were made to refinance its liabilities for $700 million. In 2004 the assembly approved the sale of Hylsamex, the flagship firm of the family and Monterrey itself, and in 2005 it was bought by the Italian-Argentine consortium Ternium. This led to a transformation at Alfa, which began to invest in auto parts (Anderson 28). In 2008 there was a new global economic crisis, which strongly affected the automotive industry, and sales fell by 40 percent in its auto parts subsidiary, Nemak. The company invested $637 million in financial derivatives, which with the economic crisis and exchange rate losses, made for an overall loss of $9.53 billion (Flores, Lourdes and Taniguchi 254). For Dionisio Garza, president and CEO of Alfa in 1994 the company was poorly prepared for the implementation of NAFTA (n.p., "Por la Puerta Grande" 1). In the 1990s the portfolio of Alfa comprised steel, synthetic fibers (basic industries) and red meat. Hylsamex had a production capacity of three million tons of steel per year, when in the rest of the year other players produced a minimum of 30 million tons (Anderson 32). It was under these circumstances that the president and CEO of the company proposed it be restructured. By 2014 Alfa had a presence in 23 countries in Latin America, Europe, and Asia, and ran 121 factories. In 2013 total revenue amounted to $15.78 billion (Alfa "Cifras Relevantes").

It employs 70,453 workers (Alfa "Cifras Relevantes") and is a diversified company with five principal divisions. Alpeck is its petrochemicals arm, which alone provides half of its income, as the largest company in this sector in the country and one of the largest in Latin America. Nemak, the auto parts division, is 93 percent owned by Alfa, with the remaining 7 percent in the hands of Ford. It is the world's largest producer of aluminum engine blocks and heads. The other three divisions are Sigma, with refrigerated foods; Alestra, which provides telecommunications; and Newpek, which covers hydrocarbons (Anderson 29). The current president of the board is Armando Garza Sada and the CEO is Alvaro Fernández Garza. This division of roles represents an important change, since the power of decision lies with two representatives of two of the coalition families, rather than with a single person, as was traditional. The strategies involve various levels and processes. In production, the focus was on savings in processes and on reducing the costs of raw materials. In the business model, this involved the sale of Hylsamex (the parent company) and the transformation of the company by combining cyclical sectors (auto parts) with anti-cyclical ones (food) (Anderson 30).

The global internationalization strategy of the company comprised the following components: (1) Diversification and territorial expansion into markets outside of the Americas: Asia, China, Europe; (2) Strategic portfolio restructuring: sale of Hylsamex (steel), reorientation toward automotive (monoblock head) and petrochemical industries, and seeking vertical integration expansion towards food, telecommunications and energy; (3) Innovation and technology strategy: investments were made in strategic purchases that increase production, the intellectual property rights to IntegRex technology were bought, which simplifies the production of PTA and PET plastics, enabling them to be made in a single process. Licenses for the use of this technology were sold. The investment plan is focused on organic vertical integration and on technological advantages that are difficult to replicate. The financial strategy involved placing long-term debt ($1 billion). This mode of approaching technology—purchasing and commercializing rights—represented a break with Alfa's earlier strategies, which were based on strategic associations and transfer agreements. By 2015 one of the leading strategies of the company is investment in technology and in research and development (Alfa "Estrategias").

The productive restructuring strategy in Alfa plants, such as the Aplek petrochemicals plants, comprised staff cuts, innovation in raw materials (self-generation of energy) that led to large energy savings, and reorganization of operations to make them more efficient (reengineering). With standardization of productive and administrative processes, and greater control, Alpek made savings of $40 million. Nemak made savings of 50 percent of its total costs. Altogether Alfa saved $800 million, which represents almost 10 percent of the total sales of the conglomerate (Anderson 30).

According to *Expansión* (n.p., "Por la puerta Grande" 1), the departure of Alfa's CEO was "an open secret." Family pressure for him to leave the presidency of the company combined with complaints from shareholders for the company's results in 2009. His cousin (brother of the current CEO) declared in an interview with *Expansión* that "only the Pope is for life" and asserted that the position of President and CEO should not fall to the same person (Anderson 31).

Cervecería Cuauhtémoc Moctezuma (CCM) is another of the emblematic companies that emerged from the industrialization and economic development of Monterrey at the end of the 19th century, and was a member of the Monterrey Group. This firm was the parent company of other businesses that became vertically integrated: Famosa, Titán, Malta, fabricas de Monterrey, Almacenes Silos, Fundidora Monterrey, Grafo Regia (manufacturer of labels), HYLSA, Vitro. All belonged to the Garza Sada family, which had a long-standing presence and tradition in Monterrey. Under the presidency of Eugenio Garza Lagüera, CCM became Grupo Visa (Valores Industriales), and in 1988 it became FEMSA (Fondo Económico Mexicano). In 2010 FEMSA decided to sell the emblematic firm CCM to the Dutch beer company Heineken in a deal valued at $7.35 billion (Anderson, Bárbara and Ortega 24). For Fernández Carbajal, president of the administrative board, this was less a sale than a swap of shares and debt worth $2 billion (Anderson, Bárbara and Ortega 28).

The families that control FEMSA group are Garza Lagüera, Garza, Muguerza, Garza Rangel, and Garza Sepúlveda. In 2001, José Antonio Carbajal was named president of its administrative board and CEO of the company. In 2014, in a break with tradition, the positions were divided and Carlos Salazar Lomelín was named CEO, while Fernández Carbajal took the position of president (Femsa "Conoce femsa"). FEMSA comprises several divisions: Coca-Cola FEMSA, the largest bottler of Coca-Cola products in the world, in which these families hold 47.9 percent of shares; FEMSA Comercio, which manages several chains of convenience stores, the largest of which is OXXO, and is 100 percent owned by these families; and FEMSA Negocios Estratégicos which provides logistics services, and point of sale refrigeration solutions to both FEMSA companies and external clients (Femsa "Comercio"). As a result of the sale of the flagship firm CCM, the families hold 20 percent of shares in Heineken and two non-voting seats on the board ("El Diablo Presume Trato").

In 2014 FEMSA had a workforce of 216,700 (of which 170,109 were in Mexico), a presence in 10 countries in Latin America, 64 production plants, 345 distribution centers, sells over 200 brands, and has established 12,853 OXXO stores (Femsa "Comercio"). The cause of the sale of the emblematic CCM, according to Fernández Carbajal, was its loss of customer base. In 1990 CCM began to lose its market share, falling from 55 percent to just 43 percent in 2008. According to the CEO, the small convenience stores (OXXO) were more profitable. "I told them that it had a lot of potential, that it was a shame to see it go" (Anderson, Bárbara and Ortega 26). "For my father it was a business he didn't understand, they were more interested in producing and transforming things than in stores" (Anderson, Bárbara y Ortega 26). For Fernández Carbajal, there are nostalgic members of the family (the founders) who tell those in the fourth generation that these businesses "are going to be run by other people." In his view, "I accepted that someone else ran the business for me, because I was sure they were going to do it better than me" (Huerta, Ramón "José Antonio Fernández"). For Fernández Carbajal, the competition was far better: "if we didn't open up we were going to end up isolated … successful, but isolated." For some members of this fourth generation, it is the choice between being rich or being a king; for others, what Fernández Carbajal did was to "hand over his company to Heineken in exchange for 20% of the shares (minority partner), sit on the board of a multinational and learn from the Dutch multinational" (Anderson, Bárbara and Ortega 30). It must be added that the company was in debt at the time of sale, to the tune of $2 billion (Anderson, Bárbara and Ortega 28). The sale provided liquidity and enabled it to invest in other areas of business that have now become central to the family's companies. The sale of CCM led to a redefinition of the strategy to boost the expansion of both the Coca-Cola business and the OXXO convenience stores. This implied a reordering of the portfolio, and as a result the disincorporation of CCM and the Mundet apple-based soft drinks production division. The new portfolio includes the commercialization of pharmaceutical products with the acquisition of a 75 percent share of the YZA and

Farmacia Moderna drug stores, with the goal of achieving regional coverage of this market (Femsa "Informe anual 2014"). Investments were made in information technology systems, in the HVKOF project and the Sap HVKO system for all other operations. Strategic alliances were established in research and development: funding was obtained from the National Council for Science and Technology (CONACyT) for research and development of new products that were supposedly healthier and lower in calories. A cooperation alliance was also established with the Tec of Monterrey (ITESM), and agreements with Cornell University and the UCLA for the Biotechnology Center located in the ITESM (Femsa "Alianzas Estrátegicas").

The market strategy takes advantage of market segmentation and specialization in the sale of products and brands by zone, region, neighborhood, etc. This same system is used to locate OXXO stores. The production and distribution network underwent restructuring (relocation to increase times, efficiencies and cost savings). Commercial, logistics and sales services processes were all standardized. The objective was to create synergies in all processes and make cost savings in merger processes. The use of technology in service processes seeks standardization and control over sales, products, administration, or in short, control over the working process (Hernández "Reestructuración del empresariado" 715). One of the working practices implemented by the firm in 2006–2008, before the sale of CCM, was the advanced retirement policy. All employees over the age of 55 and who had worked over 20 years in the company could retire. At the same time, the pension system changed. Previously, pensions were paid monthly, for life, and complemented the state pension granted by the Mexican Social Security Institute (IMSS) (González "Report Reserch" 75). Now, with the change, a single full payment was made, in addition to the IMSS payment. Another aspect recorded in the sustainability report is the issue of flexibility. This is defined as "a benefit for workers" although it is reduced to flexible working schemes, work from home and shorter working days (with reduced pay). According to the firm's own figures in 2014, 1,244 workers chose to follow this system. The report states that 47.88 percent of all workers are unionized and that 100 percent of these have collective work contracts (Femsa "Sustainability Report"). In 2014 the conglomerate's revenues were $17,861 million, of which $9,986 million came from Coca-Cola FEMSA and $7,432 million from OXXO. One of the points of pride of the company is the role it plays in the creation of educational, sporting, and cultural institutions, together with its role in a number of national and international foundations. Perhaps the most important in cultural terms is the creation of the Museum of Contemporary Art (MARCO) in Monterrey.

For Fernández Carvajal (Huerta, José "José Antonio Fernández"), the success of the company would have been impossible without the support of the board, and above all, a board run by family members. However, some members of this family, following the sale of the flagship firm CCM, spoke to the media to point the finger of responsibility at Fernández and to mention a loss of trust on the part of the families, just as occurred with Alfa when Hylsa was sold, regardless of the profit made.

The business vision of the state patrimonial family configuration in the North of Mexico has transformed, not only in terms of the DNA of business, but in the entrepreneurial culture and sense of work itself. The cultural, family, and regional codes that ascribed meaning to a business legend have lost legitimacy with the pressure of competitive neoliberalism, a fourth generation confrontation between tradition that they have inherited, and what drives the heirs to limit themselves to conserving their inheritance or increasing it. The head companies of the Monterrey Group were not prepared for the market liberalization and the long-awaited free market, to meet the challenges of becoming competitive and global enterprises. The story of the now weakened Monterey Group speaks of crisis, bailouts by the state, transformations, ruptures, generational changes, and disputes among family coalitions.

The year 2000 appeared hopeful, but by 2005 different pressures (debt, lack of competitiveness) resulted in the choice of renewal or death: survival for them meant selling off the iconic and non-iconic companies,[2] and establishing themselves in new business niches. This moment marked the reconfiguration of an entrepreneurial vision, at the same the re-appropriation of particular codes under new circumstances. Their skill in business, largely forged as a result of belonging to the "caste of the pioneers" ran up against its limitations upon leaving the desert and entering the global information superhighway, from the regional to the global, into the big leagues. It was no longer about doing business with their neighbors, or with entrepreneurs from the U.S., who knew them, learned from them, established strategic alliances, but did not compete with them. Thus, the code of fear appears, the doubt about heading out on their own, the competitors were very strong, they were in debt, the companies were not modernized, at least not enough to compete in the global sphere, all they were, in Garza Medina's words, "scrap metal."

It was the transition from self-sufficiency and spirit of conquest that emerged from the cowboy culture to one of fear, the decision made was to grasp the hand of someone stronger and "climbing up to globalization in the hands of international brands" (n.p. "Por la puerta grande"), or handing over the control of companies to those who have the experience and knowledge to do so. But these entrepreneurs are—contradictorily— trained for the challenges, to get ahead, and once again the reapropriation of the past, the rupture and return to the daring adventure of launching themselves into new worlds, different businesses to those of family tradition, new markets (Europe), within a business niche that generates security and profit. This process has also seen the reassertion of the professional work ethic, the recovery of the culture that values the practical, the use of science and technology, to innovate, and the desire to constantly restructure, and the taste for profit. The sense of conserving the family patrimony is reconfigured.

The patrimonialism of the corporation allowed them to reconstruct the glorious past of their predecessors, to remember and show that they were a caste of winners in Monterrey, although this reference point has disappeared, there is no longer a flagship company or a living symbol, there are new companies that are successful and pay good dividends, but what gave them identity, pride in the achievements, conquests, and a respectable morality as the founders of an industrial region, no longer exists. These companies are no longer under the control of the Monterrey families. There are new generations of entrepreneurs, who are not of the "family," a new culture of work and of the meaning of the company. The merger of capitals between families, as a value understood among equals (trust, loyalty, and shared risk) together with the idea of refusing to be subject to foreign capital, is broken, and new codes appear. Distrust comes to dominate relationships, the anger of families at the selling off of the flagship businesses results in loss of confidence in the representatives of the families who presided over the sale, regardless of the profit or having voted for the sale. Added to this, the corporate restructuring, changing of CEOs, division of power, the president of the board is different from the CEO, appointments of non-family CEOs (Vitro). In society there is disenchantment, the great generals have disappeared, their children are tired, the grandchildren have no presence, there no leaders, they no longer have the moral standing to lead social movements like before: litigation over inheritance,[3] public disputes, accusations, lost trust, broken loyalties. The ideal of the corporate patrimonial state, which was nothing but a coalition of business families centered on the ownership of their companies, related through loyalties based on patrimony and blood ties and who came to form a cohesive political force, creating a network of centralized business dealing that was culturally integrated, uniting all branches of business families in Monterrey or through chambers of commerce, undergoes reconfiguration.

The coalition of family remains, but the code of trust has changed to distrust, loyalty has changed to pragmatism, and this code plays a role, along with convenience, blood ties, and the union of capital.[4] The code of austerity is lost, corporate offices become art galleries, houses become museums, hobbies become extravagant amusements (hunting in Africa) and leisure travel replaces work, hence the assertion of Dionisio Garza's sister, "another maxim he imposed (she refers to Dionisio Garza), he least of all needs to nourish his ego with luxury." As a political force, it also weakened the ideal of being seen as the new Mexican State, as the alternative and solution to the conflicts arising from the government and to establish new arrangements with society, the church and the government through a corporate patrimonial state, is lost. They have economic power, they maintain a critical discourse against the State, they demand solutions—newspapers in the region recount all this[5]—but their voice on the national stage is not heard, is not felt: they are no longer able to weaken the State and become the patrimonial state. Regionally, they maintain economic power; politically, they are divided between the PAN and those who support the PRI.

There is a repurposing of the chambers of commerce, the surnames of the business leaders again occupy the presidencies of these, and they demand, propose and perform actions intended to substitute the local government's actions. Thus, they appropriate public space and turn it into a theme park. There is no longer any danger of communism, there is no flag to fly, so they can reduce the scope of their political action. Religious expression changes, while according to Gómez Hinojosa, "many define themselves as believers, they belong to a church and follow certain rituals, this does not translate into a personal or community calling, in other words they lack the religiosity of central Mexico, there is no tradition of saint's day festivities, municipal fairs are business and not religious holidays like in the center of the country, and there is a growing religious syncretism" (Gómez 58). Thus, according to the same author, the interlocutor is no longer the traditional church, that is to say, the bishop is no longer the interlocutor. The new religious groups or congregations are the new interlocutors (Christos Legionaries, protestants), but this dialogue is between equals, not directed to the people, to society. In the upper classes there is a strong influence from American behavior, with a strong presence of European secularism (Gómez 55). That is, there is a distancing between business leaders and the Monterrey community, the channels through which they previously acquired presence, sought influence and imposed their ideology no longer operate in the same way, and it seems that they care little for what they represent in the eyes of the population. In terms of labor relations, the type of unionism established in Monterrey companies is the so-called "white union," subordinated to the company, opposed to the corporate unionism of the state.

However, since the Fox administration, the Labor Minister, Abascal, tried to push a corporate system based on the social doctrine of the Catholic Church, which formally inspires the "white unions" of Monterrey, and included these in the discussion of the labor reform. Business leaders apparently accepted this. However, this represented the entry of these "white unions" into the sphere of national politics, something that had been carefully avoided by the management of Monterrey companies. As a result, several "white union" federations merged and the second-largest union organization in the country was created with this type of union. As a result of its growth, the dependence on the personnel departments of companies was diluted and, paradoxically, this new organization embarked on public relations with national state powers.

Recently, however, there has been a rapprochement between the unions and the government of Nuevo León, each praising the other, making invitations to each other, and declaring good industrial relations. The union grants recognition to the Governor for his support, and the union is invited to attend the inauguration of the Labor City. Moreover, when elections took place in 2006, and a minority of employers took sides with the candidate of the left, Alfonso Romo, behind the presidential candidate, López Obrador, the "white unions" spread the rumor that this entrepreneur had betrayed Garza Lagüera, his boss. That is, there is an unprecedented rapprochement between the "white union" and the government, between the union and politics, which may be a transition to another type of unionism, no longer remote from political power, as was the intention of employers in the 1930s, when they created the white unions that were subject to companies in Monterrey. Although the unionization rate has declined overall in Mexico and in Monterrey, it remains high in large industrial companies. According to the report of the representative of labor in Monterrey in 2012, "at an individual level there is conflict between labor and management, and the union plays a role in containing conflicts, not by intervening in decisions that have to do with work, but as executor of what the company decides." According to De la Garza, in Monterrey collective contracts are flexible from the outset, and if they retained certain rigidity up until the 1980s this was due to managerial cultures that in another period identified themselves with Taylorism, rather than due to resistance from unions (De la Garza 24).

In this sense, we can say that the collective agreements have never been an impediment to unilaterally imposing the conditions under which the company operates. The culture of interjected work that is reinforced in daily practice, the discourse on the role of entrepreneurs and their will to provide work and support workers, met the ideological function of indoctrination and they accepted the designs of the business leaders. At the same time, there was a reward and they earned well, enjoyed benefits, job security, and their family could enjoy these benefits. But working conditions have deteriorated, a new form of flexibility has been implemented (e.g., the "hours bank" in some companies) and business owners see this as a "benefit" for the worker. But, the pride in providing work, in creating a commitment between employer and employee, the representation of this symbolic, imaginary or real pact, would seem to have vanished. The maxims of the entrepreneurship founder generation was to believe in the boss and not in the unions, loyalty was to the employer, the worker was filled by the pride of being from the North, by this culture of discipline and hard work that gave them meaning as a region and identified them as part of a mutually constructed ethnic space. The relationships established were patrimonial, we can say that were corporate company unions, a complement to their ideal of the corporate patrimonial state of the large companies. The patrimonial is linked to the patrimony of the families, the corporate labor of the company, which are the supposed agreements between union and company. In Monterrey the state was not included in these agreements, different to the rest of the country, but it would appear that these relationships are in transition towards a closer relationship between the unions and politics (FNSI "Noticias").

The Subordination to the State Configuration in the 21st Century

The subordination to the state configuration comprises firms dating from the period of the Porfirio Díaz dictatorship (Hernández, "La cultura empresarial" 84) at the end of the 19th century, new nationalist business leaders, and the incorporation of professionals as business people. Thus, we may refer to business people whose business sense was given them by the profession and the nation (the president of Grupo ICA, Zapatos Canadá) or the business people who entered the industry as a result of the new neoliberal economic situation in the late 20th century, when the State companies were sold off (Carlos Slim, Roberto González, Harp Helu), and those who inherited major companies established in the 1940s (Televisa, with Azcárraga Milmo). However, regardless of how they came to own the company and the direction in which they took it, the relationship with the State was the same. It was not one of confrontation but rather of complicity, interest, negotiation, of mutual benefit (Hernández, "La cultura empresarial" 90). These business owners have made their fortune under the protection of the State, offering their support for government policies and receiving by way of payment concessions, influence over decisions, and the trust and friendship of the president.[6]

Another aspect that defines the subordination to the State configuration was the courtly culture. During the Porfirio Díaz dictatorship the company was pillaged by its owners, who extracted as much as they could from it (travel, days in the country, gatherings, carriages, clothing, parties, residences, etc.) in order to enjoy a palatial lifestyle, where what mattered was not work but social recognition. As a result, social origins and skills became important codes for political and economic relations (Hernández, "La cultura empresarial" 90). For a good part of the 20th century this taste for palatial lifestyles remained, though with the incorporation of new business owners dependent on the State, this became a combination of pleasure and work. In business, the notion was maintained of achieving success through personal relationships (family, kinship, and cronyism) or adulation (presents, tips) and favoritism. Belonging to a high social class, going to the best schools, and establishing relationships of friendship, in the sense of relationships that will be profitable in the future, whether because of the political influence they grant or the important jobs they provide access to.

The taste for ostentatious living and a luxurious daily life was preserved from the times of the *Porfiriato*, but brought up to date: dressing according to the latest fashions, owning a particular type of house in an exclusive area, having the latest car, looking at Europe as the ideal of culture, owning large areas of land for weekend retreats, being a friend of the president, etc. Simulation, racism, and classism are further codes present. These events, liberalization, purchase of State companies and new business leaders in new sectors (telecommunications, finance) made up the conglomeration that gave way to a process of reconfiguration, a new arrangement in business practice with a greater vocation for work, a more professional work ethic with codes such as nationalism, commitment and an end to pillaging. At the same time, in other firms the *ethos* continued of the courtly culture, with codes like loyalty, simulation, personal relations, combined with the modernization of companies, new markets and reinvestment. In the sphere of labor the corporate system of labor relations was maintained.

There was a convergence on the professional work ethic, although in the productive sphere the project continued to be based on the relationship of subordination or alliance with the State. In the next section we will examine how these codes are reconfigured and the relationship with the State is transformed. For part of the business class, this resulted in a distancing from the State, while for others the economic, political and ideological confluence has major repercussions for the firm. The cases of Slim (America Móvil-Telcel) and Azcárraga Jean (Televisa) provide examples of the hypotheses set out in the previous text (Hernández, "La cultura empresarial"). At the same time we may observe how the configurations are not static, but rather built on shifting sands, due to the relationship with the State, group interests, friends and enemies and the globalization of the economy. Faced with extreme situations they establish new coalitions that lead them to set up new configurations, or that within their configurations accommodate business owners from other configurations.

Reconfiguration of the Subordination to the State Configuration (Televisa and Telcel)

Televisa and Telcel[7] form part of this business configuration, although they have been reconfigured for the 21st century both in business and production model and their relationship with the State. Televisa has moved from maintaining a relationship of subordination to the State to form part of the State, and thus to influence in important economic and political decisions. Meanwhile, Slim has moved from a relationship of privilege (alliance) to one of tension that has seen him fall out of favor from the State. Nevertheless, both continue to depend on the State to boost their business operations and maintain their concessions and privileges, and, therefore, their growth strategies in Mexico, whether positive or negative, are not independent of the State.

Televisa is a media oligopoly. It operates four broadcast television channels in Mexico City, produces and distributes 25 pay television brands for distribution in Mexico, and exports its programs and formats to the United States through Communications, Inc. (Univision) that offers video, voice data, and high speed Internet services (Triple Play). It is involved in the publication and distribution of magazines, production and broadcast of radio, professional sports and live entertainment, production and distribution of films, and operates a horizontal Internet portal, games and raffles. It holds 50 percent of the shares in GSF Telecom Holdings, S.A.P.I. de C.V. ("GSF"), which is the controlling company of the Group (Televisa "Grupo Televisa"). It also manages a division called Televisa Foundation, which funds NGOs with a clear tendency to influence society and give guidelines to the State about the direction it should take, for example, how education should work in Mexico. In other words, what you hear in Mexico—and what is not heard or read—is defined or produced by Televisa, especially for the base of the social pyramid. For a large part of the population, Televisa is the power behind (or in front of) of the presidential chair. It is a company that was born, grew, and consolidated itself in relation to the state. This oligopoly has experienced several crises, not only economic, but also of the credibility of the population with regard to the content of the information generated and transmitted via the news, which is seen as linked to the interests of the state (Villamil 55).

It has repeatedly been and continues to be questioned for its bias in election coverage, for creating positive or negative images, and censoring presidential candidates who were not chosen by the system. In 2000, with President Fox, who made ratings, spots, and marketing a new form of government, the power of Azcárraga Jean reached its apogee. In the last two presidential elections—2006 with President Calderón and 2012 with President Peña Nieto—not only was Televisa accused of the above, but also of falsifying the news (producing information on sets and broadcasting them as if they were real), in accordance with the interests of the State, and of "making" presidents by producing a soap opera—Televisa's leading product. (Peña Nieto's wife was an actress signed exclusively to Televisa, and rivers of ink have been spilled on the fabrication of this soap-opera style romance and wedding.) Televisa has further been accused of fabricating news to conceal or present alternative versions of events, such as reenactments of police detention of kidnappers acted out for the broadcaster, the conflict resulting from the #YoSoy132 student movement and the doubts about the electoral coverage of Peña Nieto election. As a result Azcárraga received the lowest approval rates among business people (Bello 200). In other words, Televisa's best strategy for overcoming the economic crisis (though not the crisis of credibility, which continues among a sector of the population) has been to offer its services to the State, by constructing an imaginary reality that serves its interests.

The death of Azcárraga Milmo (father of Azcárraga Jean) in 1997 brought his son Azcárraga Jean to the leadership of the company. When he took over control, the company faced a debt of $1.8 billion. His strategy comprised forming his own team of directors, financial restructuring, production restructuring (development of new programs and adjustments to schedules), reducing costs by sacking staff, and reducing wages (fired staff were rehired on lower salaries and with fewer benefits). Even though Mexican federal labor law prohibits the reduction of an employee's salary this is valid for workers but not for managers. According to the CEO 5,000 personnel were fired at all levels, some 40 percent of the entire workforce (*Bello* 206). There was no protest or questions raised by the union or the workers themselves.

Those who work at Televisa are, roughly, divided into actors, represented by the National Actors' Association (ANDA); while extras and technicians have traditionally been unionized (Industrial Union of Television and Radio Workers and Artists). However, the proliferation of sub-contracting agencies is replacing the functions of the union in terms of hiring staff, leading to increasingly insecure working conditions (Feregrino 33). However, all employees are obliged to comply with Televisa culture, and actors and presenters, who are those seen by the public and define the company's image, are prescribed a form of dress and speech, and must support the political position of the company in shows. This is always connected to support for the State and upholding the codes of the Catholic Church and of nationalism, glorifying the army and the family: no dissidence is permitted. The union itself, it must be emphasized, is subordinate to the company and substituted by the loyalty of employees to the company, to the owner, and to what Televisa represents in relation to the State.

The labor relation based on loyalty remains in force, though it is now more distant; the relationship between the owner (Azcárraga Jean lives in Miami) and the workers (actors, presenters, technicians, etc.) is mediated by the executive directors of Televisa (who are known as the "Fantastic Four"), and not directly by the CEO (Villamil 62). That is, the boss-worker relationship is grounded not on a contractual relationship but on loyalty and subordination to the interests of the company. Over 15 years after having taken over the direction of company, and having balanced the books, Televisa generates its own content, which is what gives it the competitive advantage over its competitors. According to the CEO, "the team knows whether to eliminate or take a program to air ... at the lowest possible cost" (Bello 205), it is the creator of a factory that produces and sells dreams (Villamil 73).

In 2007 Televisa entered into litigation with América Móvil (Slim's Telcel and Telmex), a confrontation of the State's two most-favored titans, which made their fortunes thanks to government largesse, which now takes them to the courts, in a dispute in which they seek the State's beneficence in the form of favorable telecommunications regulation, and for their competitor to be declared at fault for holding a predominant market share. Slim won the favor of President Salinas de Gortari in 1988 with the sale of Teléfonos de México, and the concession of telephone lines and bandwidth, which he turned into Telmex, now extended to Telcel (the mobile phone provider). Televisa also benefitted from the State with the concessions of broadcast TV in 1946, permission to operate casinos (Fox), and subsequently the approval of the so-called "Televisa Law" at the end of his mandate. It was thus named due to the capacity of the group to impose its interests on political parties, the Chamber of Deputies and the Senate, to allow it to pursue monopolistic practices.[8] With Peña Nieto,[9] Mexico has a new telecommunication law and the Federal Competition Commission approved the purchase by Televisa of 50 percent of the operator Iusacell, making it the number one competitor of Slim in Telecommunications. In 2014 Telcel was declared the holder of the predominant market share, and in 2014 the whole group of companies that make up Grupo Carso (CNNExpansion "declaran agente preponderante América Movíl"), they must sell an important part of fixed capital. Televisa thus sought to become number one in telecommunications. The closeness of the state provides benefits and power, but it also takes them away from those who don't play the same game.

The team of directors who makes the decisions at Televisa, decides the route to follow and defines content, may be viewed as a coalition. However, unlike in the case of the State patrimonial family configuration, this is not the result of blood ties or the merger of capital, but comprises the owner and three friends or "brothers," as Azcarraga Jean calls them. When asked about them he says, "They are more than friends, I think they are my family, my second family, my brothers. And I believe that among friends and brothers there is a strong sense of loyalty, which ensures this functions very well and what they do they do very well, you can see the results for yourself." He adds, in response to the interviewer's question about the advantage of this group: "There is a dream that was born in 1997.... They are very well paid, indeed they are extremely well paid, because they do their job extremely well ... and there is something that is more than financial, which is the power to fulfill our dreams together" (Bello 206).

América Móvil is the jewel in the crown of the Slim empire, the second richest man in the world. It is the largest company in the telecommunications sector in Latin America and the third largest worldwide in terms of number of subscribers. It is an oligopolistic firm in telecommunications in Mexico. It provides wireless services (mobile phone and data services), fixed telephones, broadband internet and cable television, with a presence in 18 countries in Latin America and 7 in Europe. It holds shares in KPN—a Dutch company—as well as in Austria Telekom, providing mobile and fixed line telephone services. Worldwide, it provides services to more than 852 million people (Americamovil "Reporte Financieros"). In Mexico it offers cellular communications services through its subsidiary Radio Móvil Dipsa, which is known commercially as Telcel. The board is presided over by Patrick Slim, the youngest of Carlos Slim's sons, and the CEO is Slim's son-in-law, Daniel Hajj. As of late June 2014 América Móvil had 338.7 million accesses (Americamovil "Reportes Financieros"). It is a family business, shares with voting rights are distributed among Slim's sons. However, the administration and management of the business extends to the sons-in-law, brothers-in-law, and nephews, establishing a family network at the top of business and the board (Hernández, "Reetructuración del Empresariado" 715). This is made up of the family and a group of experts, ex-politicians (ex-heads of government institutions) and business leaders, as well as a body of professionals. América Móvil has the largest percentage of assets in Mexico.

The company has gone through several restructuring processes at all levels, from the corporate through the sale and purchase of shares. Expansion is via the purchase of small companies to enable them to grow and expand their market, but also through the purchase of foreign technology companies (Hernández, "Estrategias de las Macroempresas 98"). In technology, it has invested in integrating fiber optic networks linking different platforms into one, as well as in an underwater cable linking Latin America, the Caribbean and the United States, with an initial investment of $10 billion. The grand strategy that enabled Telcel to achieve high profit margins was the prepaid system it implemented, which involves prepaying for a certain amount of airtime, which is less costly for the user to acquire this package upfront, and less risky for the company (personal interview). The portfolio of businesses is aiming to expand to pay TV service, which is in open dispute with Televisa as mentioned above. Undoubtedly, one of the main strategies of the company that has a positive impact on its income is the system of distribution and points of sale, which operates under the compensation system (personal interview).

At Telcel labor and union relations are based on a flexible collective bargaining agreement (CBA). The presence of the union is subordinate to the company. Negotiations are held between the national union leader and the representative of the consortium. A worker at a call center says that "if there is a problem between the company and an employee, there is no question but the union will stick up for the company. 'They must have had a reason to fire you' would be the response of the union." Which is not to say that the union does not negotiate wage increases and benefits, which are comparatively high (personal interview).

Slim has always maintained closeness with local governments, one way of doing this is to provide funding to rescue the historic centers of towns and cities in different States, as well as in Mexico City itself. Meanwhile, the relationship with the federal government has changed, and become more distant since the beginning of the 21st century. The new PAN administration meant that Slim lost his networks of relationships and thereby his influence over the political sphere. Before, these relationships with the State allowed him to obtain state decisions in his favor, such as: favorable rates, benefits such as interconnection costs, and blocking the entry into the market of new companies. These aspects were on the table for discussion from the Fox administration, and materialized against America Movil with Peña Nieto. An important fact to highlight—that could have further influenced the distancing with Fox—was the 2005 announcement by Slim on behalf of civil society and involving different political, social, scholars, trade union, and scientific actors in a National Agreement for Unity, the Rule of Law, Investment and Employment (called the Chapultepec Agreement). With this action, the business leader behaved like a governor, according to Matilde Luna (682).

The declaration sought "points of consensus to establish State policies to delineate a short- and mid-term future for Mexico." In other words, the idea was one of a shared responsibility in taking the country forward, where the business leader placed himself at the head of this movement, calling on the president himself (Luna 683). This act, which placed Slim on view, showed that he wanted to be the State, not subordinated to it. With Peña Nieto's arrival to power he was no longer invited on presidential tours, and above all was questioned, taken to court, and punished for quality of service and for holding a monopoly. Slim's economic discourse refers to a social commitment, nationalism (defense of national capital), efficiency, quality and austerity (Martínez 89). His ideological-political position since the Fox administration was to distance himself from the State (Hernández, " La cultura empresarial" 115).

The configuration of subordination to the State has also seen ruptures, reappropriations and reconfiguration with new codes that give meaning to their vision of business and work, but always in agreement with the State, since they rely on it and its institutions, such as the decision to allocate concessions (open broadcast television, spectrum) to provide the service. We analyze two strategies, two kinds of companies. For the CEO (owner) of Televisa, the achievements of the firm—taking it out of debt, improve finances, regaining control of the shares, the Triple Play venture, and being part of the State, means demonstrating that he could drive forward "the dream" and the appropriation of a material, cultural, and symbolic heritage to serve their own "dream," thus reaffirming to society, business, and the "extended family," that he could be the "Little Tiger" Azcárraga and wield power beyond that of shareholder. He was an inheritor without his own history (he was remote from decision-making), but at the same time was part of another family, but he wanted to make his own history, and to do this had to partly break with the myth of the past (the father, the "Tiger" Azcárraga). The way to achieve this was to give a new face to the company—his own. But the great power won has been achieved in order to be part of the State, to operate as part of the state (extended concept of the state of Gramsci). Placing at the service of the state first the concessions that the State itself granted, in an age where the culture of telemarketing, of the audiovisual, forms an integral part of power.

They (Televisa) have the means, the infrastructure to influence the political preferences of viewers via the news, talk shows, entertainment, and soap operas, on the positive and beneficial aspects of economic and social reforms, what is good and what is bad politically for the population. Azcárraga Jean experienced the autocratic power of his father, experienced the company as a fiefdom where everyone must obey, the workers were objects, the owner-manager decided all: he was the company. Now, this power, this idea of the fiefdom has spread throughout Mexico, this is its new fiefdom. It (Televisa) can control the audience, can influence it, define what is good, bad, who to vote for, the positive aspects of the laws passed by the Executive and the government chambers, it produces news (real or invented), it makes and unmakes artists and presenters, just as it makes politicians, it is enough to jump-start the "dream factory." They believe that can do whatever they want, it is their business and their country.

There is disdain for institutions, the only thing that is respected is the "dream" of the dominant team members—the head is Azcárraga Jean but the three top executives (who are not shareholders of importance) share in it—certainty provides trust, the "loyalty" of these friends, who were desk-fellows (school). Thus, experiences and dreams make them brothers. But along with this, control, especially with regard to the company (in information, in the staff who work there, in what is produced, etc.) and externally, seeking to control society and the state, converting them into part of their fiefdom. The relationship to other state subjects is overdetermined by the link with the federal government, but knowing how to play on the contradictions (Villamil 71), they can equally build a good relationship with representatives of the PAN and of the PRI (regardless of ideology): their job is to produce dreams, but always within the ruling bloc. The Televisa Foundation also represents the interests of Televisa and the state, and is presided by employers or their representatives, and serves to make demands and exert pressure from within about what the state "should" do (in terms of education, administration of justice, etc.), and can claim to be the voice of society, with the clear bias of their interests. The "Televisa spokespeople are the people (artists, journalists) and for the people." In business practice, this has been reconfigured, is no longer cronyism, flattery without efficiency and without a vocation for work. The team is made up of a new generation based on professionalism, knowledge of finance, how to gain ratings, how to strategize, negotiate: they are executives without a history, without a path, everything is possible, because there is nothing to hold them down, they were not forged in relation to the previous generation of entrepreneurs, but are the new generation, professionals, where what matters is to pursue the business practice as part of that arrogant utilitarian pragmatism, although state action parameters are well-defined. The autocratic power of this clique remains, seeking to be absolute. But as it fails to transcend the Mexican border, it is a dream that comes down to the local, the domestic.

What is central and what changes in Slim is, first, the relationship with the state, the distancing by the government to the second-richest man in the world. Slim dared to want to be at the head of State, made his call, and lost. The relationship of alliance with Azcárraga Jean failed, and they became competitors. Now he is not just one of the forgotten by the state, but is scorned, to be combated as a monopoly and for distributing his wealth among large corporations. In Mexico, competitive advantage, at least in this configuration, and success, is measured by the proximity to the state: Slim himself was the example. Now it seems that Slim is closest to the configuration of the forgotten state, not in the productive sense (unmodernized medium and small companies that depend on loans granted by the state to survive or grow), but in the political and economic sense, where the business is dependent on the state grants (grants, fees, spectrum, etc.), and the state has not only forgotten Slim, but he is attacked, beaten, politically he is not welcome. Nevertheless, Slim knows that the balance can change, and at some point he may again be one of the groups that establishes alliances and forms part of the configuration of the privileged subordinates. The Slim family keeps up the PRI discipline, and has never publicly expressed the evil of the state, like the culture of the old PRI when it lost and was sent to the bench, although that PRI no longer exists. In the business vision it remains the codes of efficiency and quality applied to productivity. There is nationalist discourse and a huge array of foundations that support health, science, art, entertainment, but unlike the other foundations, these do not make public statements, and do not produce simulated or real messages, but only present the results of their foundations. That is to say, Slim stopped seeking to be the state, just as the state patrimonial family configuration did, and his vision was reconfigured solely towards business, but still looking towards the state, which he needs.

In this configuration there is an amalgam of cultural codes, generational interests, subjectivities that generate different meanings. On one hand, we find that the *ethos* of courtly culture, codes of loyalty based on personal relationships, simulation (having a dream factory, philanthropy) persists, although codes of efficiency are added, professionalism and utilitarian pragmatism. Lavish tastes (the wedding of Azcárraga Jean demonstrates this, with 1,500 guests, artists, politicians, businessmen), the branded clothing, sports cars, apartments in Miami, philanthropy, the causes for the poor people. But on the other hand, there are entrepreneurs with a culture oriented more to austerity (no dissipation), doing business outside Mexico (Slim), facing new actors and institutions, no longer in relation to the proximity to the state. In other words the ethnic space built as a courtly culture is reconfigured in the business vision of a new generation with roots in the older generation; there is professionalization together with the utilitarian pragmatism, but where the values of ostentation and personal relationships persist, so does the culture of simulation as part of that embedded culture, turned into a legitimate collective practice, not only for entrepreneurs but as an accepted part of society. But on the other hand, there are those who enter the game of globalization, and no longer depend only on the state, but also on business practices and decisions in the world. Yet, as a corporate culture, the focus remains the relationship with the state, and proximity to the executive.

Conclusions: Business Reconfiguration in Mexico, Roots of Culture and State Links

We find that in 2015, fragmented business elite in Monterrey, not content with being part of the state, but wanting to be the collective reference of society, wanted to hold the hegemony that defines life in Mexico. They were weakened, there is no longer a Monterrey Group, they are no longer the pillar that supported and legitimized an ideological and political position in relation to the state, society and the companies themselves. This means a return to legitimate representation via chambers of commerce, foundations, a presence under the cover of these organizations, but also fragmented by ideological affiliation and the interest of these entrepreneurs in different political parties, in addition to major conflicts between the heirs for the division of capital. However, they maintain a professional work ethic (training, a taste for work, doing things right); unionism is changing in their business, in possible transition towards politicization in relation to the government and, for workers, the loss of employment benefits. The Monterrey *ethos* is reconfigured, but the pride of being from the North remains, of being workers, except that the employers are no longer the generals.

In the center of the country, relations with the state were reconfigured too, great power was instituted with the media and in particular Televisa. However, there are new players close to presidential power (Group Higa linked to the construction sector, Oceanográfica to Pemex) with the same codes of courtly culture, although it is reconfigured with professionalism and utilitarian pragmatism.

The form of political participation of business becomes more complex, on the one hand, with the revival of traditional chambers of commerce, which in the 1990s had declined in influence (repurposing of these organizations, for example in Jalisco and Nuevo León and the Federal District itself), with regional scope but also, we can talk about new forms of business representation, such as civil society organizations (CSOs), funded by business owners in different formats, foundations, agencies of analysis and information generation, and citizen observatories. The proliferation of these associations ranging from alleged involvement in the design of public policies (education, justice, public security), to play the role of intermediary between the state and international organizations (Luna 676). That is, it is a new way for business leaders to do politics, through social pressure, aimed at intervening, influencing ideologically, establishing the direction towards which state policies should be directed (social, economic, educational, legal, human rights, etc.), on the basis of a supposed legitimate social representation. The profession of lobbyist also appeared on the part of business owners: approaching and convincing lawmakers of the importance of certain laws, winning their votes, etc. But perhaps most striking is the individual participation of certain business leaders in the intended career to directly form part of the government. There have been encounters, disagreements, legitimating and loss of legitimacy of various business groups of entrepreneurs (Carlos Slim) in relation to the state. This is the new politicized context, one of individual or group participation (associations) in the political life of Mexico by business leaders, which has repercussions on their decisions and on the success of their business.

Discussion Questions

1. Is it important business culture to explain firm strategies?
2. What is the difference between rational choice and configurative choice?
3. In a neoliberal economic context like Mexico, is intervention of the state in business is important?
4. From a qualitative study as this essay. can you make conclusions or this is only possible of quantitative research?
5. Is the cultural history of entrepreneurships important to explain their actual practices?
6. Is the business culture in Mexico and the United States very different?

Key Learning Terms

Business culture: Norms, values and meanings characteristics of a business.
Business strategy: Process of decision of main aspects of the business and production in a firm.
Culture business history: Change of culture of a business with time.
Neoliberal model: Economic model alternative to Keynesian model, based in free market and minimum state intervention.
Qualitative study: A style of research from qualitative data, especially for problems of compression of actor meanings.
Rational choice: Model for human action, decision for action is result of calculation of rate between utilities and costs.

Notes

1. This research was made with Configurationist approach from Enrique de la Garza ("Metodología de las Ciencias Sociales" 2010).
2. The founding companies who created the legend of industrial Monterrey have been gradually selling off businesses, a process that accelerated in 2005 with the sale of Hylsa, Imsa and Cervecería Cuauhtémoc Moctezuma, all belonging to the Monterrey Group families.
3. This may be observed in newspapers and in videos that relate these confrontations that have led to violence, even with firearms.
4. However, we are talking about large Mexican corporation, in many small, medium and even large companies in Mexico today loyalty is still the status quo. Many Mexican businesses to not have to adapt to international pressure or global markets, are so small that they do business in small circles in which the "old" Mexican management style is still present
5. In an investigation by Pussetto, Smith, et al., a comparison is made of the topics published in Monterrey newspaper El Norte between the years 1995 and 2005. Those representing the interests of business people, the state and political system occupy 17 percent and 16 percent, respectively, above companies (11 percent), followed by art and culture (14 percent), work (2 percent), and religion (1 percent).
6. President Salinas de Gortari sold Telmex to Carlos Slim with a division between shares with right to vote in the council of administration and the others, to favor Slim. Also let a new concept of rate for consumers of telecommunications ("Rate for Measured Time"). In few years Telemx recovered investments. At the same time Telmex was considerate by government like a private monopoly for several years
7. The Azcarraga family is central when we talk about Televisa. This business started with father of the actual owner, first in the radio sector, and when TV began in México grew step by step. It is the fists oligopoly in TV in Mexico no affected by last reforms of 2013. The case of Slim is different, in the eighties he was a business man with no importance. His turning point was with the purchase of Telmex in 1990. This decade was the golden age for Slim, from fixing telephone services to cellular and strong investments abroad. But, his relationship with PAN government changed.
8. When the law was approved, 93 percent of all television channels were owned by two media firms, of which 80 percent were owned by Televisa (Luna 673–674).
9. Enrique Peña Nieto was supported by PRI and was governor of State of Mexico before becoming president. He is part of a traditional elite political group "Atlacomulco."

References

Adams, Julia. "Culture in Rational-Choice Theories of State-Formation." *State/Culture: State Formation After the Cultural Turn*. Ed. Steinmetz. Ithaca: Cornell University Press, 2009. Print.
Alfa. "Annual inform Alfa." Web. 7 March 2015.
Alfa. "Alfa estrategias." Web. 23 March 2015.
Alfa. "Cifras relevantes." Web. 24 March 2015.
Alfa. "Reporte de responsabilidad corporativa." Web. 5 March 2015.
América Móvil. www.americamovil.com.mx/amx/en/.
América Móvil. "Reporte financiero y operativo del segundo trimestre de 2014." Web. 13 March 2015.
Anderson, Bárbara. "El fin de una era." *Expansión* 14 March 2010: 28–34. Print.
_____, and Adolfo Ortega. "Mi nuevo Femsa." *Expansión* 14 February 2010: 24–30. Print.
Bello, Alberto. "Tenemos el talento y el dinero: Emilio Azcárraga CEO de Televisa." *Expansión* 12 Nov. 2012:199–206. Print.
Cámara de la Industria y la Transformación (CAINTRA) de Nuevo León. "Informe 2012–2013, Presidente Eugenio Clariond." Web. 27 March 2015.
CNNExpansion. "Agente preponderante." Web. 12 April 2014.
CNNExpansión. "El diablo presume trato Femsa-Heineken." Online video clip. 8 February 2010. Web. 3 March 2015.
De la Garza, Enrique. "Estilo de desarrollo y nuevos patrones de relaciones laborales."
Ed. Dombois Rainer and Pries Ludger. *Trabajo industrial en la transición: Experiencias de América Latina*. México, D.F.: Fundación Friedrich Ebert de México—El Colegio de Puebla-Editorial Nueva Sociedad, 1993. 13–26. Print.

_____. *Metodología de las ciencias sociales*. México: Fondo de Cultura Económica, 2010. Print.
"Enfrentamiento entre hermanos Garza Laguera." Online video clip. Youtube.mx. YouTube, 25 January 2013. Web. 18 March 2015.
"An Employee of América Móvil." Personal Interview. 5 February 2015.
Femsa. "Alianzas estrategicas." Web. 5 April 2015.
Femsa. "Informe anual." Web. 17 April 2015.
Femsa. "Responsabilidad social." Web. 17 April 2015.
Femsa. "Conoce Femsa." Web. 18 April 2015.
Feregrino, Azucena. "Los extras de televisión, el arte de hacer invisible lo cisible." *Trabajo no clásico, organización y acción colectiva*, Tomo II. Ed. Enrique de la Garza. México: Plaza y Valdés, 2010. 23–68. Print.
Flores, Lourdes, and Hanako Taniguchi. "Al mal tiempo…. Invertir." *Expansión 21* June 2013: 252–258. Print.
Graglia, Diego, and Lourdes Flores. "Alfa encuentra la veta." *Expansión* November/December 2013: 252–260. Print.
Gómez, José. "Recomposición religiosa." *Nuevo León, hoy: Diez estudios sociopolíticos*. Ed. Luis Lauro. México, D.F.: La Jornada Ediciones—Universidad Autónoma de Nuevo León, 1998. 53–107. Print.
González, Mónica. "Report of Research. Facultad de Comercio y Administración." México, D.F.: UNAM, 2014.
Martínez José. *Carlos Slim: Retrato inédito*. México: Océano, 2010. Print.
Hernández, Marcela. "Productive Restructuring and Business Culture in Mexico." The Center for Latin American Studies, Berkeley. Berkeley University. 4 April 2002.
_____. *La cultura empresarial en México*. México, D.F.: Miguel Ángel Porrúa-Cámara de Diputados LIX Legislatura-Universidad Autónoma Metropolitana, 2004. Print.
_____. "Estrategias de las macroempresas y la maquila grande de exportación en el sexenio de Fox." *Revista Trabajo* 3.4 (2007): 81–112. Print.
_____."Estrategias de subcontratación en México." *La influencia de las configuraciones subjetivas y culturales*. México: UAM-Plaza y Valdés, 2012. Print.
_____. "Reestructuración del empresariado y las grandes corporaciones." *La situación del trabajo en México, 2012: El trabajo en la crisis*. Ed. De la Garza Enrique. México: Universidad Autónoma Metropolitana-Plaza y Valdez, 2012. 697–730. Print.
Hoshino, Taeko. "Industrialization and Private Enterprise in Mexico." Japan: Institute Developing Economies-Japan External Trade Organization, 2001. Print.
Huerta, José. "José Antonio Fernández Carbajal." Online video clip. YouTube.mx. YouTube, 27 January 2010. Web. 25 March 2015.
Luna, Matilde. "Las asociaciones empresariales y el estado sanista." *La situación del trabajo en México, 2012: El trabajo en la crisis*. Ed. De la Garza Enrique. México: Universidad Autónoma Metropolitana-Plaza y Valdez, 2012. 661–694. Print.
Martz, Aldo. "Pelea Garza Mercado de Plaza Fiesta." Online video clip. YouTube.mx. YouTube, 4 August 2014. Web. 1 April 2015.
Meléndez, Jorge. "Sindicalismo en el Área Metropolitana de Monterrey, 1983–1998." *La globalización en Nuevo León*. Ed. Esthela Gutíerrez. México: Universidad Autónoma Metropolitana-Ediciones El Caballito, 1999. 279–303. Print.
Nortecom. "Pelean por herencia hijos del empresario Roberto Garza Sada." Online video clip. YouTube.mx. You Tube, n.d. Web. 17 February 2013.
n.p. "Cola de León o Cabeza de Ratón." *Expansión* 1–14 February 2010:1. Print.
n.p. "Por la Puerta Grande." *Expansión* 1–14 March 2010: 1. Print.
Oviedo, Alberto. "Pleito de los Garza Delgado, socialites de Monterrey." Online video clip. Youtube.mx. YouTube, 16 February 2013. Web. 29 March 2015.
Smith Pussetto, Cintia, Nancy Janett García Vázquez, and Jesús David Pérez Esparza. "Análisis de la ideología empresarial regiomontana: Un acercamiento a partir del periódico El Norte." *Confines* 4.7 (2008). Web. 3 March 2015.
Staff de prensa. "Representantes de nuestra FNSI acuden a la inauguración oficial de la instalación de la ciudad laboral." 13 October 2014. Web. 24 March 2015. fnsi.com.mx/noticias.html.
Televisa. "Grupo Televisa." Web. 7 March 2015
"To a manager of distribution of Telcel." Personal Interview. 18 September 2014. Mexico City.

"To a worker of a Center of Clericals Telcel." Personal Interview. 25 January 2015. Mexico City.
Villamil, Jenaro. "Emilo Azcárraga Jean, las Trampas del Raiting." *Los amos de México*. Ed. Jorge Zepeda. México, D.F.: Planeta Mexicana, S.A. de C.V., 2007. 49–92. Print.
Villegas, Pedro. "El Nuevo Sindicalismo Blanco." *La situación del trabajo en México, 2012: El trabajo en la crisis*. Ed. De la Garza Enrique. México: Universidad Autónoma Metropolitana-Plaza y Valdez, 2012. 639–660. Print.

Human Capital Development in Mexico

Pramila Rao

Professional training efforts in Mexico are a collaborative effort among several key stakeholders such as the government, large organizations, banks, and universities. The integration of these various resources has helped augment the knowledge of the local workforce. Global trends, such as free trade agreements, have specifically enhanced the labor infrastructure of local companies. Today Mexican organizations compete with leading multinationals in several industries as their workforce becomes increasingly competent (Cantu de la Torre and Cantu Licón 20; Ruiz 32; Ruiz 51, 52).

The government has played a key role in employee development right from the implementation of its labor law. It has introduced important federal acts to bring about a certain standardization to organizational training (Cantu de la Torre and Cantu Licón 20; Murphy 85). Further, policy leaders in the government pursued a vibrant trade policy in the early 1990s that has largely contributed to enhancing local organization's management practices (Ruiz 32; Ruiz 51, 52). The role of national culture is also evident in the implementation of training initiatives as cultural dimensions influence training methods that locals prefer (Nathan 20; Rodrigues 611–613).

This essay provides an overview of training and development practices in the Mexican context. It begins with the definitions of concepts related to training and development. The government's systematic role in training efforts of the local talent is provided. The main outcomes on employee development that emerged as a consequence of the free trade agreements are identified. The predominant trends in training in the Mexican corporate world are discussed. The role of national culture on training methods is also showcased. The last section details some best practices from the industry. The essay concludes with a reiteration of the key stakeholders in this process and also recommendations for further improvement.

Training can be defined as providing individuals sufficient knowledge, skills, and abilities (KSAs) to perform their current jobs adequately. For example, offering frontline employees training on how to provide customer service for their customers. On the other hand, development focuses on providing employees KSAs that may be required subsequently in their careers. For instance, providing mid-management employees leadership training as they may be assigned upper-level positions sometime in the future (Gomez-Mejia, Balkin, and Cardy 246).

The next sections will discuss the role of the key stakeholders (government, free trade agreements, and large organizations) who have contributed in enriching the skill sets of the local workforces.

The Role of the Government in Training and Development

The government has been very supportive in supporting human capital development. The *Ley Federal de Trabajo* (Federal Labor Law or FLL) established in the Mexican constitution in 1931 was introduced to provide employees protection in several employment-related practices. In 1978, this law included a specific article on training and development. The government mandated firms provide two weeks of training to their employees. The law clearly stipulates that organizations will face punitive consequences if they do not provide the required training (Cantu de la Torre and Cantu Licón 20; Murphy 85; Arias-Galicia 185, 186). In 2012, additional revisions were made to the FLL for making organizational training programs more accountable to the government. Organizations now are required to provide comprehensive details of their training programs specifying content, methods, participants, duration, and goals. The training programs should be evaluated and any outcomes in organizational productivity should also be reported. The close interaction with the government on organizational training makes human capital development a very strategic initiative (Heylman 16). Blue-collar and white collar employees are required to receive approximately three and six training contracts respectively. Employees who do not meet the required skill sets in this period can be terminated. This recent modification in the labor laws should substantially enhance the knowledge capital of employees (United-States Mexico Chamber of Commerce "Mexico's new labor" 42, 43; OECD "Economic surveys"). The fact that Mexican firms receive such support from their government has been one of the predominant reasons that Mexican organizations have bolstered their employment skills to those of global standards (Cantu de la Torre and Cantu Licón 20).

However, there is a large concern that local organizations usually find many loopholes just to provide nominal training to comply with training audits of the governments. Most organizations seem to provide the bare minimum professional development to employees merely to stay compliant with the law. Employees with technical backgrounds receive training more favorably than non-technical personnel. However, most organizations do not invest in elaborate training to enhance the knowledge capital of their employees. Very few organizations actually budget funds for training of management employees as organizations do not like to invest elaborately in its employees (McKinsey Global Institute 33–51; Arias-Galicia 185, 186; Wharton University of Pennsylvania).

The government further has established several resources to enhance the skills of its labor force. In 1978, it launched *Servicio Nacional de Empleo* or SNE to offer vocational training programs and financial assistantships for individuals to augment their employment skills. The SNE offices, located throughout the country, offer various kinds of professional development programs for individuals free of cost. For example, professional online courses or PROCADIST (PROgrama de CApacitacion a DIstancia para Trabajdores) established in 2006, offered by the SNE, provide individuals competencies on a variety of topics (Villar, Linas-Audet and Escardbul 313). PROCADIST provides distance education learning modules for different kinds of learners. In 2013, approximately 25,468 online courses were offered ranging from technology to leadership to commerce among several others. These modules provide skills from primary school to doctorate educational levels covering a wide repertoire of skills requirements (STPS "Cursos por estado"). In 2013, the maximum number of distance education programs offered were individuals seeking "*licenciatura*" (17,193) followed by "bachillerato" (3018) levels (STPS "Subdirección de Tutoría"). Table 1 provides details of the number of programs offered in various educational categories.

Table 1. Online Education Courses Offered by the Government (SNE)

Escolaridad	2013
Primary School / Primaria	21
Secondary School / Secundaria	701
Bachelor's Degree / Bachillerato	3018
Vocational Training / Carrera técnica	2780
Degree / Licenciatura	17193
Master's Degree / Maestría	1695
Doctorial Degree / Doctorado	60
No data / Sin dato	0
Total	**25468**

Source: STPS (Secretaria del trabajo y previsión social). Coordinación de Capacitación a Distancia. Subdirección de Tutoría en Línea. 2013. Web. March 2015.

These federally-aided public distance programs have been very successful in attracting and training a lot of individuals. For example, from 2006 to 2010, PROCADIST offered training to almost 10,000 employees from approximately 5000 companies (Villar, Linas-Audet and Escardbul 313). A global report on successful training programs of several countries identifies this program as very effective in its implementation. From 2010 to 2012, PROCADIST offered 38,000 individuals training with a variety of choices from 1800 courses. This suggests this government training program is widely popular among individuals and companies (G20 Taskforce on Employment 102, 103). The Mexican government offers this generous investment in education and training as it realizes that many Mexicans may not have the finances to become academically or technically skilled. For instance, only 33 percent of Mexicans who have high school diplomas pursue college degrees (McKinsey Global Institute 15).

Becate, another successful government program established in 2002, has been very effective in training unemployed individuals into private companies or for entrepreneurship. Almost 1.5 million employees were able to find employment with this educational and training partnership program (OECD "Economic surveys"). A global report on best training practices in different countries suggests that Mexican's *Becate* does an excellent job in providing a variety of professional competencies. For example, from 2010 to 2013, this program offered approximately 40, 000 training courses for 800,000 individuals (G20 Taskforce on Employment 112).

In 2000, the government established the e-Mexico portals that made a significant leap on human capital improvement both at the macro (government) and micro (organization) levels. The four aspects of this federal venture are e-learning (*e-aprendizaje*), e-health (*e-salud*), e-economy, (*e-economia*), and e-government (*e-gobierno*). The e-learning component had a strong orientation towards enhancing the skill levels of government employees via online classes. The government realized that most of the federal employees do not have adequate management and technology training. Their e-portals addressed these skill inadequacies by providing these programs (Luna-Reyes, Gil-Garcia and Cruz 58–59).

This e-project also received external funding from World Bank to bolster the skill levels of employees of small and medium size organizations. These organizations (small and medium) form the backbone of the Mexican economy, yet their employees do not have adequate skill sets to compete neither at the national nor international levels. Such government initiatives towards knowledge development will have a tremendous impact in upgrading the competencies of these micro entrepreneurs who do not have resources for getting such skills. In 2004, this government initiative received the Stockholm Challenge global award from Sweden reflecting its extremely positive outcomes for the local workforce (OECD "e-government studies").

The Role of NAFTA on Training and Development

External trends, such as NAFTA, and subsequent free trade agreements have made local companies cognizant of the importance of professional training as they have to compete at international levels (Petrick and Rinefort 228; Ruiz 32; Ruiz, 51, 52). NAFTA (North American Free Trade Agreement), signed in 1994, laid the first foundation for local firms' increased awareness about multinationals practices. NAFTA also mandated that organizational training and development efforts are audited frequently so that employees' skills across the domestic regions are comparable (Ruiz 32; Ruiz 52).

In a qualitative study with senior public employees on the implications of NAFTA on training, employees unanimously indicated the important role of this trade agreement on human development. First, it gave Mexican companies, small and large, access to one of the world's largest consumer markets. This preferential access made local companies become aware of their labor skills and product quality. Second, the government realized that organizations were providing just the bare minimum required for employee training and development and not investing in it abundantly. Third, this made the government take a proactive step to offer several training programs to enhance the skills of the labor capital at various levels (both management and technical) (Ruiz 32).

In a recent interview with the researcher, the NAFTA minister for trade, Mr. Ramos, indicated that one of the predominant outcomes of the implementation of NAFTA was that it made Mexican companies invest considerably in their training practices to become comparable to global standards. For instance, the increased presence of U.S. multinationals in Mexico has made their supply chains completely integrated with those of the Mexican firms. This integration put a tremendous stamp on the quality of the products or services requiring a skilled capital across the board (Villareal and Fegusson 15). He discussed this point with special relevance to the automobile industry where the various by-products for the automobile industry have to be produced at standardized quality from both sides of the border. This pursuit for excellence has made global automobile companies bolster its training initiatives to ensure quality finished products (Ramos 117).

These industry-specific training programs have been a win-win situation for both the automobile manufacturers and local employees. The auto companies frequently provide technical and language training programs for assembly line workers making them very attractive places for employment. Employees are naturally attracted to these companies making recruitment of locals an easy task for employers also. The cities of Saltillo and Ramos Arizpe are commonly referred to as the "mini–Detroits" as job opportunities for assembly line workers abound. The Big Three have firmly established their presences in these cities with robust internship and training programs. Local universities have partnered with the global manufacturers and offer tailored courses for workers to pursue either technician or engineer programs. After completion of these educational courses, local technicians and engineers on an average earn $900 and $1200 respectively. Thus, these educational/training programs become very lucrative opportunities for assembly line workers (Daniels). Further, multinationals that offer state-of-the-art professional development programs will ensure positive outcomes such as employee engagement and retention (Dávila 139).

The implementation of NAFTA has also made organizations increase their commitment to various forms of training other than industry-specific or technical training. The trade agreement has specifically addressed areas of safety and environment to be implemented by organizations. As the maquiladoras or border-plants are a source of great pollution, Mexican organizations have started to invest a lot to ensure green practices are practiced. In an empirical study of 220 maquiladora managers, it was identified that lower-level employees received substantial investment in environmental training. Mexicans also indicated they like to work in teams for training towards any common organizational outcomes (Daily, Bishoup and Massoud 641–643). Similarly, worker safety and training has become an important priority among manufacturing intensive industries. Mexican organizations now invest to provide their employees substantial training in workplace safety that is comparable to that of their U.S. and Canadian counterparts. The labor statistics in Mexico (such as safety, environment) is constantly compared to those of the U.S. and Canada making locals even more aware of what they should do to reach global standards (Petrick and Rinefort 228).

Mexico further expanded its trade portfolio and currently is a member of thirteen free trade agreements (bilateral and multilateral) with 44 countries. This has made their domestic firms extremely aware of and absorb best practices from different cultures and regions. As local companies cross new borders, they are bound to learn new skill sets from their professional interactions with various countries. In 2012, Mexico signed the Trans-Pacific Partnership with 12 countries in its relentless pursuit to constantly seek for learning opportunities beyond its boundaries (Villareal and Fergusson 15; Villareal 3–13).

The Role of Organization Size on Training and Development

The size of the organization usually determines its policies towards training and development. A majority of Mexican companies are usually small (under ten employees) or mid-size (between eleven and 500 employees). These organizations generally follow unstructured HRM (human resource management) practices as they do have adequate financial or labor resources to provide formal programs. Most of the small and mid-sized firms are also family-owned which might lend to environments of informal management styles. In these organizations, training new employees may usually involve job shadowing their superiors or peers at work to learn any work-related practices. These organizations usually have unstructured formats of job shadowing where employees just follow what the other employees are doing (Cantu de la Torre and Cantu Licón 20).

Small and medium-sized organizations, however, find different strategies to strengthen the skill sets of their workforces. First, these organizations seek managerial and technical training via government initiatives (such as the e-portals, PROCADIST) which are offered free. These programs have helped these companies upgrade their labor skills. Second, a predominant number of these companies are a part of the supply chains of larger companies. These large companies commonly offer to train employees from these smaller companies so that they can get quality products and services. The classic example of this supply chain model can be observed in the auto-industry which has small firms supply products for the bigger companies (McKinsey Global Institute 9). Third, employees from these firms can benefit from recent government programs such as the National Institute for Entrepreneurs that has as its primary goal to develop and enhance the entrepreneurial spirit of small and mid-size firms (United-States-Mexico Chamber of Commerce, "It is time to move" 25).

However, small sized companies still have minimum capital and labor resources to augment the skill sets of their employees. Thus, the productivity of small companies (employers with less than ten employees) fell by 6 percent annually over a ten year period (1999–2009). Small companies may need much more investment by key stakeholders in bolstering their skills. For example, small companies do not have easy access to financial resources. They are largely overlooked by the Mexican banking industry which caters to large and mid-sized firms. Banks that do offer loans to micro firms tend to charge high rates of interests making it difficult for these owners to borrow capital for any investment purposes (McKinsey Global Institute 7).

On the other hand, large firms (500 employees and more) generally follow robust and progressive HRM practices as their capital and labor resources allow them to invest in such programs. This striking contrast between the traditional and modern firms has been referred to as "the tale of two Mexicos" (McKinsey Global Institute 5). The distinct role of employee training on labor productivity is evident from some comparative statistics of large and small firms. Large companies (more than 500 employees) such as Grupo Bimbo, Grupo Alfa, among several others have increased their labor productivity by 5.8 percent annually over a ten-year period (1999–2009). This efficiency has contributed to the nation's GDP (gross domestic product) and also enhanced the images of these local firms. These companies have invested in state-of the art technology, process improvements, elaborate employee training to ensure their firms provide superior and quality products (McKinsey Global Institute 7, 10).

Professional training efforts of large firms include a variety of opportunities for employee development such as internal training programs, absorbing best practices from other multinationals, collaborating with universities, and also teaming up with professional vendors (Arias-Galicia 185, 186; Cantu de la Torre and Cantu Licón, 20).

Large Mexican organizations offer a variety of in-house training and development programs (Arias-Galicia 185, 186; Murphy 85, 90). Grupo Bimbo, a successful bakery firm, provides specific functional, technical and product training to employees at every level in their organization as it strives to be a global leader in the region. Its executives are provided opportunities for continuous education and also receive international training in the U.S. Grupo Posadas, a hospitality leader, empowers it employees with e-learning modules provided by both internal and external trainers. Telmex, a monopoly in telecommunications, offers various kinds of cross-training to their employees so that their internal talent can be leveraged effectively across different departments ("Top Ten Strategies" 50, 51).

Large Mexican subsidiaries adopt best training practices from other countries also (Arias-Galicia 185, 186; Murphy 85, 90). For instance, the Japanese manufacturing concepts of Six Sigma, kaizen, and lean manufacturing has become the norm in many local manufacturing environments (Cantu de la Torre and Cantu Licón, 20). Mexico is the manufacturer's haven for seven of the largest multinational automobile manufacturers. All these automobile manufacturers outperform the labor productivity of their home (U.S., Japan or Germany) counterparts as these multinationals have invested heavily in skill training of local employees (McKinsey Global Institute 36). Mexican automobile firms have also embraced the principles of total quality management (TQM) and implement it rigorously in their manufacturing plants. Mexican firms have realized these international training practices have several positive outcomes. A case in point- the management of Baxter Mexico, a leader in medical services, provides six sigma, kanban, and lean manufacturing training for their employees recording $30,000 in savings (Drickhamer 1). In another example, employees in General Cable plant receive extensive manufacturing training recording a stupendous amount of $1.4 million in organizational savings (Cable 31, 32).

Large organizations also provide customized training programs for their employees by collaborating with leading universities. Several leading Mexican firms collaborate with high-profile business schools integrating the latest academic knowledge with their organizational goals ("Top Ten Strategies" 50, 51; Kastelein 48–50). This has become an important global trend in professional executive development- the strategic partnership between leading universities and business firms. Mexican organizations frequently send their executive talent for specialized education to distinguished domestic or overseas universities ("Top Ten Strategies" 50, 51; Kastelein 50, 51). These tailored educational curricula catered to different industries make them very popular and marketable (Speizer 59, 60). For instance, the Mexican business schools of EGADE of the Tecnológico de Monterrey (*The Escuela de Graduados en Administración y Dirección de Empresas*) and IPADE (*Instituto Panamerico de Alta Direccion de Empresa*) have international MBA programs that offer professionals well-rounded global perspectives. These degrees include different learning methods via virtual meetings, guest speakers, and case studies blending different formats for a comprehensive education. These graduate programs are rated very highly by both students and institutional educational reports (Buckley 23). Further, many leading business schools in Mexico also offer short certification programs for specific organizational needs (such as leadership among others) (Garrett 39, 40). The business schools of EGADE and IPADE train almost 50 percent of the Mexican executive talent population indicating the high demand for customized human capital training (Authers & Silver).

Large organizations also seek external vendors or other creative formats for professional development. Many large organizations offer off-the shelf training programs that may cost approximately from $800 to $2300. These training programs are customized and provided based on organizations' needs analysis for specific programs (Cantu de la Torre and Cantu Licón, 20). Large companies also adopt different strategies such as corporate retreats that allow for training in an outdoor atmosphere. These innovative formats combine physical activities and organizational learning in a very effective way. The outdoor activities include a variety of sports such as kayaking, balloon rides, or rafting while including some kind of learning in leadership, team, or functional skills (Gleason 54, 55).

The Role of National Culture on Training

Culture has a strong role in management practices and work-related values. This essay will use the GLOBE (Global Leadership and Organizational Behavior Effectiveness) cultural dimension's study which is considered one of the most recent cultural studies. It provides the results from 61 countries on nine core cultural dimensions of assertiveness, future-orientation, gender egalitarianism, humane orientation, institutional collectivism, in-group collectivism, performance orientation, power distance and uncertainty-avoidance (Chhokar, Brodbeck, and House 1–31). Table 2 provides the definitions of these various cultural dimensions.

Table 2. Definitions of National Cultural Dimensions

#	Cultural Dimension	Definitions
1	Assertiveness	Degree to which individuals in organizations or societies are assertive in social relationships
2	Future-Orientation	Degree to which individuals in organizations or societies plan for the future
3	Gender Egalitarianism	Degree to which organizations or society promotes gender equality
4	Humane Orientation	Degree to which individuals in organizations or societies reward individuals for positive behavior
5	Institutional Collectivism	Degree to which organizational and institutional practices encourage collective action
6	In-group Collectivism	Degree to which individuals in societies reflect collectivist behavior
7	Performance Orientation	Degree to which upper management in organizations and leaders in societies reward group members for performance excellence
8	Power Distance	Degree to which organizations and societies accept power
9	Uncertainty-Avoidance	Degree to which organizations and societies avoid uncertainty by relying on practices and procedures

Source: Chhokar, Jagdeep, Felix Brodbeck, and Robert House. Culture and Leadership Across the World: The GLOBE Book of In-Depth Studies of 25 Societies. Mahwah, NJ: Lawrence Erlbaum Associates, 2007. Print.

The GLOBE research is considered distinctive in cross-cultural research for several reasons. First, the study introduced cultural dimensions at two different levels, the organizational and societal, providing both the micro and macro perspectives. Second, this research offers two units of analyses showcasing respondents' current and future perceptions of their cultural practices ("as is" and "should be"). Third, this research also introduced two new cultural dimensions, performance and human orientation, not addressed in Hofstede's classic pioneering research. Fourth, the masculinity dimension has been differentiated into assertiveness and gender egalitarianism to reflect both masculinity-femininity and also gender equity. This expansion of the cultural dimension provides a more comprehensive understanding of these concepts (Hofstede, Hofstede, and Minkov 3–26; Gannon and Pillai 3–23; Chokkar, Brodbeck and House 1–31).

Most cultural studies in the field of business management rely on the seminal researches of Hofstede and GLOBE. Both these studies have been applauded and criticized for several methodological reasons (Tung and Verbeke 1260–1262; Gannon and Pillai 3–23). The GLOBE study is considered more current (1990s) than that of Hofstede's (1970s). The research project of GLOBE involved 150 researchers from different countries surveying managerial employees from 951 non-multinational organizations from diverse industries. Hofstede was the primary investigator of his cross-cultural research based on a single multinational that surveyed managerial and non-managerial employees from an information technology industry (Hofstede, Hofstede, and Minkov 3–26). Table 3 provides the main differences and similarities between these two insightful research studies (Rao 301).

Table 3. Primary Differences Between the Hofstede and the GLOBE Study

#	Points of Difference	GLOBE Study	HOFSTEDE's Study
1	Time Frame	1994–1997	1967–1973
2	Primary researchers involved	170	1
3	Respondents	Managers	Non-managers and managers
4	Organizations surveyed	951	1
5	Type of organization	Non-multinational	Multinational (and its subsidiaries)
6	Industries	Food processing, financial and telecommunication services	Information technology
7	Number of societies surveyed	62	72
8	Research analysis	Team effort	Single person's effort
9	Project design	U.S.-based	Dutch-based
10	Cultural dimensions identified	Nine dimensions	Four dimensions

Source: Pramila Rao, The Role of National Culture on Mexican Staffing Practices." Employee Relations 31.3 (2009): 295–311. Print.

The strength of the GLOBE cultural project was the integration of scholars from all over the world. The primary investigators of this project were distinguished researchers from schools such as Wharton School of Management, University of Maryland, among others. Each country was represented by a team of scholars (two to five members) who are natives and had extensive publications in their field. These country representatives performed both qualitative and quantitative research to obtain the cultural dimension scores (House et al. 5–7). The unique contributions of this global study are that it identified cultural dimensions (9), cultural clusters (10), and leadership dimensions (6) enriching this body of literature (Javidan et al. 97–100). The literature constantly debates and discusses the pros and cons of both these studies (GLOBE and Hofstede) implying their importance to the cross-cultural field (Tung and Verbeke 1260–1262; Gannon and Pillai 3–23).

In the GLOBE study, Mexico scored the following scores for these dimensions: assertiveness (4.45; Rank 16), in-group collectivism (5.71; Rank 12), gender-egalitarianism (3.64; Rank 16); uncertainty-avoidance (4.18; Rank 26), institutional collectivism (4.06; Rank 38), future-orientation (3.87; Rank 26), performance-orientation (4.10; Rank 32), human orientation (3.98; 34) and power-distance (5.22; Rank 30) (Chhokar, Brodbeck, and House 723–765). Table 4 provides the scores and ranks of Mexico on these various cultural dimensions.

Table 4. GLOBE's National Cultural Dimensions for Mexico

#	National Cultural Dimensions	Scores	Rank
1	Assertiveness	4.45	16
2	Institutional Collectivism	4.06	38
3	In-Group Collectivism	5.71	12
4	Future-Orientation	3.87	26
5	Gender Egalitarianism	3.64	16
6	Humane Orientation	3.98	34
7	Performance orientation	4.10	32
8	Power Distance	5.22	30
9	Uncertainty-Avoidance	4.18	26

Source: Chhokar, Jagdeep, Felix Brodbeck, and Robert House. Culture and Leadership Across the World: The GLOBE Book of In-Depth Studies of 25 Societies. *Mahwah, NJ: Lawrence Erlbaum Associates, 2007. Print.*

It is important to bear in mind when analyzing national scores that there can be a lot of cultural diversity among any local population. This could be based on demographic characteristics such as age, gender, geographical regions, occupational positions etc. Further, international trends such as globalization (presence of multinationals) and migration (leaving and returning of brain drain talent) could also create cultural differences among locals. Thus, to assume any country demonstrates truly bipolar dimensions (such as collectivist or individualistic) based on these national scores of any cross-cultural research may be an incorrect assumption (Tung and Verbeke 260–1262).

This essay will discuss only the cultural dimensions of *power-distance, uncertainty-avoidance, and institutional collectivism* which have demonstrated to influence organizational training methods. Mexican organizations have a preferences for internal trainers, structured formats, and group efforts towards their employee development (Envick, Langford, and Martinez 13–16).

Large Mexican organizations prefer to adopt internal trainers who demonstrate subject matter expertize. High power-distance cultures favor to adopt internal employees proficient in content areas to disseminate training information. These methods provide additional authority and status to the trainers. Employees from high-power-distance cultures deeply cherish any display of power in the workplace. Also, an authority providing training content in high-power-distance cultures has better learning results with the trainees as they feel a deep sense of commitment to their superiors (Nathan 18–20, Rodrigues 611–613; Edmundson 45).

Rao identified from a study of best companies in Mexico that employees preferred to learn from their own superiors as they felt their bosses might share the most authentic industry experiences. The manager from this study also indicated that internal trainers have a much better effect on training outcomes than external trainers. This could reflect the dynamics of power-distance as employees pay more attention to training programs directed by their superiors as a result of their loyalties to their bosses (33–51).

High uncertainty-avoidance cultures, with their inclination to avoid ambiguity, prefer training methods that will reduce the uncertainty in the learning process. Employees from such cultures prefer to have methods that are clearly structured with minimum ambiguity. Thus programs that have face-to-face training with clear outcomes will be compatible with local values. On the other hand, e-learning methods may face challenges as it leaves room for gray areas in the training process (Burke et al. 137–142; Reynolds 36).

Collectivist cultures prefer a participatory approach to learning as it demonstrates a collaborative spirit in learning. Individuals from these cultures exhibit a strong emphasis on group or team accomplishments rather than on solitary or individual achievements. The focus on belonging and learning in special in-groups is also cherished in collectivist cultures. Thus, providing any team formats in training is congruent with the national culture and frequently used in their manufacturing environments (Daily, Bishoup and Massoud 641, 642).

The learning styles in collectivist cultures also is quite different. The focus in collectivist cultures is towards a deductive training style, while individualistic cultures prefer an inductive training style. Deductive learners learn concepts from the general to the specific principles, while inductive learners learn from the specific to the general principles (Nathan 20). Deductive methods tend to be informative or instructional, while those of inductive training emphasize problem-solving and critical thinking skills. In a deductive approach, the trainer is usually the subject-matter-expert, while in an inductive approach the trainer serves as either a facilitator or an expert (Lohman 437–440). In Mexico, there is a preference for didactic or instructional training formats as the educational system has fostered a passive learning approach among individuals (Dávila and Elvira 14).

Scholarly studies have reflected the local culture's values towards training methods and formats. In an empirical study of 83 U.S. affiliates (joint ventures and wholly-owned) in Mexico (Envick, Langford and Martinez 11–15) classroom training was identified as commonly used method to train employees. This method of training allows for both an instructive (reduces uncertainty-avoidance) and a discussant format (encourages collectivism) that the culture prefers. Training videos in this study included Mexican employees performing the main roles and identifying important cultural values to make the learning modules culturally appealing and realistic (Envick, Langford and Martinez 11–15).

Best Training Practices of Domestic and Multinational Subsidiaries

This final section will showcase several best practices from various Mexican companies from different industries.

The Mexican retailer Liverpool was a pioneer in offering e-learning services to its employees. It won the Society of Human Resource Management award, for providing rigorous e-learning at a time when most domestic organizations were not offering such innovative training practices. E-learning practices are an emerging trend in Mexico as the collectivist culture commonly prefers face-to-face structured interactions for training. E-learning is usually a solitary learning experience for learners and technical glitches may lead to moments of uncertainty (Moss 50–52; Rianhard 57). In 2002, the firm established the Liverpool Virtual University (LVU) that offered employees opportunities to master several work-related skills. The management observed that learning opportunities enhanced their employee retention especially in an industry that is marked with frequent job-hopping. This retail organization has become a model in the business community as other retailers seek their guidance on professional development. LVU also offered blended methods of e-learning modules with both synchronous (live instructors) and asynchronous (learners train at their own pace) formats so that cultural preferences of personal interaction is also fulfilled (Moss 50–52). The company has graduated almost 5000 employees from this university since its inception (Liverpool).

Cemex, the Mexican leader in cement industry, provides various methods of professional development right from the time employees are inducted into their organization. In their orientation programs, in-house trainers introduce the company's business model to ensure new employees understand the company's strong focus on superior quality from the very first day. The orientation programs are also customized to different employee levels so that the training sessions are more meaningful to new employees. Employees are constantly expected to take advantage of the numerous online courses offered by the company in various subject disciplines. The company was also awarded for its superior safety training programs that it provides via e-learning modules (Fernandez; Wilson and Chang 28–30). Further, new employees are frequently relocated overseas as international experiences are considered valuable forms of learning and education (Fernandez). Cemex also customizes education for their senior talent by collaborating with leading business schools providing individualized developmental programs. The company is a global leader in cement as it operates in several emerging economies, successfully understanding their local markets thoroughly through a well-trained workforce (Wilson and Chang 28–30).

Grupo Bimbo, the leader in bakery products, has invested in elaborate human capital development via external coaching consultants. The company wants its executive cadre to navigate its various international markets efficiently and successfully. Over the past eight years, the company has enrolled 420 executives with international consultants to receive intense development on cross-cultural skills to ensure they become inspiring global leaders in their own markets (Development Dimension International).

Several multinational subsidiaries act as role models in their efforts towards providing professional development. For instance, Unilever, the European company, in Mexico offers "*Aprendizaje de Univeler*, that provides more than 7600 distance education learning modules. Management employees have taken advantage of these educational programs with almost 95% of their employees participating in this learning system. McDonald's offers entry-level employees professional development opportunities at their international Hamburger University. The German automobile industry, in conjunction with the local government, offers high quality vocational training for employees at their automobile factories in Puebla, Mexico. This system of providing occupational training specific to the industry is an excellent method to address specific skill inadequacies. The German organizations are definitely duplicating their nation's method of employee development and skill enhancement" (McKinsey Global Institute 88).

Rao identified superior training practices in a qualitative study of six "best" companies from diverse industries of hospitality management, medical services, foods and beverages, financial services, and air delivery and freight services (33–51). These organizations offered programs such as authentic leadership training that included organizational leaders sharing actual leadership experiences (successes and failures) with their employees. This "live" format of learning offers employees a hands-on experience of actual situations in their own industries. This kind of learning is also very meaningful in Mexico as subordinates view their superiors as absolute experts. Peer coaching was provided by high-performing employees to other employees offering realistic perspectives of their TDRs (tasks, duties, and responsibilities). This team-based learning has positive outcomes in Mexico as its culture endorses any collective kind of training. Educational certifications were offered to employees from distinguished international universities on completion of relevant learning modules. Any distinction among employees in the workplace based on titles or certifications is appreciated in the local culture. Youth training was provided to integrate the economically disadvantaged applicants by providing them in-house training and identifying their developmental needs. Mexican employees like to get engaged with their local communities via any corporate social initiatives which again ties in with their collective spirits (Rao 33–51).

Mexican firms have initiated innovative training initiatives to reach out to individuals at the "bottom of the pyramid (BOP)." These BOP employees are usually low-skilled employees who are trying to upgrade their skills for economic advancement. For example, CEMEX has empowered low-skilled employees by providing finance and training so that they can become micro-entrepreneurs in selling cement. These corporate practices ensure that individuals are not marginalized based on their socio-economic statuses and also demonstrates strong communal spirits that organizations should portray (C.K. Prahalad 6–11).

Conclusion

Professional training efforts in Mexico are a result of close collaboration among the governments, its institutions, universities, and large organizations. The federal government has been very instrumental in providing support for training and development through employment laws and several educational initiatives making professional learning a very important agenda. (Luna-Reyes, Gil-Garcia, and Cruz 58, 59; OECD "e-government studies"). Large organizations have the potential and resources to offer various forms of internal and external training methods. Universities also play a very significant role in specialized training and coordinate with leading organizations to provide valuable industry-specific training (Buckley 23).

External trends such as the establishing of free trade agreements (FTAs) and globalization (presence of multinationals) has also contributed significantly to the development of the knowledge capital of the local talent. FTAs have made local companies increasingly aware of the quality of their products that they have to export and thus have invested in enhancing skill development of their employees. The presence of several multinationals in Mexico has allowed local companies to absorb best practices in training. Multinationals also invest in elaborate employee development to ensure they have a qualified workforce (Villareal and Fegusson, 15; Villareal 3–13).

Cultural norms of power-distance, uncertainty-avoidance, and in-group collectivism may contribute to locals' preferences for specific formats of instructional design (Nathan 20; Russell, 42–44). Employees may prefer group training as the local culture enjoys harmony and camaraderie in any organizational initiatives. These preferences also could be strengthened by Mexicans' indirect communication styles which makes trainees more open with their peers rather than with their superiors (Edmundson 45). However, individual training via personal leaders is also a norm as subordinates in Mexico are extremely loyal and respectful to their bosses. Thus any learning from their own leaders becomes more meaningful and engaging (Rao 40).

Today several of the large Mexican companies have received international awards for their distinguished efforts towards human capital expansion (Moss 50–52; Wilson and Chang 28–30). The Mexican government also has been identified for its exemplary dedication to enhance the knowledge capital of its labor force (OECD "e-government studies"). The small and medium size companies that form the predominant proportion of the market share do not have adequate resources to invest in their employees' skills. Policy makers should identify additional strategies to enhance the skill sets as the nation's overall productivity depends on all its actors performing well (McKinsey 16, 17).

There are several additional strategies that key stakeholders can implement to enhance the knowledge capital of Mexican employees. First, organizations should be encouraged to form partnerships with universities for aligning their talent requirements with tailored educational curriculum for both mid and senior levels. Currently, in Mexico, a focus of this kind of collaboration exists predominantly for executive education. These academic outreach initiatives should be broadened to include other management levels also (Speizer 59, 60; Kastelein 48–50). The phenomenal success of the Indian IT industry is built on creating strategic relationships between universities and organizations to develop qualified talent pools *at all levels* (Cappelli et al. 49–85).

Second, universities should be encouraged to establish *diplomados* (short tailored courses) for employees in small and medium (SME) firms also. These firms form the backbone of the nation's economy and yet their employees are not qualified or trained enough to global standards. These employees will benefit with specific certifications from universities that will allow them to develop basic managerial or technical skills (United States Mexico Chamber of Commerce "Helping small businesses" 42, 43). Currently most universities offer *diplomados* for upper-level managers of large organizations (Kastelein 48–50; Garrett 39–40). The topics of these *diplomados* should be broadened to capture the interests of employees from SMEs as well (United-States Mexico Chamber of Commerce "Helping small businesses" 42, 43).

Third, organizations should frequently conduct a comprehensive needs analysis to identify and develop specific training programs. A needs analysis is a structured organizational practice that allows managers to get a holistic idea of what precise skills sets their employees lack, offer such precise programs, and evaluate its effectiveness (Dessler 134, 150; Cantu de la Torre and Cantu Licón 20). Most Mexican organizations fail to do a thorough needs analysis which is considered the preliminary step for a robust training framework. They also rarely evaluate the results of their training initiatives on productivity or profits (Gurchiek).

Fourth, organizations that have the resources should create virtual universities as it will help develop idiosyncratic talent specific to their industries. A case in point, Liverpool, a very successful retailer in Mexico, offers customer service, sales management, and merchandise administration classes to enhance its employees' professional profiles. This organization has witnessed tremendous success in terms of productivity and retention in its industry (Liverpool, Moss 50–52).

Fifth, organizations that can provide vocational training for lower-skilled levels should offer such programs. These employees definitely do not have the financial resources to attend university education (OECD "Education policy outlook"). Most subsidiaries of multinationals in Mexico do offer this kind of training to entry-level employees. The German model of education and business revolve around the concept of developing individuals' occupational skills and integrating such skilled talent into their workforces. Large Mexican organizations that have the resources and capital should invest in such skill development for lower-level employees (Daniels; McKinsey 72). In 2011, only 4 percent of Mexican students had completed vocational training compared to the global average of 47 percent (OECD "Education policy outlook").

Finally, banks and large organizations should be encouraged to play stronger roles in the promotion of SMEs. For instance, they can lend capital to these small firms as their lack of monetary resources often impedes them from investing in robust HRM practices. For example, Alibaba, a leading Chinese online retailer, promotes the growth of micro companies by offering them substantial financial help. This collaborative spirit among companies benefits the entire economy and ultimately enhances the productivity of the nation (McKinsey 17).

Thus, the enhancement of Mexico's human capital requires a *stronger* collaboration of all its key stakeholders—the government, private sector, universities, and banks. This investment also requires policy makers to reexamine its educational system and standards. A qualified workforce is also dependent on a robust academic curriculum. While the Mexican government has invested considerably in public training platforms, this investment still lags behind Scandinavian and western nations (Villar, Linas-Audet and Escardbul 13; OECD "Education policy outlook"). Multinationals have also invested considerably in providing vocational training to lower-skilled employees (McKinsey 9).

Mexico has become a regional and global leader in various industries because of its talented workforces. It has been recognized by Goldman Sachs, a leading consulting firm, as one of the emerging nations that will show a lot of economic promise in the next decade. The MIST (Mexico, Indonesia, South Korea and Turkey) nations will show a lot of potential as their business and government leaders proactively invest in their labor to showcase their best knowledge capital to the business world (Brent 21). A well-trained and developed workforce is a definite passport to organizational success and sustained competitive advantage. An economy of any nation finally hinges on the competencies of its employees and their knowledge capital (Hatch and Dyer 1156–1158).

Discussion Questions

1. Distinguish between the concepts of training and development.
2. How has the government supported initiatives for training and development in Mexican organizations?
3. How has NAFTA shaped training and development of employees in Mexico?
4. What is the difference between inductive and deductive training styles?
5. Do you learn inductively or deductively? How do you prefer to be trained?
6. Which national cultural dimensions impact training? How?
7. Identify how your local culture has impacted your learning style?
8. Explain some best practices identified in Mexican companies for training and development?
9. Why do you think customized education for executives is so much in demand in Mexico?
10. What are some additional recommendations you have for Mexican stakeholders to enhance their efforts for organizational training and development?

Key Learning Terms

Deductive learning: Deductive learners learn concepts from the general to specific principles.

Development: Development focuses on providing employees KSAs that will be required in their careers for the future.

Future-orientation: The degree to which individuals in organizations or societies plan for the future.

Gender egalitarianism: The degree to which organizations or society promote gender equality.

Inductive learning: Inductive learners learn from the specific to general principles.

In-group collectivism: The degree to which individuals in societies reflect collectivist behavior.

Needs analysis: A process that allows organizations to understand their business strategies and their employees' KSAs to identify the required training programs.

Power-distance: The degree to which organizations and societies display differentiation of power among its members.

Training: Training can be defined as providing individuals sufficient knowledge, skills, and abilities (KSAs) to perform their current jobs adequately.

Uncertainty-avoidance: The degree to which organizations and societies avoid ambiguity and uncertainty.

REFERENCES

Arias-Galicia, Fernando. "Human Resource Management in Mexico." *Managing Human Resources in Latin America*. Ed. Anabella Dávila and Marta Elvira. London: Routledge. 2005. 179–190. Print.

Authers, John, and Sara Silver. "Sights Set on Foreign Students: The Two Schools Have Educated Almost Half of Mexico's Senior Executives." *Financial Times*, May 27, 2002. *ProQuest*. Web. 24 March 2015.

Brent, Paul. "A Few Bricks Short of a Load?" *Canadian Business* (November 23, 2009): 21. Print.

Buckley, Tom. "Top of the Class." *Business Mexico* 15.2 (2005): 23. Print.

Burke, Michael, et al. "The Role of National Culture and Organizational Climate in Safety Training Effectiveness." *European Journal of Work and Organizational Psychology* 17.1 (2008): 133–152.

Cable, Josh. "Operators Lead the Way." *Industry Week* (January 2010): 31–32. Print.

Cantú de la Torre, Ismael, and Liliana Cantú Licón. "Focus on Mexico." *Training* 46.2 (2009): 20. Print.

Cappelli, Peter, et al. *The India Way: How India's Top Business Leaders Are Revolutionizing Management*. Boston: Harvard Business Press, 2011. Print.

Chhokar, Jagdeep, Felix Brodbeck, and Robert House. *Culture and Leadership Across the World: The GLOBE Book of In-Depth Studies of 25 Societies*. Mahwah, NJ: Lawrence Erlbaum Associates, 2007. Print.

Daily, Bonnie, John Bishop, and Jacob Massoud. "The Role of Training and Empowerment in Environmental Performance." *International Journal of Operations & Production Management* 32.5 (2012): 631–647.

Daniels, Serena. "Twenty Five Years After NAFTA, a Mini Detroit Rises in Mexico." September 2014. Web. 22 March 2015.

Dávila, Anabella. "Meet the Person Perspectives." *HRMexico: Human Resource Management in Mexico: Perspectives for Scholars and Practitioners*, 2d ed. Ed. Pramila Rao. Charlotte: IAP Publishing, 2015. 137–142. Print.

Dávila, Anabella, and Marta Elvira. "Culture and Human Resource Management in Latin America." *Managing Human Resources in Latin America*. Ed. Marta Elvira and Anabella Dávila. London: Routledge, 2005. 3–24. Print.

Dessler, Gary. *A Framework for Human Resource Management*, 6th ed. New York. Prentice Hall, 2011. Print.

Development Dimension International. "Grupo Bimbo's Story: On Growing Global Leadership." Interview with Lucy Chauvet, HR Director of Grupo Bimbo. 2014. Web. 22 March 2015.

Drickhamer, David. "Baxter Mexico: IW Best Plants Profile 2008." *Industry Week* (December 12, 2008): 1–2. Web. 20 March 2015.
Edmundson, Andrea. "Culturally Accessible E-Learning: An Overdue Global Business Imperative." *Training and Development* 63.4 (2009): 40–45. Print.
Envick, Brooke, Margaret Langford, and Zaida Martinez. "International Training and Development: A Study of U.S. Parent-Mexican Affiliate Practices." *Latin American Business Review* 3.2 (2002): 1–16. Print.
Fernandez, Jose. "CEMEX Takes the High Road." *NYSE Magazine* (October/November 2006). Web. 22 March 2015.
Gannon, Martin, and Rajnandini Pillai. *Understanding Global Cultures: Metaphorical Journeys through 29 Nations, Clusters of Nations, Continents and Diversity*. Los Angeles. Sage, 2010. Print.
Garrett, Kelly. "Creating Capable Business Leaders." *Business Mexico* 15.5 (2005): 38–40. Print.
Geert Hofstede, Gert Jan Hofstede. and Michale Minkov. *Cultures and Organizations, Software of the Mind: Intercultural Cooperation and Its Importance for Survival*. New York: McGraw-Hill, 2010. Print.
Gleason, Megan. "Escape Artists." *Business Mexico* 15.12 (2005): 54–55. Print.
Gomez-Mejia, Luiz, David Balkin, and Robert Cardy. *Managing Human Resources*, 6th ed. New York: Prentice Hall, 2010. Print.
G20 Taskforce on Employment. "Job Creation and Labor Activation Policies in G20 Countries." 2013. Web. 22 March 2015.
Gurchiek, Kathy. "Mexico HR Group Create Certificate Program." Society for Human Resource Management, March 2014. Web. 22 March 2015.
Hatch, Nile, and Jeffrey Dyer. "Human Capital and Learning as a Source of Sustainable Competitive Advantage." *Strategic Management Journal* 25.12 (2004): 1155–1178. Print.
Heylman, Susan. "Mexico Employers Must Have Employee Productivity Training Programs." *HR Magazine* 58.1 (2013): 16. Print.
House, Robert, et al. "Understanding Cultures and Implicit Leadership Theories Across the Globe: An Introduction to Project GLOBE." *Journal of World Business* 37.1 (2002): 3–10. Print.
Javidan, Mansour, et al. "In the Eye of the Beholder: Cross-Cultural Lessons in Leadership from Project GLOBE." *Academy of Management Perspectives* 20.1 (2006): 67–90.
Kastelein, Barbara. "Tailored Learning." *Business Mexico* 10.5 (2000): 47–51.
Liverpool. Fact Sheet. 2015. Web. 22 March 2015.
Lohman, Margaret. "Deductive and Inductive On-the-Job Training Strategies." *Advances in Developing Human Resources* 3.4 (2001): 435–441.
Luna-Reyer, L., R. Gil-Garcia, and C. Cruz. "E-Mexico: Collaborative Structures in Mexican Public Administration." *International Journal of Cases on Electronic Commerce* 3.2 (2007): 4–70.
McKinsey Global Institute. *A Tale of Two Mexicos: Growth and Prosperity in a Two-Speed Economy*. March 2014. Web. 22 March 2015.
Moss, Desda. "A Lesson in Learning." *HRMagazine* 52.11 (2007): 50–53. Print.
Murphy, David. "Global Leadership Potential in Mexican Firms." *Management Research News* 29.3 (2006): 80–91. Print.
Nathan, Edward. "Global Organizations and E-Learning: Leveraging about Learning in Different Cultures." *Performance Improvement* 47.6 (2008): 18–24. Print.
OECD (Organization for Economic Cooperation and Development) OECD e-Government Studies Mexico. 2005. Web. 22 March 2015.
OECD. Economic Surveys Mexico. May 2013. Web. 22 March 2015.
OECD. Education policy outlook: Mexico. November 2013. Web. 22 March 2015.
Petrick, Joseph, and Foster Rinefort. "The Challenge of Managing Mexican Workplace Safety." *Business & Society Review* 111.2 (2006): 223–234. Print.
Prahalad, Krishnarao. *The Fortune at the Bottom of the Pyramid. Eradicating Poverty through Profits*. Upper Saddle River, NJ: Pearson Education, 2010. Print.
Ramos, Kenneth. "Meet the Person Perspectives." *HRMexico: Human Resource Management in Mexico: Perspectives for Scholars and Practitioners*, 2d ed. Ed. Pramila Rao. Charlotte: IAP Publishing, 2015. 115–122. Print.
Rao, Pramila. *HRMexico: Human Resource Management in Mexico: Perspectives for Scholars and Practitioners*. Charlotte: IAP Publishing, 2012. 33–51. Print.

_____. "The Role of National Culture on Mexican Staffing Practices." *Employee Relations* 31.3 (2009): 295–311. Print.
Reynolds, Penny. "Yearning for E-Learning? The Pros and Cons of the Virtual Classroom for Your Call Center." *Customer Inter@ction Solutions* 27.1 (2008): 36–37. Print.
Rianhard, Carl. "E-learning." *Business Mexico* 12.9 (2002): 57. Print.
Rodrigues, Carl. "Culture as a Determinant of the Importance Level Business Students Place on Ten teaching/Learning Techniques: A Survey of University Students." *Journal of Management Development* 24.7/8 (2005): 608–622. Print.
Ruiz, Carlos. "The Impact of NAFTA on Training and Development in Mexico: The Perspective of Mexican Senior Government Agency Officials." *New Horizons in Adult Education and Human Resource Development* 23.4 (2009): 51–66.
_____. "The Impact of NAFTA on Training and Development in Mexico: The Perspective of Mexican Senior Government Agency Officials." 2008. Web. 22 March 2015.
Russell, Roxanne. "Training for Innovation in India: Cultural Considerations and Strategic Implications." *Performance Improvement Quarterly* 21.2. (2008): 37–49. Print.
Shepard, Lorrie. "The Role of Assessment in a Learning Culture." *Educational Researcher* 29.7 (2010): 4–14. Print.
Speizer, Irwin. "Custom Fit." *Workforce Management* 84.3 (2005): 57–63. Print.
STPS (Secretaria del trabajo y previsión social). Coordinación de Capacitación a Distancia. Cursos por estado. 2013. Web. March 2015.
STPS (Secretaria del trabajo y previsión social). Coordinación de Capacitación a Distancia. Subdirección de Tutoría en Línea. 2013. Web. March 2015.
"Top 10 strategies: Training." *Business Mexico* 10/11.2 (2001): 50–53. Print.
Tung, Rosalie, and Alain Verbeke. "Beyond Hofstede and GLOBE: Improving the Quality of Cross-Cultural Research." *Journal of International Business Studies* 41.8 (2010): 1259–1274. Print.
United States Mexico Chamber of Commerce. "Helping Small Businesses." *Alliance Business Magazine* (October 2011): 42–43. Print.
_____. "It Is Time to Move Mexico Forward—Enrique Pena Nieto." *Alliance Business Magazine* (March 2013): 21–25. Print.
_____. "Mexico's New Labor Law: A Step Forward to Greater Competitiveness." *Alliance Business Magazine* (March 2013): 42–43. Print.
Villar, Alejandro, Xavier Llinàs-Audet, and Josep-Oriol Escardíbul. "International Briefing 31: Training and Development in Mexico." *International Journal of Training and Development* 17.4 (2013): 310–320. Print.
Villareal, Angeles. "Mexico's Free Trade Agreements." Congressional Research Service, 2012. Web. 22 March 2015.
Villareal, Angeles, and Ian Fegusson. "NAFTA at 20: Overview and Trade Effects." Congressional Research Service, 2014. Web. 22 March 2015.
Wharton University of Pennsylvania. "How Culture Affects Work Practices in Latin America." Knowledge at Wharton, 2005. Web. 22 March 2015.
Wilson, Deirdre, and Calvin Chang. "CEMEX Promotes a Sustainable Approach with Manufacturing Excellence." *Environmental Quality Management* 12.4 (2003): 23–34. Print.

Perceptions of Ethical Decision Making in Mexican Business
State of the Literature and an Exploratory Study

Miguel R. Olivas-Luján

Ethics is a word that generates disconcerting—and sometimes impassionate—reactions when applied to cross-cultural interactions between Mexico and the United States. As the study of moral principles and associated behaviors, its wide variety of philosophies and frameworks creates an environment ripe for misunderstandings, especially when these two countries share one of the longest borders in the world and their interactions have increased exponentially in recent years.

Popular press in the U.S. often portrays Mexico as a country with ubiquitous corruption, where the rule of law has been overpowered by drug cartels, and the line between big business interests and political advantages has been blurred. Unfortunately, well-publicized cases within Mexico that include politicians at the highest level getting astoundingly rich a few months after their elections, U.S. companies getting caught breaking laws from both sides of the border and a never-ending onslaught of violence spreading throughout the country, contribute to this gloomy perception that ethics in Mexico are close to non-existent. In parallel, most Americans who have interacted with Mexicans in the United States are likely to have perceived the "Mexican work ethic," described as taking the toughest jobs, for less pay and at the highest performance levels. This seems to be noticed by automakers and other manufacturers, which have been increasing their investments in Mexico thanks to the fact they find "First World productivity and quality at Third World wages" (UC Berkeley's Professor Harley Shaiken, quoted by Miroff).

The popular view of U.S. ethics from the Mexican side is equally ambiguous. Many Mexicans perceive the U.S. as a materialistic, hedonistic country whose affluence has created a (paraphrasing a now famous phrase in a slightly different context) "giant, sucking demand" for drugs. If it were not for such a demand, the narrative goes, Mexico would not have the violence stemming from the organized criminals fighting to serve that market—as well as the domestic markets of imitators of all that is perceived as "hot" in the USA, be it illegal drugs, clothes, fast food, technology, and most, if not all things American. Still, Mexicans working with U.S. citizens open their homes and their hearts to them, and admire the country's organization and technical prowess. In spite of all the perceived problems, the "American dream" is still attractive to Mexicans immigrating both legally and illegally into the United States.

Interest in business ethics within Mexico has increased in the past years, due in part to the economic integration that the North American Free Trade Agreement (NAFTA) has created for this region. For example, moral implications of the *maquiladora* industry in particular, and of economic integration in North America in general have been analyzed by many (e.g., AFL-CIO; Barrera Bassols; LaDou; Moure-Eraso et al.; Sanchez; Sargent and Matthews; USITC). Political, drug trafficking scandals in Mexico (as well as other countries) are obstacles to expecting ethical practices within the region (Arruda). The perception that Mexicans do not strongly value or support ethical standards undoubtedly affects the development of legitimate international business relationships. This perception may even attract business ventures whose aim is to profit from an environment seen as having bendable standards.

However, little evidence currently exists to clarify whether or not such perception is true, or it merely reflects prevalent stereotypes about the Mexican culture (cf. Arruda). Almost two decades ago, Husted (referenced by Dunfee and Werhane) stated that business ethics in Mexico is just emerging as a focus of interest in both the business and academic domains. Most of the academic activity on ethics in Latin America has been unfortunately focused on teaching, primarily using case studies (cf. Schmidt). The need for research-based evidence on ethical decision-making and similar strong influences of management on society appears clear and pressing.

The purpose of this essay is threefold: first, it includes a summary of the limited amount of research on ethical decision making in Mexico to date published in the business ethics journals at the individual level of analysis. Second, it presents the results of an empirical study on business ethics at the aggregated, organizational level of analysis. Third, exploratory empirical results about the ethical environment construct used in the study are presented to encourage more research efforts on this topic.

Individual-Level Ethics Studies About Mexico

A few individual-level studies about business ethics in Mexico have appeared in the academic literature, comparing Mexican subjects to samples from other nationalities. To summarize, these studies have not found large differences between Mexican decision-makers and their counterparts from other nations. One exception is a study by Volkema, who found that graduate business students from Mexico had a greater disparity than their U.S. counterparts in their likely use and perceived appropriateness of unethical negotiation behaviors, but in a counterintuitive fashion: specifically, Mexican MBA students rated questionable negotiation behaviors as *less* appropriate than their U.S. counterparts did. This empirical finding contradicts the stereotype that ethical standards of U.S. respondents are higher than those that can be found in Mexico. It would be easy to dismiss Volkema's findings as a difference stemming from social desirability (the tendency that respondents have to answer polls in ways that are more socially acceptable), but the data collection method was robust enough to endure anonymous peer review before being published.

On the other hand (and consistent with the stereotype), Tadepalli, Moreno and Treviño found statistically significant differences in perceptions about questionable practices for purchasing managers. The American respondents showed a higher level of ethical concerns toward seven situations that are typical to commercial transactions, such as accepting free trips, gifts and meals from salespersons. The differences in magnitude, however, were relatively small: only one item ("it is acceptable to make exaggerated statements to a supplier in order to gain a concession") had an average score that differed by more than one point in a Likert scale (1.37 for American managers versus 2.50 for Mexicans). The other items differed by .89 or less and the standard deviations did not exceed 1.19 (on a sample of 150 managers). Tadepalli and his colleagues stressed the need to consider their findings within the cultural, political and economic contexts in which their respondents are located, rather than identifying one group as more ethical than the other. As a noteworthy contribution, they propose a model that takes into consideration the stage of evolution in which the professions are in the U.S. and Mexico to explain the differences in perceptions they found.

Marta, Heiss and De Lurgio ran another study focused on perceived ethical problems among marketing professionals in both countries. In contrast with the study by Volkema, U.S. respondents scored higher in terms of religiousness and corporate ethical values—which were hypothesized as predictors of perceived ethical problems—and also were significantly more likely to consider problems as "ethical" than their Mexican counterparts. On the other hand, this study showed consistency with Tadepalli et al.'s in that Marta and colleagues suggest that the differences in findings are likely to stem from the countries' differences in economic development. In many other cultures—particularly in Asia and the Middle East, but even European cultures are very accepting of this—customs such as gift giving, after hours entertaining and similar customs that would be frowned upon in the USA are considered an integral part of business (Morrison and Conaway); these divergent findings are likely to reflect cultural differences in interpretation. As Coria-Sánchez writes in his essay, neither country's preferences can be categorically classified as more ethical than the other's; they are simply different.

Earlier, Husted, Dozier, McMahon, and Kattan had found significant differences in moral reasoning of U.S. versus Mexican MBA students. Mexican (and Spanish) MBAs used "lower" levels of moral reasoning stages (Kohlberg) than their U.S. counterparts did, when tested by using Rest's Defining Issues Test. Despite some significant differences in the forms of moral reasoning of their samples, Husted and his colleagues reached the conclusion that "a consensus is emerging around a core of moral judgments or attitudes regarding questionable practices" (406).

Similarly, Etheredge and Erdener examined differences in adherence to three ethical philosophies (non-consequentialist orientations, rule utilitarianism, and act utilitarianism) between undergraduate students from China, South Korea, Mexico, and the U.S. Their results for Mexico and the U.S. revealed statistically significant differences in act utilitarianism only. Significantly different responses from South Korea and China suggest that cultural components (in particular religion, as the results from a small Hispanic-American sub-sample similar to the Mexican sample in the study indicate) influence preferences in ethical orientation.

Finally, Elahee and Brooks empirically found that Mexican business people show lower trust levels when they negotiate cross-culturally than when they do so with fellow Mexicans, in addition to endorsing the use of more competitive (or ethically "dubious") negotiation tactics. Elahee and Brooks also report previous research findings that Mexican negotiators have a more favorable perception of Spanish counterparts than they have of those from the U.S. From a social identity theory perspective (Tajfel and Turner), this result is not surprising, as people regardless of nationality—tend to treat more favorably those that are perceived as members of the "in-group" when compared to those perceived as members of the "out-group." These differential levels of trust affected the type of negotiation tactics considered acceptable: the more distant (from a cultural perspective) the opposing negotiator, the more acceptable the questionable negotiation tactics (e.g., competitive bargaining or haggling, false promises, positional misrepresentations, etc.).

On the other hand, Mexicans have been documented to exhibit "*malinchismo*" (a reference to Malintzin, Malinalli or "Doña Marina," a Native Mexican woman whose language and cross-cultural skills helped conquistador Hernán Cortés subdue the Aztec empire with a relatively small group of Spanish soldiers in the 16th century). Mexican *malinchismo* in business translates into preferring foreign brands, suppliers and most things foreign to national ones. This phenomenon has been well documented (Ueltschy and Ryans) and coexists with "Lo Hecho en México Está Bien Hecho" (which literally means "What's made in Mexico is well done"), "buy national" campaigns.

Although scant, research on individuals' ethics on business decisions suggests little differences between Mexico and the U.S. One can offer several interpretations from these findings. First is that given the limited amount of research, conclusions should wait until more evidence is gathered. This interpretation emphasizes the pressing need for research on this topic. Second is that perhaps individuals in these two cultures are more similar than dissimilar on their ethical decision-making. This would be consistent with studies that hint "cultural convergence," such as Allmon, Chen, Prichett and Forrest's. They state that the agreement in perceptions of ethical business practices among their respondents (proceeding from Australia, Taiwan and the U.S.) tips the balance more toward universality of perceptions than toward "national relativism" (DeGeorge).

Organizational-Level Ethics Studies

A third interpretation to existing perceptions of business ethics in Mexico is that perhaps the critical differences between these two cultures do not exist at the individual level, but at the organizational level. Unfortunately, the literature reviewed as a basis for this article did not produce any studies at this higher (i.e., aggregated) level of analysis (cf. Rousseau). This distinction is critical, given that business ethics researchers attribute ethical behavior to two major classifications of predictors: individual and organizational level determinants (e.g., Treviño; Treviño and Youngblood; Stajkovic and Luthans). For example, Wimbush, Shepard, and Markham ("An Empirical Examination") demonstrated a relationship between ethical climate (an organizational level construct) and individual decision-making behavior.

The work of Victor and Cullen provides another example of an organizational level study. They empirically found five different "ethical climates" within and between organizations. Their Ethical Climate Questionnaire (ECQ) has been used extensively (e.g., Cullen and Bronson; Deshpande; Victor and Cullen; Weber; Wimbush et al.), both as an overall measure of the Ethical Environment construct, and also to explore the relationship between organizational and individual level outcomes.

A final example that was essential for the current study is Treviño, Butterfield, and McCabe's ("The Ethical Context"). Treviño conceptualized "ethical culture" as a component of organizational culture capable of promoting ethical (or unethical) behavior. Treviño et al. ("The Ethical Context") tested the discriminant validity of ethical culture and ethical climate, using items from both Victor and Cullen's ("The Organizational Bases") ECQ and Treviño's ("A Cultural Perspective") empirical work. Factor analysis of the combined items revealed ten factors with eigenvalues greater than one. Treviño and her colleagues labeled the first and more general of such factors "ethical environment"; it accounted for 20.22 percent of the variability. The other nine factors referred to company stakeholders more specific in nature: employees, the community, authority, codes of ethics, and so forth. None of these other factors accounted for more than 4.6 percent of the variation in the scores.

Corporate Social Performance

A related theme to ethical decision-making in the business ethics literature is corporate social performance (CSP; for a review of the development of this construct, readers are referred to Clarkson). Electronic searches of studies about CSP and corporate philanthropy in Mexico yielded no results. The present study explores the importance given to one of the basic dimensions of CSP known to exist in Mexico: corporate philanthropy.

Codes of Ethics

Academic and practitioner interest on codes of ethics has developed exponentially in the U.S. since the issuance in 1991 of the Federal Sentencing Guidelines (FSG).[1] No equivalent legal incentive is present in Mexico. Nevertheless, this research tested the existence of corporate codes of ethics or value statements to test whether any relationships between this and other indicators of ethical environment emerged empirically. As precedents for this inquiry, McCabe, Treviño, and Butterfield (1996), found an influence of codes of conduct on ethical behavior, and Harrington (1996) found little effect of company or information systems codes of ethics on computer abuse judgments and intentions (albeit not in Mexican firms). Within the Mexican context, Miceli Méndez wrote a master's thesis on the use of codes of ethics within large food-manufacturing companies. None of the companies in his study reported having codes of ethics per se, but other official documents (e.g., company statements such as their mission, vision, corporate values or policies, etc.) analyzed in his study showed evidence of intent to explicitly generate an ethical environment. Stronger ethical environments are thus to be expected in companies with a code of ethics, than in those without corporate ethical guidelines.

Method

Data collection. Human resource (HR) managers have been examined in the academic literature as a qualified source of information on ethical issues (e.g., Bartels, Harrick, Martell, and Strickland; Mitchell, Daniels, Hopper, Falvy, and Ferris; Driscoll and Hoffman). Compliance with labor law and follow up to employment relation issues normally are an important responsibility of the HR function. HR department employees are consequently among the most qualified for this type of study. The researcher had also observed that the allocation of ethical responsibilities in Mexican companies generally fell within the scope of HR managers' functions. Based on this information, five hundred four-page survey forms accompanied by a cover letter were distributed at the 1999 annual Conference and Exposition of AMERI (Spanish acronym for Mexican Association for Industrial Relations Executives), which is now known as AMEDIRH (*Asociación Mexicana de Directores de Recursos Humanos*). This is the largest and geographically most extended Mexican HR manager's organization. Two hundred and seventy attendants to the two-and-a-half day conference composed the main sample, but some questionnaires were also placed in the exposition area to include HR managers that attended only the exposition. This attendance pattern is customary for this kind of event. The author collected 47 usable surveys, for a 17 percent response rate.[2] The greatest value of this database arguably resides in the composition of its respondents (see below).

Sample. The average manager in the sample is 37 years old (S.D. = 7.96), with 15.76 years (S.D. = 8.36) of work experience, 12.23 years (S.D. = 7.96) of HR experience, 6.43 years of company tenure (S.D. = 6.63), and 4.88 years of tenure in their current position (S.D. = 5.17). Regarding their educational level, 66.2 percent have a bachelor's degree, 30.4 percent a master's degree and 4.3 percent report finishing at least high school. The academic area for 37 of them is business (78.7 percent); engineering studies for three (6.4 percent), law for other three respondents, psychology for two (4.3 percent), and the remaining two did not answer. Thirty-two respondents (71.1 percent) are males and 13 females (28.9 percent).[3] At least ten respondents (24.4 percent of valid answers) report titles indicative of having director's level and 31 (the remaining 75.6 percent of valid responses) indicate middle managerial positions. Twenty-four respondents (52.2 percent) report to the top manager of their company, and the remaining 22 valid responses report to higher level managers (47.8 percent).

Companies are in very diverse industries, running the gamut from soft drinks to telecommunications, from education to banks, from pharmaceutics to hotels. Grouping industries at the broadest level yielded 17 firms in manufacturing (37.8 percent), 28 companies in service industries (62.2 percent).[4] Company size is fairly large: 650 employees is the median, six the minimum and 50,000 the maximum; $12 million USD in sales for 1998 as median, $20,000 minimum and $1 billion maximum; seven locations as median, one minimum and 800 maximum.[5] Twenty-eight of these firms (59.6 percent) are Mexican-owned, 17 (36.2 percent) foreign-owned and one (2.1 percent) reported mixed-ownership. Fifteen respondents (31.9 percent) stated no union affiliation of their employees. Twenty-eight of the remaining, unionized firms (87.5 percent) stated that their employees' union is affiliated to a national organization and four more (12.5 percent) had independent or company unions.

Measures. The survey requested information on a variety of items, a subset of which was analyzed for this report. In particular, the study requested HR manager's perceptions (using a five-point anchored Likert-scale) of the importance, for the overall success of the company, that the HR department be very efficient in (1) follow-up to ethical problems in the company (especially at the executive level), (2) administrative management of disciplinary issues (fights, vocal harassment, etc.), (3) periodic distribution of laws, norms and regulations related to the firm, (4) sponsoring events for the families of employees, (5) for communities neighboring the firm, and (6) for other entities, such as schools, churches, clubs, etc. The first three items test the importance of the HR departments' ethics-related functions, whereas the last three items tap the perceived importance of corporate philanthropy for the company.

The survey also used a five-item version of the Ethical Environment factor that Treviño et al. found when they combined Victor and Cullen's ("The Organizational Bases") ethical climate questionnaire and Treviño's ethical culture instrument. The items selected from Treviño and colleagues are at the top of Table 1 (items one through five). They used seven-point, anchored Likert-scales where ascending values indicate stronger agreement and the middle point a neutral position. The researcher translated these items to the Spanish language, changing their sentence structure on several iterations, until two other native Spanish speakers with managerial experience concurred that the spirit of the items was similar to the instrument by Treviño et al. (1998). The scale's reliability coefficient (Cronbach's alpha) for this sample was 0.82, a very acceptable level of internal consistency.

Table 1. Correlations for Ethical Environment Items, Scale, Codes of Ethics, Ethical Functions and Corporate Philanthropy

(Pearson's correlation coefficients; for row 7, Kendall's tau-b)

	Item or Question	Mean (S.D.)	1	2	3	4	5	6	7	8	9	10	11	12
1	The top managers of my organization represent high ethical standards	5.76 (1.37)												
2	Unethical behavior in my company is surely disciplined	6.17 (1.02)	.54***											
3	In my company, it is perceived that those that commit ethical violations advance anyway.[rc]	2.50 (1.56)	-.45**	-.36*										
4	Ethical behavior is the norm (rather than the exception) in my company.	5.80 (1.22)	.61***	.51***	-.44**									
5	In my company, integral people, or those that behave ethically, are the ones that advance.	5.80 (1.24)	.56***	.54***	-.22	.63***								
6	Ethical environment scale (average of items 1–5, reverse-coding 3)	5.81 (.98)	.83***	.74***	-.69***	.83***	.75***	α = (.82)						
7	Company has a code of ethics or a value statement (yes=1, no=0)	69.60%	-.22	-.14	.21	-.18	-.16	-.24						

Item or Question	Mean (S.D.)	1	2	3	4	5	6	7	8	9	10	11	12
8 Follow-up to ethical problems in the company (particularly at the executive levels)	3.80 (.97)	.06	.12	-.14	.06	.16	.14	-.09					
9 Administrative handling of disciplinary issues (fights, vocal harassment, etc.)	3.07 (1.03)	-.10	.06	.13	-.37*	-.11	-.18	.17	.47**				
10 Diffusion of laws, norms and regulations related to the firm	3.27 (1.09)	.23	.19	-.03	.02	.14	.15	-.31*	.11	.28 +			
11 Sponsoring events for the families of the employees	3.29 (1.20)	.15	.23	.20	.09	.18	.09	-.12	.19	.32*	.25		
12 Sponsoring events for the community in which the firm is located	2.93 (1.28)	.30*	.33*	.01	.20	.29 +	.28 +	-.23 +	.16	.13	.23	.69***	
13 Sponsoring events for other entities (such as schools, churches, clubs, etc.)	2.71 (1.25)	.28 +	.20	-.07	.12	.22	.23	-.14	.17	.23	.32*	.63***	.77***

NOTES:[rc] Item reverse-coded to compute the ethical environment scale. Items 1–5 use a 7-point, anchored Likert scale with ascending agreement.

Items 8–13 are on a 5-point, ascending importance Likert scale. + <.10; * p<.05; ** p<.01; *** p<.001.

Results

The three questions about the importance of HR ethics-related activities indicate that, on average, Mexican HR managers consider them as "moderately" to "highly important" (rated as three and four in a five-point scale) for the overall success of the firm. In particular, (1) "following up on ethical problems in the company (especially at the executive level)" had a sample mean of 3.80 (S.D. = .97); (2) "administrative management of disciplinary issues (fights, vocal harassment, etc.)" showed a mean of 3.07 (S.D. = 1.03); and (3) "periodic distribution of laws, norms and regulations related to the firm" an average of 3.27 (S.D. = 1.09).

Corporate philanthropy questions were rated as somewhat less important, but the scores were still found within the highest half of the scale. Sponsoring events for the families of employees, a very widespread tradition in Mexican firms had a mean of 3.29 (S.D. = 1.20). Sponsoring events for communities close to the firm was rated with a mean of 2.93 (S.D. = 1.28), and events for other entities, such as schools, churches, clubs, etc., a mean of 2.71 (S.D. = 1.25). In spite of the comparatively lower ranking, it is of value to recall that a well-established tradition for many Mexican firms is for employees of all levels to get together during year-end festivities—usually for Christmas or New Year, in the form of the well-known "posadas," although company-sponsored celebrations can obviously take place at other times of the year.

The fact that many of these celebrations have a Christian component creates interesting dynamics: some year-end celebrations might include company-sponsored pilgrimages to shrines dedicated to the Virgin of Guadalupe (Mexico's national religious icon *par excellence*), prayers and religious ceremonies in some cases, but in other company cultures the celebration might be completely secularized. Usually, founders' or top-manager preferences are an important influence of how the firm chooses to celebrate the end of the calendar year, Mother's day, the anniversary of the organization's foundation, etc. Many firms also sponsor summer picnics or offer other opportunities for employees of all levels to share time outside the workplace, including, but not limited to sponsoring sport teams (classic examples include "football"—known as soccer in the U.S.—bowling, softball, baseball) or athletic events (5K, 10K, half-marathons, etc.). As Mexico's per capita income has increased, so have the number and quality of non-work occasions which offer opportunities for advertising or simply to support values or lifestyle choices that are consistent with company preferences. Logsdon, Thomas and Van Buren have documented that corporate social responsibility (CSR) in Mexico is not a recent innovation, a U.S. import or a reflection of CSR practices from the United States. As they stated (p. 58), "being considered a good corporate citizen in Mexico may require a different set of behaviours than would be the case in the home country."

Continuing with survey results, 32 firms (69.6 percent) acknowledged having a code of ethics or value statement, and 14 said they do not have one (30.4 percent).[6] Of those with a code, 22 (71.0 percent) said that responsibility for its implementation rests on the HR area, and two more HR departments share this obligation with another area. In three firms (9.7 percent), the CEO was responsible for implementation of the code and the remaining four firms (12.9 percent) named other executives.

Table 1 shows means, standard deviations and correlations obtained for the five items that compose the scale (rows one through five), the ethical environment scale (row six), the existence of a code of ethics (row seven), ethical-related functions (rows eight through ten), and corporate philanthropy items (rows 11 through 13). The only marginally significant correlation ($p<.10$) with the ethical environment scale is with the importance assigned to sponsoring events for the community in which the firm is located (row 12), and the coefficient is rather weak (.28).

Discussion

In general, the strongest items in the scale and the lack of a strong relationship between the ethical environment and codes of ethics (row seven, column six) support the notion that what matters for ethical behavior in Mexico is not so much "the talk," but "the walk," in particular the walk of top management. The first item of the scale ("The top managers of my organization represent high ethical standards") emerged as the most influential, as it may be seen from the statistically significant correlations with corporate philanthropy rows 11 and 12 in Table 1. Additionally, if the item were erased from the scale, the reliability coefficient would fall to .75, which is the lowest magnitude for the possible combinations for four-item scales.[7] In other words, if this item (or item four) were removed, the measurement of the Ethical Environment loses internal reliability; the scale would be barely acceptable for research purposes. It is noteworthy that this particular item is in line with Hofstede's study that Mexico as the country with the highest "Power Distance Index," or propensity to accept differences between employees at the different hierarchical levels of the firm. In Mexico, top management seems to be the most influential stakeholder for ethics in the organization.

An interesting finding is that neither company size nor origin of ownership seems to be related to any of the variables or items in the study, with the exception of number of employees and existence of a code of ethics ($r = -.27$, $p<.05$). It was expected that the larger or the non–Mexican companies would show the strongest Ethical Environments, more occurrences of codes of ethics or placed a stronger importance on the ethics-related functions, but the data did not show this, perhaps due to the small size of the sample. Not even the corporate philanthropy items were strongly related with company size or country of origin.

Another interesting relationship appears between the existence of a code of ethics (column seven) and the importance reported for diffusion of laws, norms and regulations related to the firm (row 10). This relationship (significant at $p<.05$) is positive, albeit weak (.30). A possible interpretation, to be tested by future studies, is that companies that are concerned with the diffusion of relevant laws, norms and regulations use codes of ethics as vehicles for their efforts. A publicly stated corporate position on ethical behavior may be a way to promote regulations that are important to the firm.

Additional tests included a factor analysis of all items in the survey. Four of the five items for the Ethical Environment scale loaded on the same factor (item three cross-loaded in this and in another factor). This supports the findings of Treviño et al. in that the items hang together, even when other items may also be related.

Some limitations must be acknowledged. The most evident limitation of the study is the low number of respondents. Some of the relationships found may have surfaced due to biases in the sample. Single-source response may be another weakness on the study, although the Ethical Environment scale produced a very reasonable reliability coefficient, and most items were inquired through multiple items, as Spector suggests.

Social desirability may haunt any ethics related studies (cf. Randall and Fernandes). This study prevented social desirability through three design characteristics. First, the ethics-related questions amounted to only about 10 percent of the questionnaire. Second, they were interspersed throughout the survey, among a variety of HR-related issues, to decrease the salience of ethical questions. Third, surveys explicitly excluded identification of respondent or firm, and the cover letter and the survey reaffirmed that anonymity would be guaranteed for all respondents.

The ethical environment construct, which has been developed by U.S. academics (Treviño et al.) and tested in U.S. settings, has not been proven as an "etic" (universal) construct (Davidson, Jaccard, Triandis, Morales and Díaz-Guerrero). There is a possibility that the construct is specific ("emic") to the U.S. Given structural differences between both countries (e.g., laws, culture, etc.), it is possible that the most important components of an ethical environment could be different in each country, and if this were influential, the scale items should reflect it.

Given limitations in available resources for the current study, this research explores the existence of Ethical Environment in Mexican organizations through a five-item scale, derived from the items that emerged in the study by Treviño and her colleagues. Future studies should benefit by using the full instrument developed by Treviño et al. or, following Cohen's suggestions, by carefully selecting the combination of dimensions of moral climate that would be most consistent with the focus of their study. To summarize, although this study seems to be the first that deals with business ethics in Mexico at the organizational level of analysis, results should be considered exploratory, rather than conclusive.

This survey contributes to the business ethics literature in several ways. First, it offers the first empirical, organizational-level study about business ethics in Mexico. Second, it summarizes the literature available about individual ethical decision making in Mexico. Third, it presents empirical results from a unique database of HR managers that may be used as a baseline for future studies about business ethics in Mexico at the organizational level, or for cross-cultural studies that can now compare the ethical environment in Mexican organizations with that of other countries. Fourth, it provides support to the Ethical Environment scale developed by Treviño et al. in a non–U.S. setting.

Given the relative recentness of business ethics as a research topic, there is great need for extending studies using different methods and designs. Replications, multiple measures and connections with relevant literature are acutely needed if the integration of Mexican companies to the global business environment is to become a reality. Both academics and practitioners must continue searching for answers to questions that may increase trust levels for doing business with Mexico and the rest of Latin America: How different (if at all) is ethical business decision-making in comparison to their business partners?

Discussion Questions

1. What are the different terms people refer to as "ethics"?
2. What are the two main types or categories of influences that encourage ethical behavior according to the research reviewed in this essay?
3. Describe the ways in which popular perceptions at times label Mexicans as "more ethical" and other times as "unethical" vis-à-vis the United States.
4. Define *malinchismo* and why it may be of importance to people interested in working with or in Mexico.
5. Describe how corporate philanthropy relates to corporate social performance in this essay.
6. How might religion affect ethical perspectives and work ethics of Mexicans? Of people in your country?
7. Research participants from any culture may be affected by "social desirability"; find a definition of this concept and summarize the reasons why the studies reviewed are less likely to be affected by it.
8. Why are codes of ethics important for companies and employees? Bring an example from a firm with which you are familiar.

Key Learning Terms

Code of ethics: Statement issued by an organization (most often a company but may be a professional or occupational group) with the aim of guiding its members in assessing what is appropriate or inappropriate, "right" or "wrong."

Corporate social performance: The idea that business organizations have responsibilities beyond serving their owners and their consumers or merely complying with government legislation; corporate social performance deals with the extent to which organizations can be considered socially responsible.

Ethical environment: A set of conditions within a context (the "environment," often an organization, company, occupation, etc.) that promote morally principled behavior within its bounds.

Ethics: The study of principles that help determine whether actions are correct or adequate from a particular ethical perspective; work is considered a preeminent moral good.

Malinchismo: An excessive preference for what is foreign, often in detriment of national alternatives; it may apply to business matters such as brands, services, products and firms, but also in other societal contexts.

Reliability: In the social sciences, the consistency of several questions used as a set to measure a "latent" (i.e., not material) variable; for example, measuring socioeconomic status as a combination of income, education and occupation is a more reliable measure than asking a person to state to which social class he or she belongs.

Work ethic: A value system that considers focused, diligent, high-quality labor as a goal.

Notes

1. Interested readers are directed to Murphy's revision of the status of corporate ethics statements in the U.S. Ferrell, LeClair, and Ferrell describe the framework through which the FSG promote ethical compliance.
2. Studies like Bartels et al.'s and Murphy's also had comparably low response rates, polling members of HR manager associations in the USA. In addition, AMEDIRH's executive director acknowledged comparable (often lower) response rates when the association has taken similar initiatives (personal communication).
3. Two respondents did not reveal their gender.
4. Two responses were ambiguous.
5. Given the variety of companies represented in this study, medians, maxima and minima are presented, rather than means and standard deviations to describe company size.
6. One respondent did not answer the question.
7. Item four ("Ethical behavior is the norm in my company") would also reduce the reliability coefficient to .75 if it were deleted. However, it did not show the strong correlations with the other questions as Item 1 did.

References

Allmon, D.E., H.C.K. Chen, T.K. Pritchett, and P. Forrest. "A Multicultural Examination of Business Ethics Perceptions." *Journal of Business Ethics* 16 (1997): 183–188. Print.
Arruda, M. C. "Business Ethics in Latin America." *Journal of Business Ethics* 16 (1997): 1597–1603. Print.
AFL-CIO. *Exploiting Both Sides: U.S.-Mexico "Free Trade."* Washington, D.C., 1991. Print.
Barrera Bassols, D. *Condiciones de trabajo en las maquiladoras de Ciudad Juarez: El punto de vista obrero.* Mexico, DF: Instituto Nacional de Antropologia e Historia, 1990. Print.
Bartels, L.K., E. Harrick, K., Martell, and D. Strickland. "The Relationship Between Ethical Climate and Ethical Problems Within Human Resource Management." *Journal of Business Ethics* 17 (1998): 799–804. Print.
Carroll, A. "Corporate Social Performance Measurement: A Commentary on Methods for Evaluating an Elusive Construct." *Research in Corporate Social Performance and Policy* 12 (1991): 385–401. Print.
Cavanagh, G.F., D.J. Moberg, and M. Velasquez. "The Ethics of Organizational Politics." *Academy of Management Review* 6 (1981): 363–374. Print.

Clarkson, M.B.E. "A Stakeholder Framework for Analyzing and Evaluating Corporate Social Performance." *Academy of Management Review* 20 (1995): 92–117. Print.

Cohen, D.V. "Moral Climate in Business Firms: A Conceptual Framework for Analysis and Change." *Journal of Business Ethics* 17 (1998): 1211–1226. Print.

Cullen, J.B., and J.W. Bronson. "The Ethical Climate Questionnaire: An Assessment of the Development and Validity." Annual meeting of the Academy of Management, August 1993, Atlanta. New York: Academy of Management, 1993. Print.

Davidson, A.R., J.J. Jaccard, H.C., Triandis, M.L. Morales, and R. Díaz-Guerrero. "Cross-Cultural Model Testing: Toward a Solution of the Etic-Emic Dilemma." *International Journal of Psychology* 11 (1976): 1–13. Print.

DeGeorge, R.T. *Competing with Integrity in International Business*. New York: Oxford University Press, 1993. Print.

Deshpande, S.P. "The Impact of Ethical Climate Types on Facets of Job Satisfaction: An Empirical Investigation." *Journal of Business Ethics* 15 (1996): 655–660. Print.

Driscoll, D.M., and W.M. Hoffman. "HR Plays a Central Role in Ethics Programs." *Workforce* 77.4 (1998): 121–123. Print.

Dunfee, T. W., and P. Werhane. "Report on Business Ethics in North America." *Journal of Business Ethics* 16 (1997): 1589–1595. Print.

Elahee, M., and C.M. Brooks. "Trust and Negotiation Tactics: Perceptions About Business-to-Business Negotiations in Mexico." *Journal of Business & Industrial Marketing* 19.6 (2004): 397–404. Print.

Erdener, C.B. "Ethnicity, Nationality and Gender: A Cross-Cultural Comparison of Business Ethical Decisions in Four Countries." *The International Journal of Human Resource Management* 7 (1996): 866–877. Print.

Etheredge, J.M., and C.B. Erdener. "Ethical Decision Patterns in Four Countries: Contrasting Theoretical Perspectives." *International Business Ethics: Challenges and Approaches*. Ed. G. Enderle. South Bend: University of Notre Dame Press, 1999. Print.

Ferrell, O.C., D.T. LeClair, and L. Ferrell. "The Federal Sentencing Guidelines for Organizations: A Framework for Ethical Compliance." *Journal of Business Ethics* 17 (1998): 353–363. Print.

Fritzsche, D.J., and H. Becker. "Linking Management Behavior to Ethical Philosophy: An Empirical Investigation." *Academy of Management Journal* 27 (1984): 166–175. Print.

Harrington, S.J. "The Effect of Codes of Ethics and Personal Denial of Responsibility on Computer Abuse Judgments and Intentions." *MIS Quarterly* 20 (1996): 257–278. Print.

Hofstede, G. *Culture's Consequences: International Differences in Work-Related Values*. Beverly Hills: Sage, 1980. Print.

Husted, B.W., J.B. Dozier, J.T. McMahon, and M.W. Kattan. "The Impact of Cross-National Carriers of Business Ethics on Attitudes About Questionable Practices and Form of Moral Reasoning." *Journal of International Business Studies* 27 (1996): 391–411. Print.

Kohlberg, L. "Stage and Sequence: The Cognitive Developmental Approach to Socialization." *Handbook of Socialization Theory and Research*. Ed. D.A. Goslin. Chicago: Rand-McNally, 1969. Print.

LaDou, J. "Deadly Migration: Hazardous Industries' Flight to the Third World." *Technology Review* (July 1991): 47–53. Print.

Lewicki, R.J. "Lying and Deception: A Behavioral Model with Applications to Negotiations." *Negotiating in Organizations*. Ed. M.H. Bazerman and R. J. Lewicki. Beverly Hills: Sage, 1983. Print.

Lewicki, R.J., and R.J. Robinson. "A factor analytic study of ethical and unethical bargaining tactics." Columbus, OH: Ohio State University, Unpublished manuscript. 1995. Print.

Lewicki, R.J., and R.J. Robinson. "A Factor Analytic Study of Ethical and Unethical Bargaining Tactics." Unpublished manuscript. Ohio State University, 1995. Print.

Lewicki, R.J.. and G. Spencer. "Ethical Relativism and Negotiating Tactics: Factors Affecting Their Perceived Ethicality." Annual Meeting of the Academy of Management, August 1991, Miami. New York: Academy of Management, 1991. Print.

Logsdon, J.M., D.E. Thomas, and H.J. Van Buren, III. "Corporate Social Responsibility in Large Mexican Firms." *Journal of Corporate Citizenship* 21 (2006): 51–60. Print.

Marta, J., C.M. Heiss, and S.A. De Lurgio. "An Exploratory Comparison of Ethical Perceptions of Mexican and U.S. Marketers." *Journal of Business Ethics* 82.3 (2008): 539–555. Print.

Mccabe, D.L., L.K. Treviño, and K.D. Butterfield. "The Influence of Collegiate and Corporate Codes of Conduct on Ethics-Related Behavior in the Workplace." *Business Ethics Quarterly* 6 (1996): 461–476. Print.

Miceli Méndez, E. "Estudio exploratorio de códigos de ética en la industria alimentaria Mexicana." MA thesis, Tec De Monterrey, 2000. Web. 29 April 2015. http://biblioteca.itesm.mx.

Miroff, N. "With Mexican Auto Manufacturing Boom, New Worries." *Washington Post*. Washington Post, 1 July 2013. Web. 10 May 2015. http://www.washingtonpost.com.

Mitchell, T.R., D. Daniels, H. Hopper, J.G. Falvy, and G.R. Ferris. "Perceived Correlates of Illegal Behavior in Organizations." *Journal of Business Ethics* 15 (1996): 439–455. Print.

Morrison, T., and W.A. Conaway. *Kiss, Bow or Shake Hands: The Bestselling Guide to Doing Business in More than 60 Countries*. Avon, MA: Adams Media, 2006. Print.

Moure-Eraso, R., M. Wilcox, L. Punett, L. Macdonald, and C. Levenstein. "Back to the Future: Sweatshop Conditions on the Mexico-U.S. Border." *American Journal of Industrial Medicine* 31 (1997): 587–599. Print.

Murphy, P.E. "Corporate Ethics Statements: Current Status and Future Prospects." *Journal of Business Ethics* 14 (1995): 727–740. Print.

Randall, D.M. and M.F. Fernandes. "The Social Desirability Response Bias in Ethics Research." *Journal of Business Ethics* 10 (1991): 805–817. Print.

Rest, J.R. *Guide for the Defining Issues Test*. Minneapolis: Center for the Study of Ethical Development, 1987. Print.

Rousseau, D.M. "Is There Such a Thing as Evidence-Based Management?" *Academy of Management Review* 31 (2006): 256–269. Print.

_____. "Issues of Level in Organizational Research." *Research in Organizational Behavior*. Ed. L.L. Cummings and B.M. Staw. Greenwich, CT: JAI Press, 1985. 1–37. Print.

Sánchez, R. "Contaminación de la industria fronteriza: Riesgos para la salud y el medio ambiente." *Las Maquiladoras: Ajuste estructural y desarrollo regional* Ed. B. González-Aréchiga and R. Barajas Escamilla. Tijuana: El Colegio De La Frontera Norte, 1989. Print.

Sargent, J., and L. Matthews. "Exploitation or Choice? Exploring the Relative Attractiveness of Employment in the Maquiladoras." *Journal of Business Ethics* 18 (1999): 213–227. Print.

Schmidt, E. "Ethical Formation That Makes Sense for Business Men and Women in Latin America." *International Business Ethics: Challenges and Approaches*. Ed. G. Enderle. South Bend: University of Notre Dame Press, 1999. Print.

Spector, P.E. "Method Variance as an Artifact in Self-Reported Affect and Perceptions at Work: Myth or Significant Problem?" *Journal of Applied Psychology* 72.3 (1987): 438–443. Print.

Stajkovic, A.D., and F. Luthans. "Business Ethics Across Cultures: A Social Cognitive Model." *Journal of World Business* 32 (1997): 17–34. Print.

Tadepalli, R., A. Moreno and S. Treviño. "Do American and Mexican Purchasing Managers Perceive Ethical Situations Differently?" *Industrial Marketing Management* 28 (1999): 369–380. Print.

Tajfel, H., and J. Turner. "The Social Identity Theory of Intergroup Behavior." *Psychology of Intergroup Relations*. Ed. S. Worchel and W. Austin. Chicago: Nelson-Hall, 1986. 7–24. Print.

Treviño, L.K. "A Cultural Perspective on Changing and Developing Organizational Ethics." *Research in Organizational Change and Development* 4 (1990): 195–230. Print.

_____. "Ethical Decision-Making in Organizations: A Person-Situation Interactionist Model." *Academy of Management Review* 11 (1986): 601–617. Print.

Treviño, L.K., and S.A. Youngblood. "Bad Apples in Bad Barrels: A Causal Analysis of Ethical Decision-Making Behavior." *Journal of Applied Psychology* 75 (1990): 378–385. Print.

Treviño, L.K., K.D. Butterfield, and D.L. Mccabe. "The Ethical Context in Organizations: Influences on Employee Attitudes and Behaviors." *Business Ethics Quarterly* 8 (1998): 447–476. Print.

Ueltschy, L.C., and J.K. Ryans, Jr. "Employing Standardized Promotion Strategies in Mexico: The Impact of Language and Cultural Differences." *International Executive* 39.4 (1997): 479–495. Proquest. Web. 12 May 2015.

USITC. *The Likely Impact on the United States of a Free Trade Agreement with Mexico*. Washington, D.C.: United States International Trade Commission, Publication 2353, 1991. Print.

Victor, B., and J.B. Cullen. "The Organizational Bases of Ethical Work Climates." *Administrative Science Quarterly* 33 (1988): 101–125. Print.

_____. "A Theory and Measure of Ethical Climate in Organizations." *Research in Corporate Social Performance and Policy*. Ed. W.C. Frederick. Greenwich, CT: JAI Press, 1987. 51–71. Print.

Volkema, R.J. "A Comparison of Perceptions of Ethical Negotiation Behavior in Mexico and the United States." *International Journal of Conflict Management* 9.3 (1998): 218–223. Print.

Weber, J. "Influences Upon Organizational Ethical Sublimates: A Multi-Departmental Analysis of a Single Firm." *Organization Science* 6 (1995): 509–523. Print.

Wimbush, J.C., J.M. Shepard, and S.E. Markham. "An Empirical Examination of the Multi-Dimensionality of Ethical Climate in Organizations." *Journal of Business Ethics* 16 (1997): 67–77. Print.

Wimbush, J.C., J.M. Shepard, and S.E. Markham. "An Empirical Examination of the Relationship Between Ethical Climate and Ethical Behavior from Multiple Levels of Analysis." *Journal of Business Ethics* 16 (1997): 1705–1716. Print.

Communication in Mexican Business

John T. Hyatt

Although Mexico and the United States share a symbiotic and crucial economic relationship through trade, foreign investment and immigration, many aspects of Mexico's business culture are understudied, underestimated and undervalued among those in academia and business. The way in which Mexicans communicate in business and everyday life, albeit a crucial element of the nation's business culture, is no exception to this lacking trend. Although solid communication skills and understanding in cross cultural communication are extremely advantageous when doing business outside of one's own borders, those looking to explore the way in which Mexicans communicate in a business environment are left with few tools to improve their knowledge. The ubiquitous trade books and international business websites describing Mexican business culture are quite redundant in generalizing the way in which Mexicans communicate in written and verbal forms. These sources list the same age-old anecdotes and situations describing the ways in which Mexicans can be expected to communicate with their foreign counterparts in business such as "The Mexican will never tell you no," "They won't tell you anything you don't want to hear," "Communication is indirect," "If they say, 'I'll get back to you on this offer' that's their way of saying no," "The official language is Spanish, you'll have to hire an interpreter if you go to Mexico on business." The list is extensive from these trade books and websites with such short tips on Mexican communication which serve as useless and in many instances inaccurate advice for doing business in Mexico. It is safe to say that with the exception of a handful of well-researched studies like those of Tebeaux and Ortiz, and possibly a few others, there is a scarcity of serious academic research dedicated to the ways Mexicans communicate in the workplace. LaBahn and Harich even highlight and explain the lack of empirical research and reliance upon a few personal encounters when analyzing business culture in general: "The complexity of culture seems to discourage empirical research and promote anecdotal accounts. It is not surprising, then, that the channels literature provide little insight into what dimensions of culture international business partners must adapt to first in order to enjoy mutually rewarding business relations" (30).

Despite the scant academic research on the topic of communication in Mexican business culture, I have chosen to utilize existing research on the topic along with historical, anthropological, psychological sources on Mexico and the way Mexicans communicate while joining such sources with interviews of Mexican businesspeople and my personal lived experiences to create a more in depth look at the way in which Mexicans communicate in business with each other, and with those from outside their borders. As a result of this research, the final findings shown in this essay demonstrate that while there are different forms of communication in Mexican business when compared to Western nations, these communication styles vary distinctly based upon the Mexican employee or business owner's socioeconomic level, education, international experience, position in the firm, and the position and status of whom the individual is communicating within a given instance. Furthermore, there is a young generation of Mexican professionals who are eschewing traditional Mexican communication trends in the workplace in favor of the more direct, linear forms of communication as seen in today's global business community. In summary, to describe or expect one universal code of business communication among Mexicans throughout the nation is utterly useless and pernicious.

Examples of Trade Books' Personification of Communication in Mexican Business Culture

While speaking with almost any American, Canadian or European who has visited Mexico for the purpose of business, vacation or education, there is a common initial response from the Westerner in regards to his initial impression of Mexicans. "All the people were so kind to us!" the Westerner is nearly guaranteed to exclaim. "Everyone was always smiling and happy" is another common analysis of Mexican demeanor and culture. The businessman will often return to his home country to exclaim to his family, "My Mexican host was so kind and hospitable. He picked me up from the airport and stayed with me in the lobby of the hotel until I was checked in and took me to some of the finest restaurants in town the entire time I was in Mexico," while the vacationers opine, "Everyone at the hotel was so nice and hospitable," and a foreign exchange student will almost certainly exclaim, "My host family was wonderful and wouldn't stop feeding me, they spoiled me and treated me like their own child!" All of the aforementioned anecdotes are accurate and commonplace experiences for the millions of foreigners who visit Mexico for a limited time. Most are overwhelmed by Mexicans' hospitality, smiles and kindness during a short visit.

Furthermore, such anecdotes are ubiquitous material found in many of the trade books highlighted by Coria-Sánchez in the introduction to this book. Also underscored by Coria-Sánchez and aforementioned in this essay, these books demonstrate little academic research in regards to why Mexicans comport themselves in various ways while offering sweeping generalizations in regards to customs and culture. In *Cultura gerencial: Mexico—Estados Unidos*, Eva Kras simply states, "One must remember that due to the sensitiveness of the Mexican, his first concern is to avoid confrontations ... thus meaning that one cannot always expect a direct response or a completely true response to a direct question" (38). Historical, anthropological and psychological research does indeed demonstrate that Mexicans in general tend to avoid conflict and prefer to communicate in more indirect ways, and such phenomena will be further examined in this essay. Nevertheless, Kras commits just a few dangerous errors with this broad cultural generalization of Mexican managers. Primarily, Kras gives no research or evidence to defend her point of view. Should this indirectness even be the case, the Westerner reading her book is left to only guess as to why the Mexican manager may behave in such a way. Second, Kras gives no specific cases, case studies or interviews to defend her argument. Furthermore, the third and perhaps most egregious aspect of such a generalization is that the reader is left to assume that *all* Mexican managers will behave in such a uniform manner. While once again recognizing that indirectness and conflict aversion are cultural trends in Mexican society, it is utterly absurd to believe that in today's global economy Mexican attorneys from a top international trade firm in Mexico City and their Mexican clients should be blindly expected to lie and speak in an indirect manner to their American counterparts when finalizing a multimillion dollar international contract. At the same time it would be equally preposterous for us to assume that a Mexican manager or director at an international company in Mexico who holds an MBA from a U.S. or European university could be expected to beat around the bush or be misleading while on a conference call from Monterrey with a group of executives at the company headquarters in Lower Manhattan.

Unfortunately, the foreigner who only spends a short time in Mexico or the international manager who embarks upon reading a trade book may not delve deep into Mexico's culture in regards to communication, especially as applied to business. He or she may return to their homeland with the understanding that Mexicans are respectful, warm and cheerful above and beyond anything else. It is imperative that the foreign businessperson understand that a chief root of the overall "kindness" that they may experience is that Mexicans by nature mostly strive to avoid conflict in interpersonal relations. However it should be noted that conflict aversion is not of the same intensity or scale throughout socioeconomic groups and regions in Mexico. It is also advisable for the Westerner doing business in Mexico to understand the root causes of such aversion.

Mexican Culture of Conflict Aversion

It is vital that we examine this cultural trait from a more historical, anthropological, sociological and psychological point of view than simply random observations on the part of the author as could easily be the case.

This overall strive to avoid conflict has existed in Mexico since the Spanish conquest of the indigenous empires and should be understood from an in depth perspective. The Spanish conquest of the Aztec empire in 1521 was one of the most brutal and humiliating conquests in world history. The fact that Spanish Conquistador Hernán Cortez was able to leave Cuba for Mexico in 1519 with only 550 men and 16 horses and in only two years conquer and subjugate an entire empire is something that even today plays a roll on the Mexican psyche. Immediately following the fall of Tenochtitlan (now downtown Mexico City) in 1521, the Indians were enslaved and relegated to second class citizen status by their new colonizers from Spain (Skidmore and Smith 19). This humiliating defeat dealt a blow to the natives along with other national defeats, according to multiple scholars, created a national inferiority complex and defeatist psyche in which Mexicans have come to identify themselves as perpetual victims (Castañeda Kindle version). This overall psyche of self-victimization has led Mexicans, especially those in the lower classes to choose to avoid conflict with others as a means of survival. Or as Carlos Fuentes stated, "Mexicans choose to avoid conflict as opposed to defending oneself against aggression" (quoted in Castañeda). As mentioned, the Spanish conquest was the first in a series of events throughout Mexico's turbulent past in which Mexicans have come to feel shortchanged and exploited first by the Spaniards and in subsequent centuries by their own government and the United States. According to Rodríguez and Ramírez, the nation has suffered eight traumas throughout the centuries or "Los 8 traumas a lo largo de los Siglos":

1. The Military Conquest (1521) (Rodríguez and Ramírez 25).
2. The Spiritual Conquest (conversion of the natives to Catholicism) (Rodríguez and Ramírez 25).
3. The "Mestizaje" or mixing of Spanish and indigenous blood to create the "mestizo" race. The mestizos were considered to be a race in no man's land without a mother as they weren't Indian or Spanish (Rodríguez and Ramírez 25).
4. The Secularization when Charles III ordered the withdrawal of many of Roman Catholic missions in Mexico, thus leaving the oppressed indigenous populations that were paternalistically controlled by the Catholic Church as spiritual and psychological orphans (Rodríguez and Ramírez 27).
5. Independence (1810): After Mexico's independence the same socioeconomic system remained in place giving the vast majority of Mexicans no new opportunities or privileges (Rodríguez and Ramírez 28).
6. Neocolonial Conquest from U.S. Mexican War of 1848: The United States took nearly one-third of Mexico's territory (Rodríguez and Ramírez 29).
7. The Reform (1854–1857): Political reforms intended to modernize Mexico while freeing it from its tragic past did little of the sort (Rodríguez and Ramírez 29). Furthermore this attempted denial of the past was better summarized as "the Mexican does not want to be Indian or Spanish. Nor does he want to descend from either of the two. The Reforma is a great breaking from the mother" (quoted from Rodríguez and Ramírez 29).
8. The Revolution: The Mexican Revolution culminated in 1917 with Mexico's current constitution, which explicitly guarantees extensive political, social and economic rights to all Mexicans. In reality this revolution and constitution did little more than usher in the Institutional Revolutionary Party (PRI) to 70 consecutive years of outrageously corrupt rule which included ubiquitous and rampant bribery, theft of public funds, rigged elections and multiple economic crises. Thus most Mexicans feel that the revolution of 1917 did little more than put another corrupt group in power to rule the country and benefit at their expense (Rodríguez and Ramírez, 30).

Although not one of the official Mexican traumas lived through the centuries, many Mexicans feel that neoliberalism, free trade and especially NAFTA is the nation's latest national tragedy, and that it has forced the nation to become an economic colony of the United States as American foreign investment is now key to Mexico's economic well-being while the Gringos have imported their consumer and pop culture into Mexico with no end in sight.

These aforementioned national "traumas" have been considered to contribute to the Mexican psyche in which the Mexican feels he cannot win, that there is no use in putting up a fight. Or as better described with direct links to the conquest: "The trauma imposed by the Conquest on the Indian was so great that his possibilities of struggle under the new culture were annulled; ... The Indian eludes conflict with the cultural elements found above him, be they friendly or aggressive" (Rodríguez and Ramírez 72, as quoted in Castañeda). This national psyche fuels this general desire to avoid conflict in day to day interactions. Furthermore, Mexico's history teaches its people that putting up a fight usually backfires. The Aztec emperor Cuauhtémoc put up a fight against Cortez and the

Spaniards and was executed while his empire was conquered. The ring leaders in the Mexican Revolution, including Emiliano Zapata, were all executed. The students who protested the PRI dictatorship in 1968 in Mexico City ten days before the opening ceremonies of the Summer Olympics were stifled and killed, between 30 and 300 (exact numbers are unavailable and historical accounts vary greatly), while more than 1,000 were arrested by security police. Hundreds if not thousands of others who opposed the PRI dictatorship disappeared in Mexico's Dirty War of the 1960s and 70s. Those wishing to challenge Mexico's largest business conglomerates, monopolies and oligopolies and their back room relationships with government have nearly always come up short either in the courts or in the case of smaller businesses being crushed in the "free market" by the unfair advantage of the national giants. The list goes on and on through Mexico's history.

Although Mexicans as a culture have traditionally chosen to avoid conflict, it is sometimes inevitable among humans. And when conflict often arises among Mexicans, the nation's cultural focus on the present becomes conspicuous. With the onset of harsh conflict or disagreement among Mexicans be it in personal, or business matters, the Mexican often feels that reconciliation is not an option. As expressed by Jorge Castaneda, "In the Mexican mind, there is no solution after confrontation; there is no walking back from a fight. In an altercation, things are said and done that cannot be silenced or undone; after a quarrel, the wounds or damages cannot be healed or dismissed" (Castañeda, Kindle version). Once things have "destapado" or hit the fan, a Mexican often wants to end the relationship, friendship, partnership or whatever it may be after an intense fight. This is often described in Mexican Spanish with the term "Me mandó a la chingada y lo mandé a la chingada" or "He sent me far away and I sent him far away" (cordially put). This desire to end things once conflict occurs goes back to the mentality in which many do not look to the future, in this case to resolve a problem for the long term benefit of both parties rather than the short sighted termination of a relationship through anger.

One of the most telling examples I have seen in regard to this short sightedness in Mexican business when conflict arises has to do with retention and termination of employees. I can recall dozens of cases in Mexico City in which someone had been terminated. On nearly all of these occasions I recall asking someone in the firm what happened to an employee. The answers were all different but all similar. I always received responses such as "He and the boss didn't agree on a marketing strategy," "He and the boss had a disagreement on how to organize the next trade show," "He and the boss couldn't agree on a new purchasing strategy," or "He was having problems getting payment from a client." No matter what the business or level of employees the stories were similar. In regards to resolving a problem or disagreement, a resolution which in the long term may allow the company to grow and be stronger, the Mexican prefers to terminate the employee and start from scratch. This extremely near sighted phenomenon in and of itself is a paradox of the national culture of conflict aversion. Why would a manager or owner within a conflict aversion culture tend to fire people at will? But it is feasible to at least understand when realizing that once conflict and disagreement arise, the Mexican sees no tomorrow in such a relationship. Or as one anonymous American employee at a Mexican business once described the company's policy if an employee had job performance problems or differences with clients, co-workers or management, "They don't work with people here, they deal with people here." The idea of tomorrow in and of itself is another cultural phenomena that must be analyzed when looking at business communication in Mexico.

Another reason that Mexicans tend to avoid conflict on a direct basis is that they live for the moment, seeing the future as something not worthy enough to fight for. Public opinion polls in Mexico and the United States show sharp contrasts between the two nationalities on the purpose of life. While 86 percent of Americans feel that life is to be enjoyed, 63 percent of Mexicans express the fatalistic sentiment that life is to be endured and to simply survive (Rodríguez and Ramírez 36). This fatalistic approach on the part of Mexicans (once again this is far more acute in the lower classes) has direct links to the nation's traumatic past, yet it also speaks to the way in which many of its citizens view the future. Research and more polling suggest that as a result of the nation's past, many Mexicans today feel such an uncertainty in regards to the future, thus causing them to live to enjoy each day (Tebeaux 59). Simply put, in the Mexican psyche, arguing with someone in a business or personal relationship about a disagreement may not be worth it. It's better to go home at the end of the day without having fought or stood up for oneself. Mexico's history and the Mexican psyche demonstrate that tomorrow may or probably will be worse than today, so let's just keep things as civil as possible at least for today. As described by Carlos Fuentes: "The Mexican mañana does not mean putting things off till the morrow, it means not letting the future intrude on the sacred completeness of today" (quoted in Tebeaux 63). These philosophic contrasts, which emphasize the present on one hand and the future on another are no different in business communication and will be later highlighted to examine the American and Mexican cases. On the contrary, the United States is a country that has always held the future in more esteem than the past or present (Tebeaux 59). This is even obvious in America's founding documents and the speeches and platforms of American presidents through the centuries. America and Americans have always seemed to be concerned with the future while Mexico and the Mexicans tend to be concerned with today. Although this is a generalization, we will later discover that this trend is more prevalent in lower classes in Mexico while the nation's younger generations possess evolving views on fatalism and the future.

This avoidance of conflict on the part of Mexicans also extends to communication styles in business and personal encounters. While such styles of portraying one individual's sentiments to another tend to be more ambiguous and courteous in Mexico, a foreign businessman in Mexico cannot presume any one form of communication as the status quo throughout Mexican society without taking into account his Mexican counterpart's education, background and business experience.

The Word "No" and Indirect Communication in Mexico

While interviewing an anonymous, successful owner of a market research firm in Mexico City, she directly opined, "Mexicans don't always know how to say 'No' because we were conquered. As a subjugated nation from the Spanish conquest we aim not to offend others. Therefore a Mexican might say "Yes" to you when he or she really doesn't mean it." This same entrepreneur went on to use the age old tale of when Mexicans throw a party. "Whenever we have parties in Mexico we might invite 50 people and they all say 'Yes.' Then on the night of the party only 20 show up. No one wants to offend the host by saying they can't come." Citing this example, it is worth stating that in Western culture we will be more offended when someone chooses to RSVP and fails to show up to our event or party. That may mean wasted food, drinks, etc., that we had planned on having for that guest. However according to this Mexican businesswoman, it is far more offensive to the Mexican host to hear the word "No" as opposed to being stood up by guests at his or her party. Once again the concepts of short-term appeasement and the present are evident. Gerardo Fernandez, an attorney in Mexico City who practices civil and business litigation opined, "Mexicans just don't know how to say no, they're scarred that someone might get too upset when hearing the word." The Mexican anonymous marketing firm owner and Fernandez make the same point with similar statements: Mexicans in general prefer to please the individual or individuals that they are talking to in that moment, regardless of the long-term consequences and is directly related to the national cultural trend of living for the present day. Although these are broad generalizations of Mexican culture, these trends are not as acute among high level Mexican managers when communicating with foreigners as will be further explained in this essay.

This overall lack of ability for many Mexicans to say "No" is of course directly linked to the culture of conflict aversion. There are many Mexican folk tales regarding the word no and Mexican lack of desire to offend with this word. One of the most famous, which has happened to several people, is when someone asks a Mexican for directions when a bit lost while in the city or perhaps the countryside. The Mexican, with no knowledge of how to get to the other's intended destination, extemporaneously makes up a route to send this person on his way, albeit the wrong way. In the Mexican psyche, the direct confrontation and possible offense involved with simply stating that he has no knowledge of the requested destination outweighs the hardship that the traveler will face when becoming even more lost in just a matter of minutes. With the aforementioned interviews and anecdotes it is important to re-emphasize the cultural value of the present in Mexican society in contrast to the futuristic approach of Westerners, specifically Americans.

Aside from avoiding the word "No," Mexican dialect has always included heavy use of ambiguity, indirectness as well as a plethora of pleasantries in order to show respect, keep the conversation as upbeat as possible and of course to avoid conflict. The indirectness occurs in traditional Mexican speech more often when there may be bad news to express. This is even more the case among the lower classes. Furthermore, in business culture Mexican employees at the lower end of the hierarchical ladder are nearly guaranteed to communicate with their superiors in not just a more respectful manner with less direct dialect. To further highlight the indirectness that is often persistent in his nation's business culture Javier Degollado, a professional in the financial industry in Mexico City, opined, "In our culture, if you do not treat people in a sweet, kind way, they will get offended. In Mexico, we are indirect as a way to soften things up on the job. We want to minimize conflict as much as possible." Or as Veronica Veliz, an IT engineer in Guadalajara, put it: "We have a nicer way to say things in Mexican Spanish than you do in English." Below is a list of examples of ways in which Mexicans have been observed "softening things up" in their speech. The reader should take note that socioeconomic, hierarchical and geographic positioning can greatly affect these forms of communication. A Canadian CEO visiting Mexico should probably not expect such speech from his Mexican counterpart in Monterrey, however such protocol may be more commonplace among a Mexican secretary in the office when speaking with him.

Commonplace Samples of Indirect Communication in Mexico (Author's Mexico City Lived Experiences)

Question or Initial Situation	American Response/ Statement	Mexican Response/ Statement (English/Spanish)	Actual Situation	Cultural Analysis of Difference In Responses
Do you have blue cheese dressing?	No. Sorry, we have Ranch, Thousand Island, honey mustard, Italian and French.	Uhm, we have Ranch. Este, tenemos Ranch.	No. The restaurant does not offer blue cheese dressing.	The Mexican is unwilling to say no directly and instead evades the reality by offering a close alternative.
Are we watching the game this weekend?	No, I can't, I have to do something with my kids.	Yeah, maybe, we'll talk on Friday. Sí, puede ser, hablamos el viernes.	No. The person already has plans for the weekend.	The Mexican would rather avoid the unpleasant experience of having to directly reject his friend's invitation to watch the game. Therefore he chooses to eschew the issue by proclaiming that they will speak on Friday. Note that the issue is further avoided by not proposing a specific time or deadline to talk on Friday. There is no "I'll let you know by Friday night at nine." Simply a general day and proposed communication.
Will your company need our services?	I don't think we are able to move forward at this time.	It's complicated. Está complicado.	The prospective client will not contract the provider's service at this time.	The Mexican simply states that things are complicated possibly leaving a Western client to wonder what this means. The Mexican is again avoiding the direct unpleasant of rejecting the provider's offer.
Will I return for a follow-up appointment in a week as planned?	I don't know if one is necessary at this point based on our company situation. What would be the purpose of the appointment?	Let me check and I will call you later. Dejame checar y te marco después.	The client sees no real reason for a follow-up and would prefer not to have one unless absolutely necessary.	As in the example of the proposal to watch a game on the weekend, the Mexican client is unwilling to state that he sees no need for an appointment at this time.
Do you have an extra cigarette?	Sorry, I don't have enough to spare and last me through the night. They have them at the bar.	They are selling them up at the bar. Se venden en la barra.	The individual is unwilling to spare an extra cigarette.	The Mexican in this case finds and offers an alternative to a rejection of the request and points the other person in the direction of the bar for a cigarette.

Question or Initial Situation	American Response/ Statement	Mexican Response/ Statement (English/Spanish)	Actual Situation	Cultural Analysis of Difference In Responses
Is the order ready for me to pick up today?	No, I'm sorry. The merchandise won't be here until Monday.	It still hasn't arrived to me. Todavía no me llegó.	The merchandise is late and will be in on Monday at the earliest.	The Mexican in this case uses a dual strategy to avoid conflict by first using indirectness by not saying no, and secondly by using sentence structure to exonerate himself from blame thus avoiding conflict and maintaining civility. The sentence "It hasn't arrived to me" of course avoids the direct, offensive statement "No." Furthermore, the Mexican flips this sentence to make the merchandise the subject. For the Mexican to say, "I don't have it yet," as he being the subject further indicts him as a culprit as it would signify his responsibility for the shipment. Stated by the Mexican the merchandise is arriving late to *him* and infers the fault of others, thus avoiding direct blame and conflict.
Are you still serving food?	No. The kitchen closed at 11, sorry. The bar is still open.	It's that the kitchen is closed. The bar is open. Es que la cocina está cerrada. Hay barra.	The kitchen closed at 11pm and there are only drinks available from the bar.	The Mexican again avoids use of the word "No" in effort to not offend and also uses the common sentence starter "It's that" or "Es que," which is often used to open a sentence which will contain bad news.
Have you been able to call the client to change the appointment?	I have called several times and left voice mails and sent two emails with no response.	It is that, he isn't found. It's that I called him several times all the more I sent him two emails. Es que, no se localiza. Le marqué varias veces. Además le mandé 2 correos.	The secretary has made multiple attempts with concerted effort to contact the client but the client has not responded.	Once again is the use of the term "It's that" or "Es que" preceding bad news. Also, like the example with the delayed shipment, the Mexican secretary makes the client the subject of the sentence to remove herself from direct blame. Furthermore the secretary uses the verb "find" in passive voice to make the sentence indirect.

Question or Initial Situation	American Response/ Statement	Mexican Response/ Statement (English/Spanish)	Actual Situation	Cultural Analysis of Difference In Responses
Do you have Diet Coke?	No, I'm sorry, we're out. We'll have some tomorrow.	No sir, we don't have it now. It's that we ran out. No señor, no tenemos ahora. Es que se nos terminó.	The store is out of Diet Coke and will not have any for the rest of the day.	In this common case the Mexican was able to say "No." However, he followed the no with an affirmation that there is none at this time which is meant to ease the shock of the word no but may be interpreted as redundant by a Westerner. More interestingly, the Mexican goes to the past to further explain the shortage by saying, "We ran out" coupled with "It's that" for an extra pleasantry. This emphasis on the past event of running out is interesting as the Mexican past can often justify the present as the employee is doing here. Interestingly enough, in this situation the Mexican will almost never exclaim that he will have more in by a certain date as that delivery (as is the future in Mexican culture) is in itself uncertain while the American employee already has tomorrow planned.

In all of the above samples there are several recurring themes including the avoidance of the word "No," use of the passive voice, a lack of willingness to make a direct statement that may come across as too harsh as well as vague parameters (or no parameters in some cases) of future times and plans. This being said, there are several things that the reader of these examples of Mexican communication should take into account. First and foremost, these are merely observations on the part of the author through lived experiences that are seen as commonplace. Second, nearly all of these repetitive observations have taken place in Mexico City. While Mexico City is the nation's capital and its largest city, one cannot infer that all cultural practices and norms in Mexico City are representative of all Mexicans any more than someone visiting New York City may legitimately conclude that the comportment of New Yorkers must be the norm in Mississippi and Wyoming. The reader must understand that sentence structure, choice of vocabulary, verb tenses and overall communication can vary greatly from one region of Mexico to another. For example, I have worked with and interviewed several people from Northern Mexico in states such as Nuevo Leon, Durango and Sonora. All of those interviewed in those regions of Mexico come across as more direct with different grammar, vocabulary and sentence structure when speaking. These same Norteños, as they are called, have also complained that Mexicans residing in central and southern Mexico (Mexico, City, Guadalajara, Oaxaca, and nearly all the Mexican states that do not share a border with the United States) are far less direct and ambiguous in their speech in comparison to their own Northern comfort zone. Third, these forms of indirect speech are more commonplace among those in lower, working classes, especially when speaking to a superior or someone whom they think holds a higher socioeconomic status than they. It is for this reason that many trade books are irresponsible in proclaiming universal cultural traits that all Mexicans, especially Mexican businesspeople possess. It would therefore be foolish for a Western businessperson to assume that Mexican company partners, executives and managers would be guaranteed to speak to them in such forms while speaking in person or on the phone or by email.

Corporate and Social Hierarchy, Education and Communication in Mexican Business Culture

I have repeatedly stated in this essay that Mexicans communicate differently among one another depending on socioeconomic status in and out of work as well as education levels and professional status while on the job. In the same interview in which he spoke of Mexicans speaking in over polite and indirect forms to "soften things up" on the job, Javier Degollado also recognized that "our manner of communication in business absolutely depends on who we are with." Degollado went on to explain that managers and business owners, when speaking with one another will be far more direct, confrontational and assertive when speaking with one another within or across companies as opposed to a lower level employee communicating with his superior. Gerardo Fernandez echoes Degollado's point of view stating, "Direct, intense communication is far more commonplace among us managers, law firm partners and business owners. Lower level employees and those in the lower classes often find mangers, owners, and most foreign businessmen to be demanding in our forms of speech. However, our forms of speaking to each other aren't seen as demanding or rude as it is par for the course. My partners and I have to be clear and to the point with our clients, especially since many of them are affluent, influential businessmen. They will not tolerate me beating around the bush or trying to bull shit them even if I want to."

In another anonymous interview with a 27-year-old graphic designer in Mexico City, I learned that she had just received a promotion in which she would be the head of all corporate graphic design as opposed to just one department. Yet the biggest challenge for her in this promotion wouldn't be her new design workload. Her most significant career adjustment in this ascendency up the corporate ladder would be going from having a direct supervisor who was around her age to answering directly to the company president who could pass as her father. My primary interest was how this employee, a college educated millennial would make suggestions and objections to a Mexican business owner on design and marketing. Let it be noted that in the "old, traditional" Mexican culture she would be expected to bow to the owner's wishes even when not agreeing on his marketing and design strategies and say nothing more than "Sí señor," regardless of her true thoughts on a project. When confronted with this question in the interview, the young lady calmly explained, "When I disagree with him and I feel that it is best for the company that we do things in a different way I will explain it to him in a respectful, diplomatic way. I will tell him that it's my opinion and give him the final decision. That is my obligation as a professional to give my insight based on my experience and talents." These comments were surprising and at the same time interesting. Most of all, they are evidence, that in today's age of globalization, many young, talented, educated Mexicans are not doing business or behaving in the ways that their parents and grandparents may have or as portrayed by trade books and other general analyses of Mexican culture. This employee's remarks and plans are bi-products of a Mexican psyche that is slowly changing in which fatalism, concern only for the present, indirect communication and conformity are slowly being replaced by a more globalized mindset.

While having documented through research, interviews and lived experiences that in higher level positions and negotiations, traditional Mexican standards of communication cannot be expected, it is apparently even more the case in dealing with large corporations. In an interview with a Mexican CEO who chose to be interviewed under the condition of anonymity, we spoke extensively about his ideal profile for a female marketing manager who would sell to major national and international retailers in Mexico such as Wal-Mart, Sams, Cosco, and Comercial Mexicana among others:

> I need my main marketing girl who deals with those huge retail purchasing departments to be a bitch, I can't have a girl who is all sweet and docile and beats around the bush. Otherwise they will kill her on price and I won't sell anything to them. Those companies are complete SOBs and try and squeeze everything they can out of you when it comes to price. I have to have a girl who is firm and to the point and won't let them push her around. The one I have now I really like because she says things to them so directly and cuts them off so quick when they try and pull the wool over her eyes that it pisses them off. I don't care if they're pissed off at her, I don't mind it at all as long as those purchasing people get the idea that they're not going to manipulate her.

This series of interviews demonstrates that Mexico, in an era of globalization is changing rapidly and just as a foreign businessperson cannot expect all Mexicans to arrive 45 minutes late to a meeting, assuming that all Mexicans in the corporate world will communicate with the same ambivalence is rather preposterous. While it is clear that traditional communication methods still exist in Mexico among those in certain socioeconomic groups and career positions, it is clear that stark contrasts exist in communication styles based upon many other factors.

Furthermore, a Mexican businessperson who communicates with a foreigner is forced to take up a different tone when speaking or writing. Juan Portilla, a Mexican entrepreneur who previously worked in large organizations, stated, "Mexicans have to adapt to US communication culture if they want to have success in the US market. Communication is less efficient here in Mexico among Mexicans, they love to BS. But when they deal with foreign clients and markets, they have to be more direct and no nonsense." Not only are communication styles among Mexicans shown to change when doing business internationally, studies demonstrate that the foreigner in Mexico is likely to change his or her communication style to adapt to the Mexican as well. In border regions especially, a transnational, hybrid culture of communication has arisen within Mexico in which both Mexicans and foreigners are adapting to one another's communication styles and needs (Ortiz 32).

Written Communication in Mexican Business

Mexico, being a culture that tends to stress the value of relationships, has distinct trends in written communication that reflect such values. A Westerner who reads a formal business letter or email from a Mexican colleague, client or provider for the first time may be taken aback at the structure and content of the text. Because of the value of a relationship building that tends to be strong in Mexican business culture, an email or formal letter from a Mexican manager generally begins with an opening sentence or paragraph, which serves the purpose of warmly greeting the reader in effort to establish and/or cultivate a strong relationship.

In her 1999 study, Tebeaux distinctly and profoundly analyzes the trends that exist in style, structure and choice of words from Mexican businesspeople in written communication while linking them back to Mexico's history, politics and culture. In her analysis of one of many of Mexican business letters, the idea of relationship building is self explanatory. Tebeaux's primary source:

> Estimado Lic. Ortiz:
> Because of the relationship that exists between us, it is my pleasure to greet you and present for your consideration the special services in Consulting and Executive Training that is offered by Grupo Empresarial SIA, which have as their object to support your organization in the achievement of the objectives of competitiveness and leadership that are demanded by the economic and social environment in which we actually live ... [65].

As explained by Tebeaux throughout her work and evident in many or her other primary documents, the importance of a relationship between the two parties is specifically mentioned at the beginning of the letter. In this and many other cases, the reader does not encounter the specific purpose or necessary details of the letter until the second or third paragraph of the letter.

Because Mexico is a high context culture, written as well as verbal communication is usually ubiquitously sprinkled with words of pleasantry and respect. Or as also stated, "Thus the high context nature of Mexican culture is reflected in written communication, which often is dominated by courtesy, dignity, tact, diplomacy and protocol of honor" (Tebeaux 78). Along with the high text cultural values and relationship building, the cultural concept of conflict aversion is alive and well in written forms of communication in Mexico. The general trends of pleasant greetings sprinkled with words of politeness and respect in written communication goes hand in hand with the Mexican's desire never to offend and thus avoid any potential conflict with his or her business counterpart.

It is my recommendation for foreign businesspeople who embark upon business in Mexico to understand the aforementioned cultural values in written communication and how they contrast from a Western, more linear brand of communication. Without such an understanding, a Western businessperson may read a letter or email from her Mexican counterpart and assume that the Mexican is buttering her up, just a smooth writer who does not get to the point or care about the details, or possibly not even serious about business. Such cultural misunderstandings could lead to lost business opportunities on both sides. We chose to embark upon the task of writing this book with the hope of creating more business and commerce between Mexico and other countries through a greater cultural understanding of Mexicans. And those foreign business people who choose to read written communication from Mexican counterparts with a cultural awareness of the nation's values will only enhance their chances of successful business endeavors with Mexicans.

Mexican Business Communication in Person and Through Modern Technology

One of the many generalizations of traditional Mexico is that Mexicans only do business face to face. Any trade book or experienced foreign businessperson in Mexico will claim, "The Mexicans have to know you first. You have to have a relationship before they will do business with you." This statement, while a broad generalization, is still true in many, if not most Mexican business circles, depending on the industry, among a myriad of other factors. Yet to highlight one of the most pernicious examples of this generalized rhetoric through trade books, let us examine the opening anecdote of Paula Heunsinkveld's *Inside Mexico:* "José Luis Ibarra, a successful Mexican businessman who had just arrived to the United States, was given an appointment from 4:00 to 5:00 p.m. with Fred Lawson, an important potential contact. Mr. Ibarra arrived at 4:45, excited and ready to do business. Great were his disappointment and bewilderment when he was received coldly and dismissed fifteen minutes later" (1). Heusinkveld goes on to explain different concepts of time to the reader as Mr. Ibarra had arrived within a one hour window to do business and Mr. Lawson was expecting his Mexican contact to arrive at 4 p.m. sharp. Hernandez-Pozas and Madero further analyze the concept of time in Mexican business culture in their contribution to this text. Yet I would like to take this excerpt to highlight a few irresponsible cultural stereotypes with regard to Mexican business practices that Heusinkveld chooses to highlight. Heusinkveld first infers to the reader that the hypothetical or better put stereotypical Mexican in this case is probably only willing to do business face to face. Second, she goes on to stress the old stereotype of relationship building in doing business in Mexico as Mr. Ibarra had planned to stay at Mr. Lawson's office for the duration of the evening. While relationship building and face-to-face meetings are still key in many realms of Mexican business culture, this trend is rapidly changing in contemporary Mexico along with many other aspects of the nation's culture.

It appears as if Dr. Heusinkveld has not stepped foot into a modern office of an international company in Monterrey, Guadalajara or Mexico City where employees communicate with their Mexican and foreign suppliers and clients through Go to Meeting, Skype, WhatsApp and iMessenger while surfing LinkedIn for talented candidates to fill positions and updating the company's website and Facebook pages while Tweeting several times a day to keep the company's new products and services fresh in prospects' and clients' minds. The idea that all Mexican businesspeople must take an entire afternoon and evening at a prospective contact's office as a pretext to doing business only exacerbates negative stereotypes of Mexicans in the minds of foreigners while once again giving them no real insight on doing business in Mexico.

In today's era of technology and globalization, Mexico is undergoing a revolution of sorts in which e-commerce, social media and marketing, and technology are revamping the way in which Mexicans communicate in business. If planning on traveling to a major Mexican city on business, a foreigner can assume that his Mexican clients, colleagues or providers have already looked him up on Facebook and LinkedIn, and will be texting with him by the time he gets to the airport to check on his pick up and hotel accommodations. In Mexico's major business cities, iPhones and Samsung Galaxies are a commonplace. As of 2014 the nation had over 50 million smart phones (just under one for every two individuals in a nation with a population of 120 million) with this number expecting to increase dramatically in the coming years (Alvarez). Additionally, of the over 50 million Internet users in Mexico today, 90 percent use at least one social media website or application (Melendez and Enriquez). These 50 million plus Mexicans connected to social media with their smartphones and laptops, or in an Internet café are obviously signs of a dynamic trend toward communicating online in the business world. Furthermore, email communication is the preferred method of correspondence in most medium and large Mexican firms just as it is in the United States and other Western countries.

Conclusions on Culture Communications and Business in Mexico

While Mexico's past and traditions cannot be forgotten or ignored, contemporary Mexico and the nation's future economic and business potential must also be recognized. It is imperative that foreign businessmen, women, and students understand the overall differences in cultural values when traveling to or doing business in Mexico as Mexicans indeed tend to be less direct and precise in expressing themselves in business due to Mexico being a high context culture in the realm of communication coupled with the traditional Mexican psyche which focuses on immediate and present pleasure in contrast to a more Western, futuristic approach (Tebeaux 78). High-context simply refers to the cultural trend in a nation such as Mexico in which contexts outside of the spoken or written communication can affect business. These contexts can include personal relationships, family issues, hierarchy, etc., which may mean more than the words themselves. On the contrary, in Anglo-Saxon cultures the words themselves carry more weight than outside contexts (Tebeaux 78). Mexico's turbulent history and a mindset of victimization have played at least some role in traditional and contemporary Mexican communication behavior. Nevertheless, communication styles in Mexico are changing, especially among the nation's younger, more educated and cosmopolitan generations. As more Mexicans are expected to educate themselves, travel, and be logged into the world on their smartphones, tables and computers in the future, these changing trends are only expected to intensify. Finally, it is conspicuous through interviews and research that management in Mexico incorporates contrasting communication styles when compared to those in lower level positions in society.

When venturing into Mexican business endeavors, it is essential that the foreign business person take into account centuries old communication traditions that are engrained into Mexican society while understand that a new, young, educated group of dynamic professionals will likely change the landscape of business in Mexico far beyond the ways in which they express themselves.

Discussion Questions

1. What are some of the broad, general stereotypes of Mexicans and the way they communicate in business as portrayed in trade books and websites on business in Mexico? Why are these generalizations dangerous for someone planning on doing business in Mexico?

2. What are some of the reasons why Mexicans, in a traditional sense, view themselves as victims?

3. What socioeconomic class, educational and geographic contrasts are described in the essay in regards to Mexican communication? Be specific with your descriptions.

4. Describe the different concept of the present vs. the future in Mexican society. Compare it to how the same concepts are described in Anglo-Saxon cultures. How do these Mexican values affect communication?

5. What are some of the examples of indirectness in Mexican communication?

6. How is today's technology changing the way Mexicans communicate and do business?

Key Learning Terms

Class differences and communication: Although there is a cultural trend toward indirect communication in Mexico, such tendencies are far more concentrated in lower socioeconomic classes in the nation's society.

Conflict Aversion: The Mexican cultural trend to avoid any conflict in interpersonal relations as Mexicans feel that there is little use in putting up a fight or defending oneself against aggression.

Hybrid communication styles: Styles of communication in which Mexicans and foreigners have each come to change their communication styles in order to better accommodate the other's culture of expressing his or her thoughts. Such forms of communication are more commonplace in the U.S.–Mexico border regions.

Fatalism: The concept in which many Mexicans feel that there is little hope or opportunity to change the future. This idea of fatalism goes in line with the concept of mañana as well as the idea of the victimization of Mexico and the Mexicans.

Indirectness: The cultural phenomenon in Mexico in which Mexicans (especially of lower classes) do not speak or write in direct, linear terms when communicating and instead convey their points in what can be viewed as "coded" speech

Mañana: According to Fuentes, the concept of mañana is that Mexicans prefer to leave things until tomorrow in effort not to sacrifice the enjoyment of the present. This concept goes in line with fatalism as many Mexicans feel that the future will be no better or worse than today and therefore choose to live in the moment.

Short term appeasement: The Mexican concept in which Mexicans often prefer to appease the individual or individuals that they are with in the short term as opposed to taking a futuristic approach by analyzing the future consequences of their actions. This also goes in line with the concepts of mañana and fatalism and the overall concept of the present versus the future.

References

Alvarez, Raúl. "Un Crecemiento imparable de smartphones en México reporta 52.6 millones de dispositivos en 2014." *Xataka México*. 21 February 2105.
Anonymous. Personal interview, September 18, 2012.
Anonymous. Personal interview, April 20, 2015.
Castañeda, Jorge. *Mañana Forever: Mexico and the Mexicans.* New York: Alfred A. Knopf, 2011.
Degallado, Javier. Personal interview, March 30, 2015.
Fernandez, Gerardo. Personal interview, April 7, 2014.

Kras, Eva. *Cultura Gerencial: México–Estados Unidos*. Mexico: Grupo Editorial Iberoamérica, 1990.
LaBahn, Douglas W., and Katrin R. Harich. "Sensitivity to National Business Culture: Effects on US–Mexican Channel Relationship Performance." *Journal of International Marketing* 5.4 (1997): 29–51.
Melendez, Pedro, and Erika Enriquez. "Estudio sobre los hábitos de Usuarios de Internet in México 2014." *Asociación Mexicana de Internet*. 2014.
Oritz, Lorelei A. "Cruzando los fronteras de la comunicación professional entre Mexico y los Estados Unidos." *International Journal of Business Communication* 42.1 (2005): 28–50.
Rodríguez, Mauro, and Patricia Ramírez. *Psicología del Mexicano en el Trabajo*. Mexico: McGraw-Hill Interamericana Editores, 2004.
Skidmore, Thomas E., and Peter H. Smith. *Modern Latin America*. New York: Oxford University Press, 2005
Tebeaux, Elizabeth. "Designing Written Business Communication Along the Shifting Cultural Continuum." *Journal of Business and Technical Communication* 13.1 (1999): 49–85.
Veliz, Veronica. Personal interview, October 2006.

Looking at Time and Business with the Mexican Lens

Olivia Hernández-Pozas *and*
Sergio Madero-Gómez

Mexico, being the second-largest economy in Latin America, and the eleventh largest economy worldwide (World Bank) has the potential to experience a prosperous future and become a global player. Like many other Latin American countries, Mexico has long been a land of paradox and contrasts (Eyzaguirre 9). According to Vassolo, De Castro and Gomez-Mejia, while currently facing many challenges to economic, political and social growth, Latin America is the second most important emerging market region in the current global economy (22). Among challenges facing the region according to Vassolo are national institutions, the macroeconomic environment and widespread regional income inequality (22–23). Furthermore, low productivity is a traditional yet persistent strain on Latin American economic growth (Eyzaguirre 9). Mexico is not exempt from the rest of Latin America in being forced to confront the aforementioned challenges. In recent decades, however, like other countries in the region, it has implemented profound reforms that have triggered influential achievements. Today Mexico is a country open to international trade, characterized by economic stability, abundant with natural resources and boasting a domestic market of over 112 million people. In the last decade, Mexico has notably reduced poverty and experienced an expansion of its middle-class. Its talented engineering workforce is the largest in the Americas. From 2013 to 2014, Mexico moved up four places in the World Bank's Ease of Doing Business ranking. It is therefore not surprising that domestic companies are internationalizing their operations while foreign investment is on the rise in Mexico. According to Reuters (2014), Mexico drew a record of $35.2 billion USD in foreign direct investment in 2013.

For foreign investors and managers not accustomed to business in Mexico, the experience could be challenging and difficult because of cultural differences. One of the most common misunderstandings is related to the notion of time. According to Lewis ("How Different Cultures Understand Time"), the United States and Mexico employ time in such a different manner that it may cause friction between the people of the two nations.

In the first essay of this collection, Coria-Sánchez highlights that there is an anthropologic explanation that contextualizes the concept of time, which unfortunately is not taken into consideration by trade books. He argues that this misunderstanding frequently triggers negative stereotypes about Mexicans. For example, Kenna and Lacy state the following: "Mexicans are more casual toward time than Americans and this includes negotiating meetings which can run up late or even be cancelled at the last minute.... It may take months to conclude a business deal" (37–51). Also, Engholm and Grimes emphasize this unconstructive stereotype about Mexicans and their priorities: "Mexican concepts of time are fundamentally different from American. In practice, this translates into Mexicans frequently being late for appointments or failing to show up at all" (15). The differences in the conceptualization of time are noticed by Mexicans too, who complain about the obsession for time of the Americans. More recently, Ned Crouch supports the following idea: "Americans are slaves of time and casually dismiss more relaxed attitudes toward the clock as convention, outdated tradition, or simply lethargy.... The notion of time we carry around in our heads explains why Mexicans think we're anxiety-ridden and why we see them as laid-back" (33–34).

In this essay, the concept of time and the rationale behind behavior is discussed from the Mexican standpoint. Its purpose is not only to highlight what is important for Mexicans when doing business, but also, why it is so vital, and how non–Mexican business people can better adjust to such differences. The aim of this essay is to build a more solid understanding among cultures. The cultural intelligence theoretical framework of Earley and Ang is used to support recommendations.

Concepts of Time

What is time? There are a wide variety of conceptualizations of time. According to Ancona, Okhuysen, and Perlow different cultures describe time in different ways. For example, Americans, influenced by the Protestant work ethic, see time as precious and as truly money. On the other hand, Spaniards, Italians, and Arabs, don't necessarily share this Anglo-Saxon view (514–515). These non–Western cultures allocate less importance to the passing of time in day to day life be it in social or business environments especially in the case that important conversations may be left unfinished (Lewis).

Most common types of conceptualizations of time include the following: clock or linear time and cyclical or event time. Clock or linear time considers time as infinitely divisible into objective, quantifiable units. This is the most common way to see time in developed countries of the Western hemisphere. Cyclical or event time refers to time in which events repeat over and over and time may be continuous and indefinite.

In *When Cultures Collide: Leading Cultures*, Richard Lewis distinguishes between two fundamental types of people: linear-actives and multi-actives. Linear-actives are those people who plan, schedule, organize, deal with one thing at a time and pursue action plans, such as the German and American. Multia, on the other hand, are those people who do many things at once. Multi-actives also plan activities not according to a time schedule, but according to the importance that each appointment brings with it. Lewis' distinction relates to the one previously proposed by the anthropologist Edward Hall (quoted in Vinton, 10).

According to Hall (quoted in Vinton, 8) beliefs and attitudes about time are hidden, therefore they can't be easily recognized and managed by people. To help with this task, Hall makes a distinction between two time styles: monochronic and polychronic. Monochronic people focus on one thing at a time, place importance on schedules, tasks and procedures, while polychronic people focus on many things at a time and place more importance on people and relationships.

Different conceptualizations of time can also be explained by religious beliefs. Arcona explains that time is socially constructed and religion influences the concept of time. In societies with a Judeo-Christian history, time is seen as a straight line. Arcona and his colleagues discuss that according to this view, and especially after the industrial revolution, time is a resource that can be measured, therefore optimized, bought and sold (514). American, Anglo-Saxon, Germanic and Scandinavian cultures often hold a linear, clock vision of time (Saunders, Van Slyke and Vogel 21). Lewis ("How Different Cultures Understand Time") explains that, in a profit-oriented society, as the American one, time flows fast and it is scarce. That's the reason Americans cannot be idle. They need to be active and producing. The more they work, the more money they make, and the more successful they become. However, other societies, with different convictions do not see time in such a way.

According to Saunders, Van Slyke and Vogel in the Hinduism and Buddhism tradition, time is continuous, cyclical, recurrent, long-term, abstract and epochal (22). In "How Different Cultures Understand Time," Lewis explains that in the Buddhist culture, not only time, but even life goes around in a circle. For Buddhism only the instantaneous sensation is real, while duration in contrast, is pure imagination. Saunders and his colleagues discussed that with this conception of time, it is illogical for an individual to stress over decisions, since opportunities and risks will eventually return.

In addition, these authors explain that philosophical systems such as Confucianism and Taoism, advocate a harmonic way of life. In this view, people are supposed to seek temporal harmony within the person, among individuals and with nature. In cultures based on this, the pursuit of harmony and maintenance of good relationships influence the way people relate to the notion of time. For example, in China, at the end of a meeting, it is customary to thank participants for their contribution of time. Chinese take arrival time very seriously. They can arrive 15 to 30 minutes earlier as a gesture of respect for their counterpart's time (Lewis).

Another distinctive case is Japan. The Japanese are meticulous when they segment time. However, according to Lewis, their segmentation is different from the American or German ones. For the Japanese, properness, courtesy and tradition are the key criteria to choose how to see and manage time.

Another difference in concepts of time depends on what is called time horizon. Time horizon refers to the given importance to the past, present and future (Vinton 9). Some cultures focus more on the future rewards than others. Those which focus more on the future are known as long-term societies, while those which focus more on the present are known as short-term ones (Saunders, Van Slyke and Vogel 20).

It is evident that perceptions of punctuality vary depending on culture (Vinton 8). Compliance with deadlines will also be affected by culture. Cultural variables such as power distance and collectivism will influence the way people manage time. According to Hofstede, power distance is the extent to which the less powerful members of institutions and organizations within a country expect and accept that power is distributed unequally. In cultures scoring high on power distance, people will find difficulty in rushing off from a meeting with a powerful individual to attend another one with a person with less power. In power distant societies, people will also find it difficult to say "No" to someone powerful. Naturally, one can expect that this behavior will have implications on punctuality and compliance. Furthermore, in collectivistic cultures, individuals expect other members of their in-group to look after them in exchange for unquestioning loyalty. Thus, since people feel obliged with other members of their in-group, punctuality and compliance with deadlines will vary depending on an individual's affiliation.

Communication is another influential factor that can be intertwined with the cultural concept of time. For some cultures communication is not direct, but indirect and depends on the context. People characterized by high contextual communication avoid verbalizing what they take for granted. Therefore, their messages about time are not explicit, which can cause those from low contextual cultures to easily become confused. Misunderstanding about time frames can arise when interpretation and communication between individuals is not aligned because of cultural differences.

As can be seen from the previous explanation, the interpretation of time varies tremendously depending on many cultural factors. If being a few minutes late is intolerable in certain societies, the same will not have negative impact in others. In this section, cultural factors such as religion, philosophical systems, variation in the importance of task versus relationship, time horizon (past, present, future), time styles (monochronic versus polychronic), linear- or multi-active, power distance and collectivism, have been highlighted as paramount. In the next section, the cultural variables and their effect on the interpretation of time, for the Mexican-specific case, will be presented.

Using the Mexican Cultural Lens

Culture in Mexico has been strongly influenced by historical, political, economic and societal factors. In many cases, even geography has impacted Mexican behavior. Thus, the objective for this section is to provide alternative interpretations and explanations of the concept of time using the Mexican cultural lens. As Coria-Sánchez states in a personal interview: "When referring to the notion of time, Mexican business culture shouldn't be portrayed as inferior or limited by their own forces of irresponsibility. On the contrary, foreign and Mexican people must be brought together by accepting each other instead of demonizing one of them, as the other."

Mexico, with a population of 112 million people, is a highly diverse county on a myriad of fronts. People in the north, center and south of the country do not behave the same and often hold varying systems of values. Likewise, the customs and values of those in the nation's urban areas contrast significantly with those of Mexico's countryside. For example, business people in northern Mexico may be more prone to speak, behave, and think like their counterparts in Texas, New Mexico, Arizona and southern California since the border regions of both countries share strong historic, economic and cultural connections. Likewise, one cannot expect people from Mexico City, with almost 20 million inhabitants, to behave like people in the small towns of Oaxaca. They face different challenges and are exposed to different influential factors, in spite of the fact that both places are in Mexico. Therefore one should be cautious with broad generalizations of the country as it is not homogeneous. In fact, one can find various subcultures throughout Mexico depending on geographical location and demographic characteristics, such as education, age, economic situation and societal status.

In Mexico, it is easy to perceive how history has influenced the beliefs and behaviors of most people. Culture in Mexico is a rich mix between pre–Columbian and European traditions. In pre–Columbian times, all indigenous people subscribed to the cyclical model of time. The Olmecs, the Aztecs, the Mayas, and the Zapotecs saw time as repetitive based on seasons and phases of the moon. According to Crouch the Mexican circular view of time has its roots in the Mesoamerican view. He explains that the Aztecs were obsessed with time and believed that at some point, time would end and they would cease to exist. Circular time was in effect a way to keeping hope alive. The circular view of time was key and connected to the survival of the indigenous empires. Today many of Mexico's rural areas are still inhabited by indigenous people or their descendants, thus their traditions have not fully disappeared in the country (34–37).

With the arrival of the Spanish and the conquest of Mexico, culture started to change. Then, Spanish traditions and especially the Catholic religion became influential. Currently, much of the modern-day behavior of Mexicans is deeply influenced by intertwined indigenous and Catholic values. The Virgin of Guadalupe has long been a symbol representing the Mexican faith. She represents both Catholic and indigenous beliefs. In Mexico, religion is important. Within the Catholic point of view, family is paramount and should deserve attention and time. Mexicans are highly collective in terms of family and interpersonal relationships. The family is considered an absolute building block of Mexican society, making it a highly valued social unit (Rosseau and Schalk 159). Collective values held by Mexicans translate to a need for harmony. Decisions about how time should be used are highly influenced by these values.

With Spanish colonization came a system of economic and social hierarchy and inequality that still exists today. Current power distance in Mexico, although not exclusively, relates to such inequalities. This power distance can also explain Mexican interpretation of time. According to Friedrich, Mesquita and Hatum Mexicans prefer clearly defined hierarchical lines and unmistaken authority roles (61). For Mexicans, the situation and the relationship indicate how late one may be to an appointment or what is an acceptable margin of completion time around an agreed deadline. In business related activities, if the relationship is hierarchical, people with less power, will often arrive on time and stay as long as needed. When arriving a bit late or needing to be excused from a meeting or appointment, it is customary to apologize or ask permission. Such a tendency to apologize for tardiness or cordially ask permission to leave early is indicative of the ubiquitous politeness in Mexico and Latin America as a whole (Lenartowicz and Johnson 271).

For Mexicans a meal can be a bonding experience. Lunch or dinner are the perfect time to strengthen family and personal relationships, and if possible, they shouldn't be rushed. This custom also extends to business and has a practical justification. In Mexico, people assume that companies do not only exist to make profits, but also provide jobs and socialization. Many Mexican business people use breakfast, lunch or dinner time to bond and build strong business relationships. Mexicans believe that mutual trust requires time.

According to Bluedorn, Kaufman, and Lane misunderstandings occur when participants, with different time views, judge intention and action (24). They cite a relative monochronic North American and a more polychronic Latin American as examples for such potential misunderstandings. Mexicans tend to be polychronic and characterized by high context communication. As polychronic people, Mexicans do many things at once, are subject to interruptions, consider commitments as an objective to be achieved if possible, often change plans and base promptness on the relationship. As high context communicators, Mexicans already have information, and their communication is not explicit. All these characteristics might cause conflict, when coming into contact with people of Monochronic and low context cultures. That's the reason it is key to understand and to learn how to manage the differences.

Jarryd Widhalm, an American professional who has studied in Mexico and is currently working in Mexico City has understood and learned how to work with Mexicans. In a personal interview, regarding the Mexican notion of time, Widhalm explains the following: "…the concept of a start time is not as fixed. By that, I mean if I have a team meeting that starts at 4 p.m. the odds are good that not everyone will be there and ready at 4:00:00. It is generally understood that as long as they get to the meeting within 5–10 minutes after 4 p.m. it won't be a problem. In order to get out in front of this, I came up with a soft start to the meeting. This way the people who arrived early or on time are not wasting their time. We go around the room, and I make everyone share good news. This can be anything positive going on in their lives, whether inside of work or outside of work. It is a soft start because it is important, but it is not a big deal if someone misses it because they arrived late. It is also a fun way to get to know your coworkers better.… I think you just have to feel it out with each person just like they will adapt to you as well."

Along the lines of Jarryd, Coria-Sánchez explains that for an American business person to arrive late or not to arrive would mean not to be at the exact time at a certain place. However, for the Mexican counterpart to arrive on time would mean to have an open window of about ten to fifteen minutes (54).

Exposure to other cultures, and familiarity with global business practices may also influence the way Mexicans approach time. For example, Nora Elia Cantu, Mexican executive of Banorte, in Coria-Sánchez's 2009 interview, stated the following: "…before globalization … to be late was like nothing happens, they had to wait for us, this attitude has changed as people these days are faced with the fact that they have to gain more clients and that being late can cause us to lose our place in business."

Two different types of situations are business and social events. Individuals should expect a greater variability regarding punctuality in social events. Coria-Sánchez, in a personal interview, mentioned, "As a matter of fact, Mexicans experience these cultural differences as well. From a personal perspective and after living in the US for more than twenty eight years, I have never understood the American way of enforcing their party hours. I am accustomed to this cultural trend by now, but still amused to this day to see the hours for beginning and ending a get-together on an invitation. Mexican invitations do not specify the time for a party to end, it is a time to be with friends and family and have a great time, what is the rush to end it?" Also, Ana Chio, IBM consultant in Mexico City, in Coria-Sánchez's 2009 interview, said, "Mexican culture is to be late fifteen or twenty minutes because the other person will also be late; it is not our culture to be on time, we are Mexicans, not English people. If someone arrives on time to a party, that's because this person doesn't have anything else to do. In other cases, however, unpunctuality can be seen as a lack of respect for others; it depends on the situation." In Mexico, the situation as well as the individual's role in the event and the relationship will dictate arrival time. For example, for a social event where the individual doesn't have a specific task to do, arrival about half an hour or even an hour late is normal. But, if the person was invited to do something at the social event or if the relationship is very strong, it means compliance with the commitment is important and therefore punctuality is expected.

In summary, in Mexico, decisions about how to manage time depend on the situation, the relationship and the individual's role. Social and business situations should be managed differently. Traditions, religion, hierarchical positions, collectivism and family matters affect the decision of being or not on time. Mexicans are polychronic people and high context communicators, so conflictive situations when managing the notion of time can be prevented with a better understanding of the cultural context. In the next section, specific recommendations about how to deal with the differences will be presented.

Recommendations

In order to avoid misunderstandings, learning about different temporal behaviors and adjustment to different cultural norms are needed. Intention and action needs to be understood with different lenses. To interpret and adjust behavior, the cultural intelligence framework is recommended (Earley and Ang 12).

Cultural Intelligence (CQ) was conceived at the beginning of the 21st century, in a moment of unprecedented globalization and interconnectedness (Ang, Van Dyne and Tan, 582). According to Earley and Ang, CQ is the capacity to function effectively in multicultural settings (12). CQ has four dimensions: knowledge (cognition), strategy (metacognition), drive (motivation) and action (behavior). Cultural intelligent individuals are those who enjoy interacting with people from other cultures (CQ drive), and not only know about cultural differences (CQ knowledge), but also plan their multicultural interactions (CQ strategy) and behave accordingly (CQ action).

The main purpose behind the concept of cultural intelligence is to identify why some people can easily and effectively adapt their views and behaviors cross-culturally, while others cannot (Van Dyne, Ang and Livermore quoted in Ang, Van Dyne and Tan 582). According to Rockstuhl, Seiler, Ang, Van Dyne, and Annen cultural intelligence is a critical leadership competency for those with cross-border responsibilities (825).

In the previous sections, an introduction to different conceptualizations of time, as well as the specific Mexican values and temporal behavior were highlighted. These previous sections are appropriate references to CQ knowledge and its importance to function well in a multicultural setting.

It is assumed that if the reader is examining this essay, CQ Drive exists already and the non–Mexican reader, not only wants to interact effectively with Mexicans, but also feels capable of doing so in a business environment. CQ drive can increase with success. It is the purpose of this essay to help the reader to be successful when interacting with Mexican business people.

CQ strategy metacognition relates to the capability to function effectively by planning, checking and adjusting using CQ knowledge. Therefore the next time you work with Mexicans we recommend that you plan such business endeavors according to explanations in this book. Check how your strategy worked and make adjustments when needed.

For CQ action, remember variables that may affect behavior. In this essay, temporal behavior of Mexicans was explained and alternative explanations for such behavior were presented. When doing business or interacting with Mexicans, it is important to recognize that Mexico is a large country where many subcultures coexist.

Mexico's current open-market policies are influencing mobility and the composition of its population. Therefore, generalizations might not apply. Be especially attentive to differences in geographical location, as well as in the education, social and economic status of the individuals. See the connection between time and family values, or between hierarchical status and punctuality. Look for patterns in the way Mexicans communicate about compliance with deadlines or the lack thereof. By doing so, you will most likely discover how difficult it is for Mexicans to say "No" and how they avoid confrontation and conflict. Plan accordingly and be ready to monitor and make adjustments.

CQ behavior includes verbal and non-verbal communication as well as speech. To fully understand and see time through the Mexican lens, pay attention not only to what Mexicans say, but also how they say it. Cultivate relationships and build trust. Be patient, remember that events and bonding are crucial for this culture. Try to understand Mexican priorities and to behave accordingly when in Mexico or when doing business with its people.

Do not be offended or get frustrated. Most likely, your Mexican counterpart is not trying to be in conflict with you. That's just the way Mexicans are. That's not because they do not have regard for others. As a matter of fact, most likely is because they do care too much. Try to be included in their group. You will see that as a foreign business person, acceptance into a Mexican's close circle of family and friends can often pay large dividends in the future. Review the factors, highlighted in this essay, and try to identify which ones are causing a particular outcome.

Take into account that Mexico is a country open to international trade, characterized by economic stability and abundant with natural resources. With an internal market of more than 112 million people, a growing middle-class and with the largest engineering workforce in the Americas, their are ample opportunities for foreign business people in Mexico. Mexicans in general terms are sociable and polite, and despite many inaccurate stereotypes, recent studies have shown that Mexicans work more hours per week on average than any nationality. Differences in priorities and interpretation of time and how it is supposed to be used explain the confusion and misunderstanding of foreign executives. When doing business in Mexico or with people from the country, try to look at time and business with the Mexican lens. Cultivate your cultural intelligence and keep in mind that this could be paramount to your success in doing business with Mexicans.

Discussion Questions

1. Why is Mexico in a promising position for foreign investment and international business?
2. What are the main differences in the notion of time between people from developed Western countries, e.g. American, Anglo-Saxon, Germanic, Scandinavian and people from Latin Europe or Asia.
3. What are the main cultural factors that make the notion of time vary around the world?
4. Explain how Mexicans understand time and what cultural factors influence it.
5. For Mexicans, what are the main differences between business and social time?
6. What is cultural intelligence?
7. What are the four dimensions of cultural intelligence?
8. How can cultural intelligence help you to avoid misunderstandings about time?
9. What are the main recommendations of this essay to be able to look at time and business with the Mexican lens?

Key Learning Terms

Clock model of time: The clock model of time is also known as linear time. It considers time as infinitely divisible into objective, quantifiable units. This is the most common way to see time in developed countries of the Western hemisphere.

Collectivistic cultures: Collectivistic cultures are those in which individuals expect other members of their in-group to look after them in exchange for unquestioning loyalty.

Cyclical model of time: The cyclical model of time is also known as event time. It refers to time in which events repeat over and over and time may be continuous and indefinite.

High contextual communication: People characterized by high contextual communication avoid verbalizing what they take for granted. Therefore, their messages about time are not explicit.

Linear-active people: Linear-actives are those people who plan, schedule, organize, deal with one thing at a time and pursue action plans.

Low contextual communication: People characterized by low contextual communication include mass information in the explicit code.

Monochronic people: Monochronic people focus on one thing at a time, place importance on schedules, tasks and procedures.

Multi-Active people: Multi-active people are those people who do many things at once. Multi-actives also plan activities not according to a time schedule, but according to the importance that each appointment brings with it.

Polychronic people: Polychronic people focus on many things at a time and place more importance on people and relationships.

Power distance: Power distance is the extent to which the less powerful members of institutions and organizations within a country expect and accept that power is distributed unequally.

Time Horizon: Time horizon refers to the given importance to the past, present and future.

References

Ancona, Deborah, Gerardo Okhuysen, and Leslie Perlow. "Taking Time to Integrate Temporal Research." *Academy of Management Review* 26.4. (2001): 512–529. Print.

Ang, Soon, Linn Van Dyne, and Mei Ling Tan. "Cultural Intelligence." *Cambridge Handbook of Intelligence*. Ed. Robert J. Sternberg and Scott Barry Kaufman. Cambridge: Cambridge University Press, 2009. Print

Bluedorn, Allen, Carol Kaufman, and Paul Lane. "How Many Things Do You Like to Do at Once? An Introduction to Monochromic and Polychronic Time." *Academy of Management Executive* 6.4 (1992): 17–26. Print.

Cantu, Nora Elia. Personal interview by Carlos Coria-Sánchez, 2009.

Chio, Ana. Personal interview by Carlos Coria-Sánchez, 2009.

Coria-Sánchez, Carlos. "Learning Cultural Awareness in Spanish for Business and International Business Courses: The Presence of Negative Stereotypes in Some Trade Books Used as Textbooks." *Journal of Languages and International Business* 15.2 (2004): 49–65. Print.

Coria-Sánchez, Carlos. Personal interview, 2014.

Crouch, Ned. *Mexicans and Americans: Cracking the Culture Code.* London: Nicholas Brealey International, 2004. Print.

Earley, Christopher, and Soon Ang. *Cultural Intelligence: Individual Interactions Across Cultures.* Stanford: Stanford University Press, 2003. Print.

Engholm, Christopher, and Scott Grimes. *Doing Business in Mexico.* Englewood Cliffs, NJ: Prentice Hall, 1997. Print.
Eyzaguirre, Nicolás. "Sustaining Latin America's transformation." *Finance and Development* (2011): 9–12. Print.
Friedrich, Patricia, Luiz Mesquita, and Andrés Hatum. "The Meaning of Difference." *Management Research* 4.1 (2006): 53–71. Print.
Hofstede, Geert. "National Cultural Dimensions." The Hofstede Centre. Web. 20 May 2015.
Kenna, Peggy, and Sondra Lacy. *Business Mexico.* Lincolnwood, IL: Passport Books, 1994. Print.
Lenartowicz, Tomasz, and James Johnson. "A Cross-National Assessment of the Values of Latin America Managers: Contrasting Hues or Shades of Fray." *Journal of International Business Studies* 34(2003): 266–281. Print.
Lewis, Richard. "How Different Cultures Understand Time." *Business Insider* 1 June 2014. Web. 20 May 2015.
Lewis, Richard. *When Cultures Collide: Leading Across Cultures.* Boston: Nicholas Brealey Publishing, 2006. Print.
ProMexico. "Reasons to Invest in Mexico. Why Mexico?" *ProMexico Trade and Investment.* ProMexico. Web. 20 May 2015.
Reuters. "Mexico Saw Record $35 bln in Foreign Direct Onvestment in 2013." *Reuters*, 23 February 2014. Web. 20 May 2015.
Rockstuhl, Thomas, Stefan Seiler, Soon Ang, Linn Van Dyne, and Hubert Annen. "Beyond General Intelligence (IQ) and Emotional Intelligence (EQ): The Role of Cultural Intelligence (CQ) on Cross-Border Leadership Effectiveness in a Globalized World." *Journal of Social Issues* 67.4 (2011): 825–840. Print.
Rosseau, Denise, and Rene Schalk. *Psychological Contracts in Employment.* Thousand Oaks: Sage, 2000. Print.
Saunders, Carol, Craig Van Slyke, and Douglas Vogel. "My Time or Yours? Managing Time Visions in Global Virtual Teams." *Academy of Management Executive* 18.1 (2004): 19–37. Print.
Vassolo, Roberto, Julio De Castro, and Luis Gomez-Mejia. "Managing in Latin America: Common Issues and a Research Agenda." *Academy of Management Perspectives* 25 (2011): 22–36. Print.
Vinton, Donna. "A New Look at Time, Speed, and the Manager." *Academy of Management Executive* 6.4 (2011): 7–16. Print.
Widhalm, Jarryd. Personal interview, 2014.
World Bank Group. "Ease of doing business in Mexico." *World Bank Group.* Web. 20 May 2015.

Mexican Government in Business
An Institutional Analysis
Juan Antonio Enciso-González

Understanding a country's culture in general and its business in particular is a difficult and complicated endeavor, even for the country's nationals, not to mention foreigners. The relationships of two or more countries have many areas or spaces of interaction as different actors perform different activities, both internally (domestically) and/or externally (internationally). Many different (cultural) perspectives and interests will emerge, representing individuals and groups, the private and the public, that interact in various ways with the rest of the actors, both nationals and internationals. Furthermore, even when the relationships (e.g., business, political, cultural) are relevant for all countries involved, multiple spaces of mutual ignorance or unawareness will always exist. It is thus no surprise that misleading or incomplete understandings lead to stereotypes, exaggerated approaches to risk, and uncertainty regarding other countries, or in the worst case a sense of superiority or discrimination. This mutual ignorance or unawareness would eventually discourage a more intense business between the two countries. As will be explained later, this essay is trying to alleviate this "distance" between Mexico and Westerners.

Mexico is a complex country to understand and decipher, even for its nationals. As with many developing countries, a modern society coexists with a traditional society. For example, today's trade openness is outstanding, with multiple trade agreements with countries across the globe, but it contrasts sharply with a border that is plagued by the smuggling of goods, arms, and people. Some cities enjoy high human development, but Mexico's poverty and inequality rates are still among the highest. The country has strong trade openness, but telecommunications and television companies operate as rigid oligopolies and are often complicit with the authorities. For example, Carlos Slim, the Mexican telecom tycoon who owns a vast majority of the Mexican telecommunications industry, owns a fortune of more than $76 billion. This contrasts with the fact that 45.5 percent of the population lives in poverty.

Although the country has seen electoral reform, its economy and development are still subject to the benevolence of the political parties and their interests, often above those of the nation. For its part, civil society remains generally unorganized and does not demand its rights. Furthermore, in general, Mexicans are poor organizers, and the business management practices are not the exception.

On the other hand, the government-business relationship is a historical relationship that is also full of contrasts, resulting in a mutual love-hate feeling. Furthermore, the government encourages the development and creation of businesses, but allows and protects oligopolies. The government allows the crossing of goods with zero or low tariff taxes, but also allows the entry of Chinese contraband and weapons from North America. Although the government defines numerous programs to promote foreign investment and trade, it fails to define real incentives to strengthen the diversification of exports. In addition, each tax scheme that is established makes the payment of taxes for those operating in the formal economy more difficult, but does little to address the millions of informal operations.

This essay presents a perspective of the business culture in Mexico, emphasizing the perspective of nationals toward the "influence" of government in business. It is intended for readers in both Mexico and other countries, especially the United States. As we will argue later in the essay, there is no simple or single "view." It is indeed difficult to draw a simple conclusion or make a final statement regarding the "Mexican perspective," as many actors are involved, all with different interests, activities, historic backgrounds, and perhaps levels of international awareness. We gather information from interviews, as well as primary and secondary sources, to describe these perspectives. With regard to the government, we present an institutional model of analysis. This model aims to depict the different actors and their perspectives toward various elements. When trying to capture the perspective of the Mexican government in business, we do so as part of a broader perspective in which the rest of the society interacts. However, before presenting and deploying the model, we present information about Mexico and its relationship with the rest of the world, especially the United States. The main intention is to explain the relevance and magnitude of the relationship between the two countries that represents the cultural best understanding.

Mexico, the World and the United States

Mexico has become an important actor in the global economy. According to the World Trade Organization (WTO),[1] in 2013 Mexico ranked fourteenth in terms of imports and fifteenth in total merchandise exports; it ranked first among all Latin American countries (even higher than the colossal Brazil, which ranked twenty second in the world in volume). An impressive 64.6 percent of the value of Mexico's gross domestic product (GDP) is related to the trade of goods and services. (The trade ratio to GDP in the U.S. is 30 percent.) From total exports, 79 percent has a destination in the U.S., and from total imports, 49 percent is originated in the United States. According to the Ministry of the Economy (Secretaria de Economía),[2] from 1999 to 2014, Mexico received total flows of foreign direct investment (FDI) of close to $380 billion U.S., with 46 percent originating in the United States; during that period, close to 64,500 foreign companies were registered, with 43.5 percent of them from the United States. Thus, one can readily see Mexico's great dependence on the United States.

Mexico and the United States not only share an immense continental frontier border (3,145 kms or 1,954 miles) but also an intense economic and political relationship. For both countries, the respective embassy is one of the most important (at least it should be), addressing many issues relevant to both nations, including trade, investment, migration, drugs, security, and the environment. Every year, millions of Mexicans cross the northern frontier, millions of tourists travel to each other's destinations, and thousands of Mexican students attend North American universities. However, Mexicans also work for the drug cartels that export illegal drugs that are used daily in the United States, while people in the United States illegally ship arms in the opposite direction. Millions of dollars in merchandise crosses daily in both directions, including machine parts, automobiles, agricultural products, and consumer products. Even so, as mentioned earlier, "there still exist multiple spaces of mutual ignorance or unawareness."

Institutional Analysis Model

Institutional analysis seeks to identify in detail the institutional arrangement of a country or sector. That is, it seeks to understand the conformation between the actors (private, public, institutional, and their organizations) and their relationships (complementary or antagonistic), the relative power of each in relation to the achievement of defined objectives (inhibit them/promote them), the applicable institutional assumptions (cooperation, opportunism, externalities, asymmetry in the relevant information, risk and motivations) that generate elements that affect institutional arrangement (bureaucracy, corruption, complementarity, forms of government, security for property and rights, common practices and rules of thumb) as well as the emergence of tangible and intangible costs (of operation, transaction, information, and follow-up). According to this definition, given that the previous elements appear in an economic sector, the formal economic, political, and social institutions necessarily arise or gain strength (legal framework of protection of industrial property, protection of national and international trade negotiations, conclusion of contracts and governance) as do the informal institutions (customs, business practices, group interests) which influence (positively/negatively) the efficiency of the sector (Enciso 59).

In that sense, institutional analysis assesses the way in which institutions affect the political or social economic activity. It is based on the concept that the institutions represent the rules of the game (North 13) (i.e., the guidelines that frame all economic and social activity). Institutions arise to minimize the risk and uncertainty that occurs in all social and economic interactions, which makes it difficult to achieve efficiency and effectiveness in this interaction (North 14). Risk and uncertainty arise due to various elements, including the different economic and political capacities of the actors, the antagonistic interests thereof, and the quality of the information they count on to carry out their decisions. Institutions can be economic, political, or social in nature, either formal, such as legal and judicial frameworks and property protection and exchange schemes, or informal, such as standards, customs, business practices, and group interests (North 15).

Theoretical models define institutional analysis as a means to analyze the process of public policies (Ostrom and Polski 5), to carry out a study of political economy (Dixit 37), to model game theory for comparative institutional analysis (Aoki 4), or to propose new institutional arrangements to promote economic development (Ayala Espino 19). Likewise, institutional analysis has been used to conduct research on the role of institutions and their impact on economic development (Rodrik 153). With respect to the role of institutions in the historical development of nations, Acemoglu, Johnson, and Robinson argued that the institutional legacy of colonialism was an important factor in determining the economic growth of nations after their independence (1262). Numerous studies have been conducted worldwide to identify the impact of institutional quality on countries' performance. Furthermore, numerous indicators of institutional quality have appeared, including among others the World Governance Indicators from the World Bank, the Economic Freedom of the World Report, the Center for Global Policy, and the Global Competitiveness Report (GCR) from the World Economic Forum. The measures of institutional quality of a country incorporate the internal and external views and perspectives on how the national institutions, their strengths and weaknesses, affect the economic, political, and social performance and outcome of a country and allow for comparison with other countries.

Under the auspices of the World Bank, Kaufmann et al. have elaborated since 1996 the aforementioned Worldwide Governance Indicators as a measure of the institutional quality of a country. These indicators aggregate six dimensions of governance from data originally obtained from polls, interviews, and other mechanisms.[3] According to the authors:

> Although the concept of governance is widely discussed among policymakers and scholars, there is as yet no strong consensus around a single definition of governance or institutional quality. Various authors and organizations have produced a wide array of definitions. Some are so broad that they cover almost anything, such as the definition of "rules, enforcement mechanisms, and organizations" offered by the World Bank's 2002 World Development Report "Building Institutions for Markets." Others more narrowly focus on public sector management issues, including the definition proposed by the World Bank in 1992 as "the manner in which power is exercised in the management of a country's economic and social resources for development" [3].

The Worldwide Governance Indicators (WGI) calculate six indicators of institutional quality: (1) voice and accountability (VA), (2) political stability and absence of violence/terrorism (PV), (3) government effectiveness (GE), (4) regulatory quality (RQ), (5) rule of law (RL), and (6) control of corruption (CC) (see Appendix 1 for definitions).

Kaufmann et al. affirmed:

> Despite these margins of error, the WGI are sufficiently informative that many cross-country comparisons result in statistically (and likely also practically) significant differences in estimated governance.... The WGI are based exclusively on subjective or perceptions-based data on governance reflecting the views of a diverse range of informed stakeholders, including tens of thousands of household and firm survey respondents, as well as thousands of experts working for the private sector, NGOs (non-governmental organizations), and public sector agencies. We rely on the reports of these stakeholders, which reflect their judgments and perceptions [3].

Before presenting our proposed model and elements of analysis, it is important to review the perspective on the quality of Mexican institutions' measures in terms of indicators of governance as calculated by the World Bank. Figure 1 shows the recent historic measures of the perspective of the WGI for Mexico, and Figure 2 presents the same indicators for the U.S. These indicators provide a first glance of the perception of the business impact of government because they capture the opinion of diverse institutional elements in which the government's regulation, enforcement, efficiency, and transparency affect in general the performance of the economy and political stability. This is another way in which the Mexican government has an indirect impact on the economic performance of businesses, mainly due to the fundamental role it plays in defining the quality of the institutions that govern the economic, political, and social life of the country. These indicators capture the perception of institutional quality by the Mexican society in general.

138 Mexican Business Culture

As we can observe in Figure 1, indicators (0 to 100) for Mexico show that the institutional quality levels are mostly in the middle range, either above or below the 50 level. Even when the general perception of institutional quality is low, the role of government and its impact on business activity are viewed a little more favorably when it refers to its effectiveness and regulatory quality, meaning that people perceive government has made efforts to improve its performance and has improved the quality of regulation. However, it has a negative impact in terms of political stability and violence, the enforcement of laws, and control of corruption. The worst indicator perceived in Mexico is the rule of law, which reflects the institutional void in terms of legal compliance and the general sense of impunity that has marked the economic, political, and social life of the country for decades.

Figure 2 shows the indicators of the United States. As expected, the numbers for this country are not only superior to those of México, but also are among the highest in the world. As for Mexico, the numbers of the United States capture the perception of its nationals and of the international organization calculating the independent indexes used to calculate the WGI. The six indicators of the perception of institutional quality of the United States range above the 90 percentile mark, except for the indicator of political stability and absence of violence and terrorism, which obtained its lowest rate in 2003, close to the 50 range.

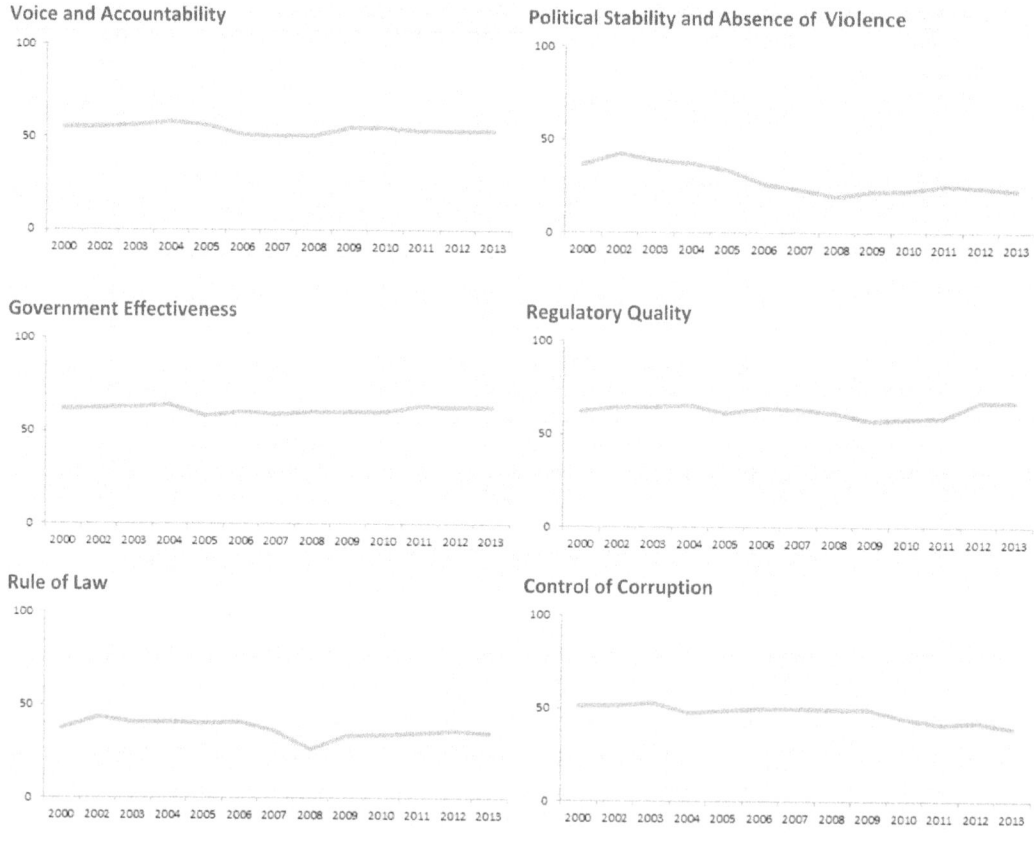

Figure 1. Worldwide governance indicators from México (percentile rank on each governance indicator), retrieved from http://info.worldbank.org/governance/wgi/index.aspx#reports.

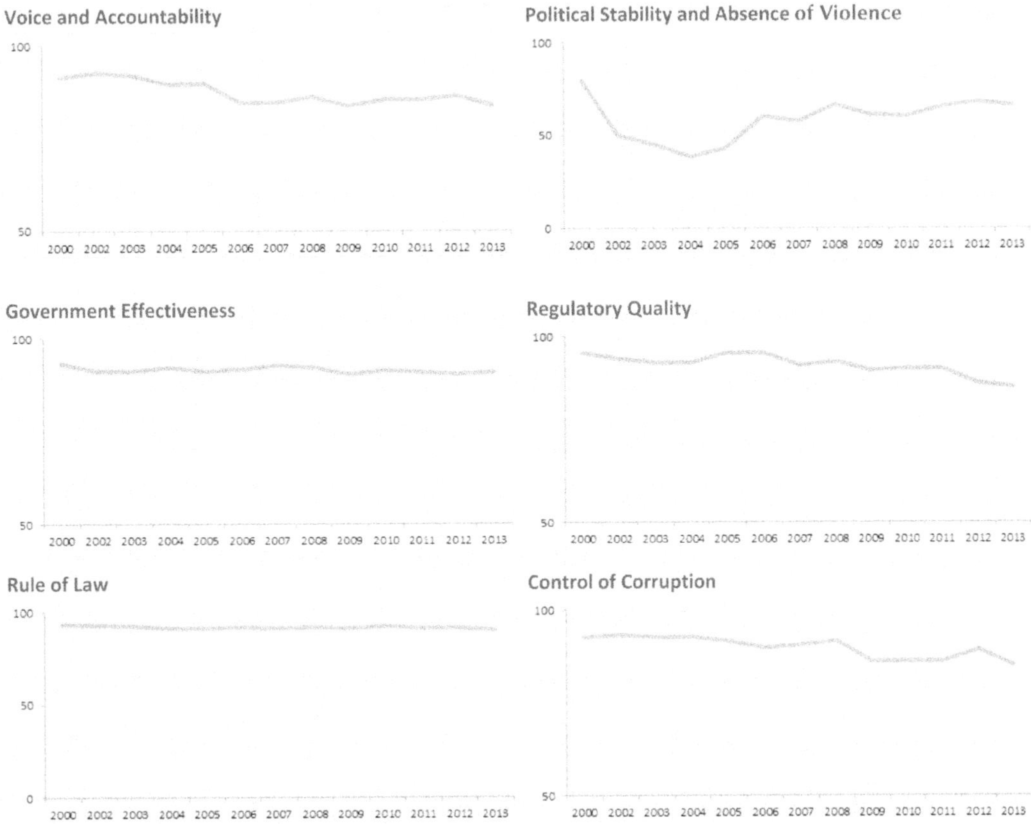

Figure 2. Worldwide governance indicators for the U.S. (percentile rank on each governance indicator), retrieved from http://info.worldbank.org/governance/wgi/index.aspx#reports.

The internal and external perception of governance differs broadly in both countries. This is relevant because, as Kaufmann mentioned, these perceptions capture the opinion of key stakeholders (3). Even though it is not the purpose of this work to enter the dispute regarding the validity of these indicators, it is important to mention that the WGI indicators have been the subject of strong criticism. For example, Voigt argued:

Some of the frequently used measures [the International Country Risk Guide, the Governance Indicators of the World Bank (Kaufmann et al., 2003), and the Polity IV measures] would neither measure policy constraints nor would they be stable; they would rather measure outcomes, i.e., policy choices. To make matters worse, the subjectivity of these measures makes it very likely that improved scores are not due to the institution being improved, but simply based on an increase in income. But if their ascertainment is influenced by income levels, they are not an adequate measure for explaining changes in income levels [3].

Government and Business

It is important to mention that the concept of government normally is used in very general terms. When most Mexicans refer to government, they make no distinction between federal, state, and municipal governments; nor do they differentiate between legislative power or even political parties. Mexicans tend to generalize.

In reality, we will not speak of a single government, but rather three levels or orders of government (federal, state, and municipal) and the various entities that comprise them. All levels will establish, according to their powers and responsibilities, schemes that encourage companies and a complicated network of regulations and requirements, including payment of taxes, duties, and rights and permissions. These are often contradictory between levels/orders/branches of government and between governments of different states and municipalities.

The governments actively participate in the Mexican economy in their role as regulators and promoters of economic activity. Ministries emerge from the federal government that regulate all economic, political, social, and cultural activity; indeed, they regulate practically all areas of life. Entities of the federal government are listed at http://en.presidencia.gob.mx/structure-of-government.

In contrast, each of the federal states in the country, as well as the municipalities that comprise them, set their own rules and incentives that affect the start-up and operation of companies, including foreign companies. It would be impossible in this space to enumerate each of the guidelines. In the report "Doing Business in Mexico 2014"[4] prepared by the World Bank Group, the competitive characteristics of each of the country's states are detailed individually. Likewise, the legislature, which is divided into the Chamber of Deputies and the Chamber of Senators, plays a role in defining the legal and institutional framework that affects the performance of companies. Appendix 2 lists changes in the institutional framework which were approved in 2013 and 2014 and that are expected to have a great influence on business economic activity.

Furthermore, understanding the impact of governments requires knowing the way in which the business sector is organized. As mentioned, according to the World Trade Organization, the trade-to-GDP ratio is 64 percent, which means that most of the activity is related to the external sector, either directly or indirectly. Mexico has a broad range of trade agreements.[5] Mexico has free trade agreements with more countries than any other country. However, it is important to mention that according to INEGI,[6] in 2012 the formal economy represented 75 percent of the GDP and 40 percent of the formal employed population. The private industrial sector is organized into industrial chambers, such as the National Chamber of the Transformation Industry (CANACINTRA)[7] by its national representation, the Confederation of National Chambers of Commerce (CONCANACO)[8] that brings together national representatives of the business sector and tourist services in the country, the Mexican Business Council for Foreign Trade, Investment, and Technology (COMCE),[9] and the Business Coordinating Council (CEE).[10] These organizations represent the interests of the business sector and serve as the liaison for negotiation (when possible) with various Mexican authorities, such as the Ministry of Finance and Public Credit and the Ministry of the Economy. For instance, the private sector has participated actively in negotiations of the free trade agreements, but has had closed doors with the federal government when defining tax policy.

Understanding the Mexican business environment requires pointing out that the relationship between the different levels of government and the private sector is not always free of friction. There are many examples of confrontation. A strong debate alludes to tax provisions relating to the payment of federal taxes, which have varied over the years, normally in an aggressive, asymmetric, and sometime incoherent tax collection strategy that does not make enough effort to increase the taxable base of the informal sector. The discussion and exchange of views continues, with periods of more convergence and others of withdrawal and distancing.

Another aspect of the relationship between the Mexican government and the private sector involves the government's purchase of goods and services provided by the private sector. There has been an effort to make this process more transparent, mainly through internet portals where tenders are carried out. For example, the site Compras de Gobierno[11] is a link where suppliers of goods and services can access various agencies of the federal government. Another area of influence is the procurement of diverse and extensive infrastructure work, such as roads, bridges, highways, buildings that are engaged by different levels of government, and private projects of public participation,[12] as well as the very different trusts that are promoted for different activities. In addition, one can observe many cases of corruption and bribery in these sectors. There is a saying that for every corrupt person inside the government there is a corrupt person outside with whom to partner. In this area of academic and political discussion, a very important question arises: Has corruption been institutionalized? For many there is no doubt about it.

As mentioned, Mexico is a country of contrasts. Faced with this ambiguous panorama, how does one come to understand the complex relationship between government and business and the business environment in general? Figures 3 and 4 depict a conceptual model that helps capture, from an institutional perspective, a general view of the (cultural) perceptions of the Mexican government.

Model Description

The relationship of government and companies is immersed in a broad model of the country and diverse actors are involved, including the following:

a) Individuals and family groups, each located in different regions of the country and each with different household income levels and expenditures.[13]

b) Government(s). As mentioned earlier, three levels or orders of government exist: federal, state, and municipal. In addition, one must consider public companies, private and public partnerships, and unions. Many other organizations are independent of the government but function under public funding, such as those regulating elections, human rights, and the environment.

c) Companies, which are classified according to INEGI as micro, small, medium, and large,[14] and their associations and chambers. We can also add the binational councils and chambers of different countries.

d) Political parties, with an orientation that ranges from left, center, and right to the environmental. These parties share power, and different parties have been elected in different parts of the country, sometimes having opposing parties in the same state (e.g., governor from one party and city mayor from another). Only recently have more parties been created and authorized to represent citizens, and for the first time in 2015 citizens can participate in legislative elections without declaring a party, proving support for a broad base of potential voters.

e) Private groups, including NGOs, foundation centers, and human aid organizations.

f) Universities and research centers, both public and private. Private centers may be profit or not for profit. Some universities are politically oriented, while others are more business oriented. The ANUIES constitutes the aggregate voice of higher education institutions.[15]

g) Other important actors whose perspectives influence general opinion include print, TV, and internet media. Again, we will find both honest and corrupt media. However, their influence is strong in the country. People may complain about them, but they keep buying the same newspapers and watching the same broadcasts.

Each of these actors has its own range of interests, including economic, political, and social; each will have a different approach toward cultural and institutional perspectives (toward governments in particular):

a) Awareness and observance of laws and regulations.

b) Knowledge and pursuit of information on markets and governments' functions and obligations.

c) Knowledge and respect for property rights.

d) Knowledge and understanding of private and public governance structures.

e) Personal interest versus social interest.

f) Family and traditions, as well as their influence in decision making. Traditionally, political views toward government are inherited.

g) Drug enforcement. This includes those who want to liberalize drug use, those who demand stronger enforcement, and those young kids who dream of becoming a drug dealer.

h) Achievement of wealth, from those who want to become rich in a very short time to those planning for the future. Each may have a different work ethic. For example, a "normal" citizen may become a wealth-seeker if holding a governmental position.

i) Political participation, including those convinced that participation is important and those who consider it irrelevant. The category also includes those who see political participation as a means to power and a way to become wealthier and those who participate from social interest. There is a growing sense of disappointment with the political parties and politicians because many in the country think that politicians protect their political parties rather than the social interest.

j) Time memory. Mexicans may react strongly (mostly arguing, and not acting) to events (e.g., Mexican peso exchange rate volatility, the discovery that the president's wife owns a $7 million house "bought" from one of the most important construction companies partnering with the federal government), but they have rather a soft memory regarding past events (e.g., corrupt parties from the past winning elections in the present, voting for popular and demagogic politicians, ignoring the signals of a potential economic crisis). The same types of events unfold over and over.

k) *Compadrazgo*. This is one of the strongest ambivalences among Mexicans. Most will complain against the government, but are willing to participate in *compadrazgo*, either selling something to governments or being appointed to a job or seat because of having a friend or relative. As it is said: Most Mexicans have a relative in the United States and a friend in government. For many, the free-rider and rent-seeking attitude may arise at any time an opportunity appears.

l) There are many different approaches and definitions of democracy, civil participation, corruption, religion, bureaucracy, and innovation.

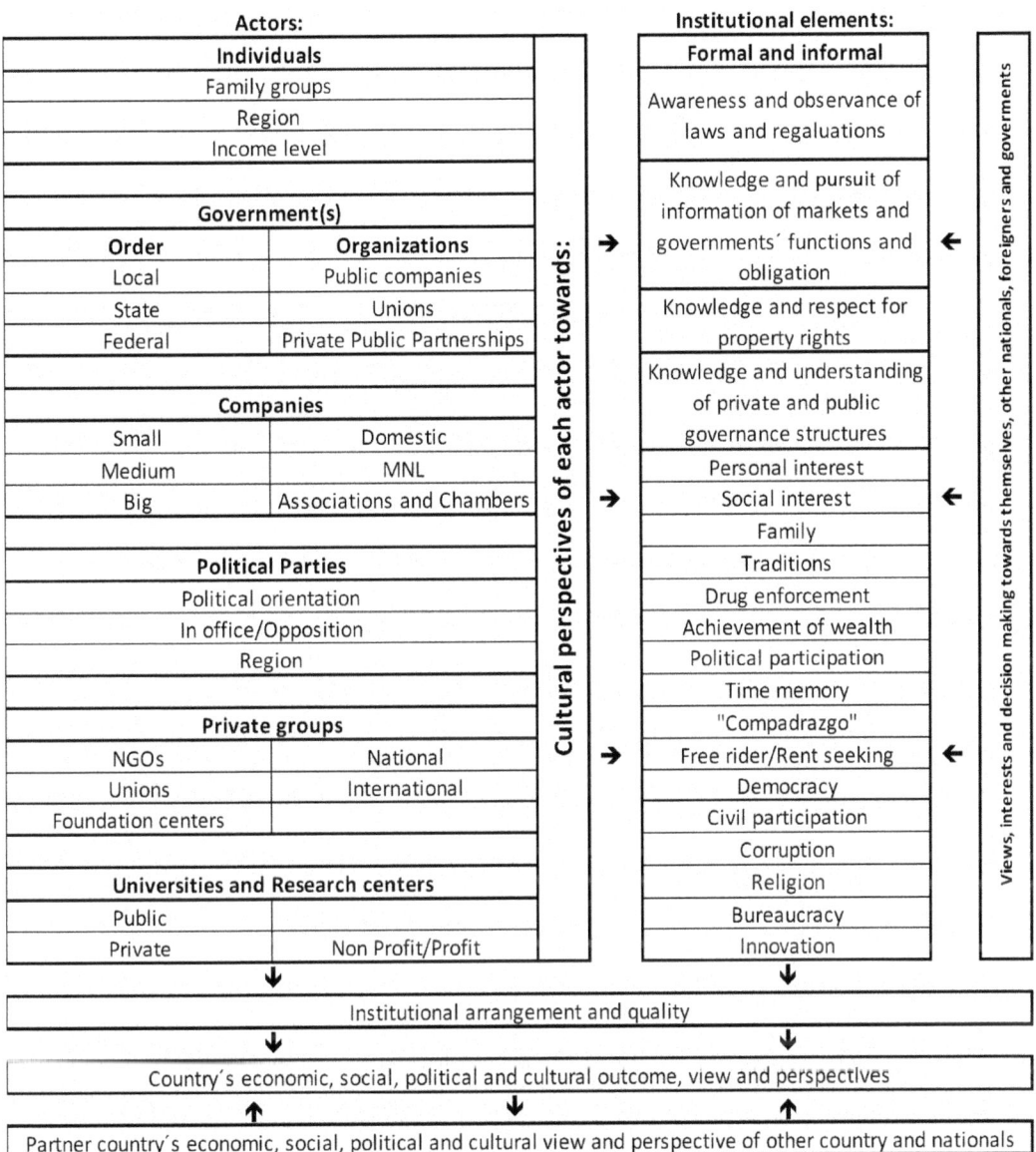

Figure 3. Institutional model of cultural perspectives and performance (a).

As mentioned earlier, each actor has a different institutional approach, to themselves and others. Mexican actors may have a clear sense of themselves, sometimes varying from rightousness to superiority, but they may also have a sense of submission and incredulity. Different actors will therefore have a different approach to government, depending on factors like whether they benefit from government *compadrazgo,* social programs, bribes, contracts, or impunity, and, for example, their sense of authority or lack of credibility and honesty.

To be specific, each actor will develop a perspective toward what he or she considers government; this may include disinformation, unawareness or irrelevance, hate, disrespect, radicalism, *compadrazgo,* friendship, a search for benefits, contracts, alliances, or power

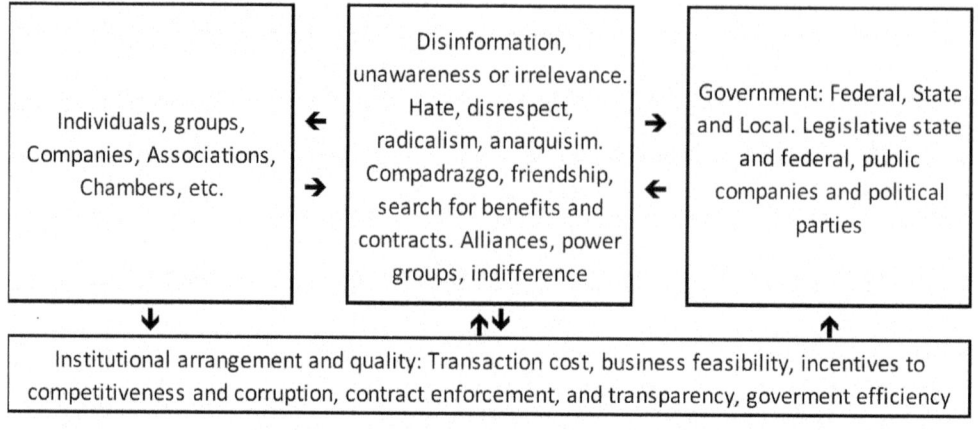

Figure 4. Institutional model of cultural perspectives and performance (b).

groups. These set or circular relationships will define the institutional arrangement and quality in which economic, political, and social relationships are formed. In addition, the institutional arrangement and quality elements take their place: transaction costs, business feasibility, incentives to competitiveness and corruption, contract enforcement, transparency, and government efficiency. This complex arrangement interacts with the equally difficult arrangements of the partner countries, in business as well as political and social interaction.

Perceptions of the Mexican Government

As previously mentioned, there is no single or simple view or cultural perspective toward the Mexican government or governments. To capture the institutional elements defined in the model, we present two complementary views. One is obtained from the annual survey that KPMG Mexico performs to capture the opinion of top management regarding different aspects of the Mexican economy, and the second view corresponds to the opinions and perceptions of business owners and directives, obtained by personal interviews, as explained later.

As mentioned, there is no single or simple view or cultural perspective toward the Mexican government or governments. To capture the institutional elements defined in the model, we present two complementary views. One is obtained from the annual survey that KPMG Mexico performs to capture the opinion of top management regarding different aspects of the Mexican economy, and the second view corresponds to the opinions and perceptions of business owners and executives, obtained by personal interviews, as explained later.

Top Management Perception

From the annual survey "Perspectives from Top Management, Mexico 2014"[16] ("Perspectivas de la Alta Dirección en México 2014"), Tables AI to AIV present the opinion of the top management regarding the question: How would you grade the performance of authorities in the country's current economic environment? (¿Cómo califica la actuación de las autoridades ante el entorno económico que está viviendo el país?) (13).

Even when this question and its responses capture the perceptions only in economic terms, it reflects that for top executives the *economic management* of the country is among the most important factors. We can argue that a cultural mindset of the Mexican directives is that government and its performance are mainly perceived and qualified by how Mexicans perceive the government's managing of the country's economy.

Tables A I to IV present the percentage of opinions regarding the economic performance of governments as *excellent, good, regular, bad,* and *disastrous* for the federal government, the state governments, the deputies or representatives (diputados), and the senators. The first surprising fact is that the categories are ranked from *excellent* performance to *disastrous* performance. This may represent the extreme positions in Mexicans' opinions.

From Table A.I., we can observe the changes in the general perception of the federal government. Note that during the period of the surveys different political parties were in office; for instance, the current president Enrique Peña Nieto (from Partido Revolucionario Institucional) took office in December 2012, so 2010 to 2012 refers to the opinions of the previous mandate Felipe Calderon (from Partido Acción Nacional). As we can observe, the previous government saw an increase in positive opinion, even extending to the first year of office of the current mandate. As said in Mexico, 2014, the second year of the mandate, normally is referred as *the end of the honeymoon*. For example, even when in 2013 the president and his cabinet were able to negotiate with the congress to approve important institutional reforms, they were not able to maintain the momentum, and the grace was lost in 2014. Then the bad and disastrous opinions about the federal government rose as never before; we can question whether that was because it became obvious that the campaign promises were only that.

Table A.I. Perception of Federal Government's Economic Performance

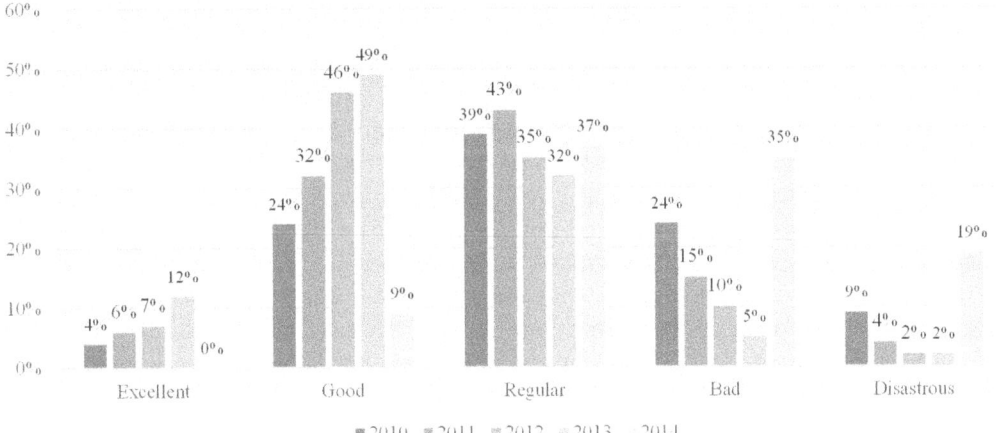

From Table A.II, we can observe that the perception of the state governments was already considered regular to disastrous. Executives can probably better envision the differences between the acts of government from different levels than the population in general. If within the federal government there was a well-marked change in tendency, no such point in time exists for state governments since there is no correspondence involving when the president versus a governor initiates the mandates. Even if the directives had higher expectations of the presidency, they have not shown confidence during the last years in local governance. How can a country and region achieve governance, economic growth, and progress in general when 30 percent of the directives perceives as disastrous the performance of local governments? Note that governors' terms do not coincide with the president's, and they belong to different parties, including Partido Revolucionario Institucional, Partido Acción Nacional, Partido de la Revolución Democrática, Partido Verde and coalitions ranging from left-wing through center to right-wing political views. Both presidential and governors' terms are six years.

Table A.II. Perception of State Governments' Economic Performance

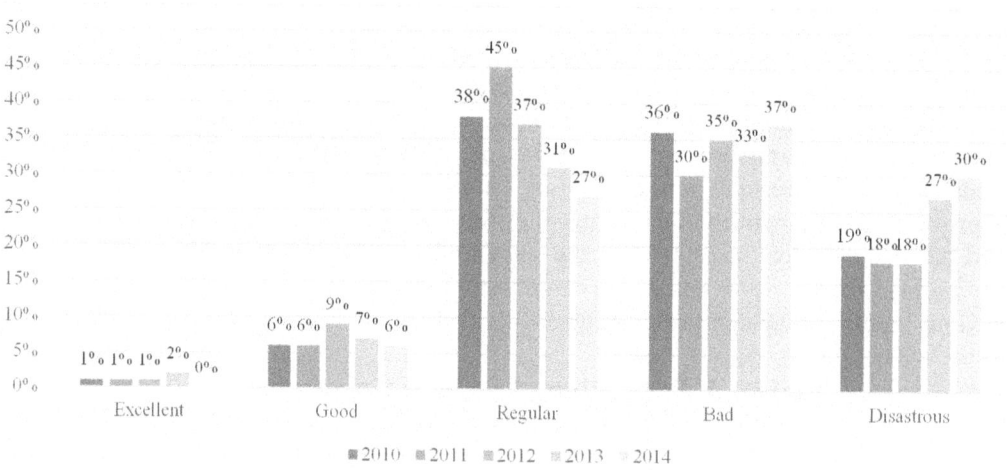

Tables A.III and A.IV show that the perceptions of both legislative chambers are even worse. Among the political actors, deputies and senators are probably perceived the worst by the directives. Scarcely a directive considers good performance; the majority ranks their performance from bad to disastrous. The fact that during 2013 important changes in legislation may have helped to improve the perception of the legislators, the directives considered only 24 percent for deputies and 27 percent or senators disastrous. That only worsened in 2014, which came with new legislation on tax increases; among other circumstances, this helped to raise the disastrous perception to 35 percent for deputies and 30 percent for senators. Like governors, legislators are from all political parties, and elections coincide only partially with presidential elections.

Table A.III. Perception of Deputies' (Representatives') Economic Performance

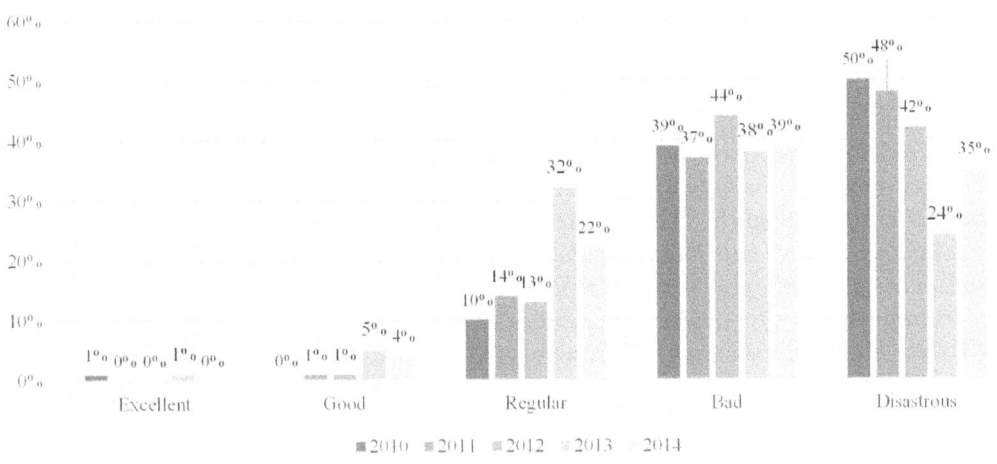

Table A.IV. Perception of Senators' Economic Performance

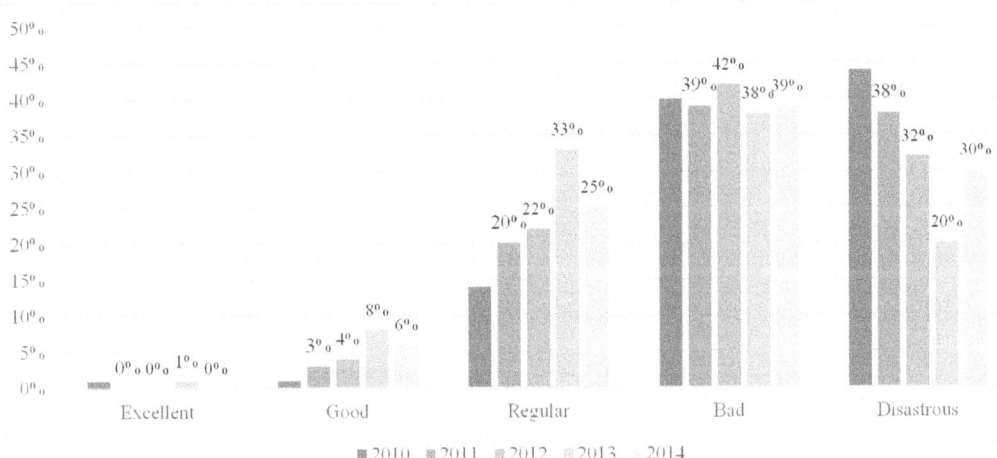

Personal Interviews of Business Actors

To complement the perspectives of business directors, a series of interviews were conducted to gather opinions firsthand from business owners and directives located in different regions of the country. Such interviews can provide fresh and "living" opinions and perspectives. All of the interviewees are currently experiencing in real life what they shared.

We presented the broad question and implications regarding their opinions (from a cultural perspective) of how the government influences the business environment. Very precise opinions were expressed. However, it is important to mention that invitations were sent to men and women, owners of small and medium-sized companies, those with a higher education degree, employees of medium-sized or large companies, and others who have worked in both government and the private sector. Note also that only men agreed to comment; some never answered, others mentioned they do not care, most promised to respond but could not find the time, and a few even responded that the best way to discuss the government is to organize a barbecue with beer, probably summarizing the ambiguity that many Mexicans feel when expressing their opinion.

The interviews were personal, but interviewees were asked to write their opinion. The text presented below highlights the conversations and is translated by the author from Spanish to English. The interviewees represent only a small group of the set of actors; however, we can infer that the institutional elements proposed in our model appear as factors of opinion and perspective. Even when it is not possible to generalize, as mentioned, the interviewees represent a sample of those who are actually dealing with government actions. As expected, responses are strongly charged with emotion.

A financial expert living in the north part of the country expressed his views of the government (or the lack of it):

> Someone there mentioned that governments are a necessary evil, I think the principal problem in Mexico is the nonexistence of a real power division, not only at a national level. Every six years, a new viceroy arrives (as governor) to make a fortune, and there is no way to prove his/her culpability of illegal enrichment, unless it comes from political initiative (revenge). The interdependence of the other two powers (legislative and judicial) to the executive (president) facilitates the incorrect use of resources, leaving the transparency in goodwill only. You can even go further, city mayors like the case in Iguala,[17] and I'm sure there are many similar (participating with cartel members); unfortunately, Mexico is full of corrupt city mayors.
>
> In the charcoal region of Coahuila, it's very difficult to obtain permits for exploration, but cartel members just take the land, and when someone is trying to denounce, authorities are afraid to confront them. Where is the law? Who protects the property right? Not the government!
>
> The governors of Nuevo Leon and Coahuila have also shown terrible administrative capacity and have used the resources freely, and even selected their successors, like the case of a former TV comedian, with no formal education, but very popular, who is already the candidate for the next governor for the Partido Revolucionario Institucional."

A business owner from the northern state of Tamaulipas, living in the U.S.[18] for the last 10 years, where he has developed a new business career, said:

> As we all know, unfortunately, the structures of the Mexican State are highly inefficient at all levels, and this is an obstacle for entrepreneurs, employees, companies, and all the economic agents. It's an obstinacy in establishing complicated paperwork (licenses, permits, etc.) which leads to corruption and bribery. The old politicians act on traditions, but the new ones for weakness, both are part of the vicious circle. We need an agile government, attentive to global trends, a facilitator and promoter of technology, education, business, exports, job creation; only then can the country walk the route of progress and the quality of life of Mexicans will rise.

He added two examples of his perspective:

> 1. In Texas, you can create a company in 24 hours. The available names can be consulted online; it's possible to obtain an IRS number as well. You can open a bank account at the same time. In Mexico, you are required to obtain a permit from the Ministry of Foreign Relations (Secretaria de Relaciones Exteriores), required to hire a pubic notary to redact the constitutive act, … it may take 30 or even 45 days to open a company and start a business. 2. The SAT (fiscal authority) has a sick plan to collect taxes, they think everyone is a potential fraudster; every year they change the fiscal laws, they change regulations again and again … it seems that economists in

the government are crazy and don't think of the potential effects for the country ... there is no seriousness in the design and planning of public policy of all the political parties. The government must allow companies to work and should intervene less in the individual allocation of resources.

An engineer owner of a technology firm located in Mexico City and conducting business for PEMEX[19] said:

> From a cultural perspective, one attached to our cultural tendencies, we should have the perception that the Mexican political class is in total and advantageous association with the large media. They are doing an excellent job to achieve their particular objectives, but neglecting the direction and objectives to lead the country to a better common reality of equity and justice. From the point of view of an increasingly smaller sector of the country that tries to produce, research, modify, and start new business, the political class is the living dead, a zombie trying to find identity in all the places except in their own roots, internal market, trade balance, education, strong institutions, and more. The answer is quite obvious; there is a bad perception of government, definitively.
>
> Bureaucracy, corruption, incoherence, confusion, and lies are the everyday in our lives; proof of this is the recent behavior of oil prices. Doing business in Mexico for Mexico and the exterior is every time more complicated, the country has been losing elements to incorporate activities with high aggregated value. The country has become a mediocre *maquiladora*[20] for the superior economies in almost all the markets. The government only deceives and manipulates information in a convincing way for the miserable interests of some power elites. The political discourse has become useless, a lie, demagogy, fraud, and simulation. Even convinced, I'm truly containing the explosion of my desire of criticism.... I'm convinced, however, that in Mexico it's possible to perform sustainable business using a well thought out strategy, with leadership.

The interviewee references a recent project where a coordinated team effort was able to import disassembled equipment for a self-designed new technology product that was sold to PEMEX and successfully installed in an ocean oil platform.

The owner of a successful logistic company located in Monterrey, but offering services to all the country and with broad experience in international business issues said:

> The government thinks that they are actually doing a favor to the business owners, they have the mentality that they own the country and not we, when they "grant" permits, licenses, public notaries, exploitation permits, custom brokerages, tenders, and construction permits that only are possible to obtain trough bribery. In the now-in-fashion financing companies only for the government's employees, a totally corrupt business, everything in the mentality of this is mine and I (government) distribute among my friends (*compadrazgo*). Not to mention the sectors like communication and energy.

He energetically questioned: "To whom does this country belong?"

Juan Manuel Quiroga Lamm,[21] a general director of the regional council of companies exporting and importing, said:

> In my opinion, the government in general, but specifically the federal, is responsible for defining the efficiency and effectiveness of public policy to influence the national economy, is a key and decisive actor in the construction of the business culture, and the fundamental actors in business, entrepreneurs, and their human capital. The other orders (levels) of government are complementary, and the other two political powers (legislative and judicial) are fundamental for the rule of law, justice, and equity that business requires.

It is possible to observe how the change in the economic model in 1986 (when the model of import substitutions changed to trade and economic openness), as Mexico joined the General Agreement on Tariffs and Trade (now World Trade Organization), represented a transformation in business culture. It moved from the captive market economy with fixed prices, where demand and competitiveness were irrelevant, to a market-oriented competitiveness and productivity. The business (environment) changed when technical, management, and directive teams were modified not only to prepare for productive activities, but also to emphasize the global environment and international intercultural relationships. This enabled companies to understand how to survive and grow among international competitors. The required orientation to competitiveness and competence, but also to globalization, has transformed the structure and goals of business plans, with new concepts of sustainable growth, and raised security for international trade to address the emergence of international terrorism. In all these actions, the government is the main actor in conducting the cultural change required for the change to gestate inside companies. The government is the first to be obligated to identify the signals of change that the world and the dominant economies require.

Unfortunately, the lack of vision and moral sufficiency of many in government positions has resulted in a burden for the rest of society, which in contrast understands clearly that the development and economic growth of this country require people to serve it and not to receive service from it.

An international manager with more than 20 years of experience as director of multinationals said:

> For the generations that are now 40 to 50 years old, the *compadrazgo* and friendship were part of everyone's culture. This is the generation that is now in directive positions, and many of them are working for multinationals. Many of them try to "over exaggerate" the problems that they deal with every day with government in order to gain power with the foreign owners or managers; they want to portray things as a lot more difficult as they are so they become necessary for the company. For some, they will try to bribe the government, but for many it will be counterproductive because of the company's regulations against bribery.
>
> Contrary to what the government may argue, there is still a sense of insecurity, which is captured quite differently from firms based in the U.S. than those in Europe or Asia. This sense of insecurity derives in the high cost of security expenses (private guards, armed vehicles, etc.).

He argued:

> Many foreigners working in the multinationals located in the country have the sense that Mexicans are very good workers, there is a culture of quality, productivity, and capacity. However, Mexicans are very prone to corruption.

In his opinion, the Mexican companies have not equally achieved these levels and practices because corruption still has strong roots. He then continues:

> History repeats itself again and again. The political parties govern for themselves instead of society. **"Fidelity is toward the party and not the people."** The government is losing its power toward the armed groups of organized delinquency (the Mexican government calls it *delincuencia organizada* or organized delinquency). Small businesses pay security to those groups because they have no option, there is an empty space that the government is not covering or protecting. The country is losing resources since many of these Mexicans are leaving the country and taking the business to the U.S., paying taxes abroad.
>
> Government promotes corruption, even in legal terms, for example, many authorizations name an "authorized" third party to obtain permits, and this is a costumed form of bribery. The media are part of the circus, and society is motionless in the middle. There is an unbalance of forces, with no ending soon; economy and politics are tied.

He finished by arguing:

There is a strong feeling of discouragement, our minds are clouded, the social pact has been broken, and even if people would like to participate more in the social movement, the question is when? Since most people have to work indefatigably just to survive.

As we can see, these representative actors of the business community expressed a general feeling of disappointment in the government. Despite multiple opinions, in general all of them share the same sense of disapproval and dissatisfaction as the directives interviewed by KPMG. This may be a combination of short term situation, but derived from the last ten years of uncertainty. For instance, since the last presidency (from now-opposing party PAN) there was a growing sense of insecurity; then the crisis of 2009 strongly affected the economy, and when the current federal government took office in 2013 it promised a change in the economy. The first year of the current president was triumphant, as he proposed many important changes in the legal framework (see Appendix 2); however, the second year in office was different, as a strong tax policy was implemented and the cases of violence did not diminish. In addition, many cases of corruption were discovered. Every day of the week, another city mayor, legislator, union leader, governor, minister, or even the president was discovered in apparent corruption, and cases such as the Iguala emerged, in which many students were killed by members of organized crime with involvement of the local authorities (the case received worldwide media attention). Worst of all, the number of cases actually prosecuted is minimal; this fosters not only impunity and corruption, but also inefficiency of the legal system.

Final Comments

We have presented an analysis based on national surveys and personal interviews that in general expresses disappointment and a belief in institutional deception regarding government performance. However, the outlook is not all negative; despite the generalized negative sense of governmental leadership, the country is actively moving and evolving. For foreigners interested in culture, traveling, or business, it is important to be aware that we have presented only a partial view of the country. As mentioned in the model, different perspectives depend on the actors. The negative perception of government by the business sector is probably shared by many countries, at least for some sectors. The perceptions of union leaders and government officials also may be different.

Institutional analysis allows us to identify Mexico as a country that still maintains low levels of institutional quality, mainly due to backwardness in different political aspects of compliance and enforcement of the legal framework. Another important aspect is the high levels of corruption that continue to affect economic activity. To understand Mexico and the relationship between government and business is to understand the complex relationship between the formal sector and the different authorities at various levels, but also the relationship between the informal activity and the governments. This relationship, which has also been a source of political bit players, corruption, and manipulation, also has served as an escape valve when the formal sector is not capable of providing all the jobs that society requires. Furthermore, the government may also be one of the main employers in the country, including those required for the technological or administrative skills, but also those that need to have to offer a job as a political compensation, many of them not working at all, known as "aviators" and those that the government prefer to have in the budget to promote the economy. One must also understand Mexico from its closeness to the United States, its increasingly regulated formal sector with pressure from foreign competition and an informal sector that despite efforts toward its integration has proved very complex to incorporate into economic, political, and social activities.

Even when we have presented an apparently not very encouraging situation of the country, its valid to mention that it seems that neither the low institutional quality nor some business sectors' disappointment in the government have discouraged foreign investors from continuing to arrive in Mexico.[22] On the other hand, the recent changes in many laws, mainly labor, tax, and telecommunications laws and mainly from the energy sector, represent a great opportunity for the development of the country. The federal government has shown that in the coming years foreign direct investors will have great business opportunities because, unlike in previous years, it will be possible to participate in a wide range of activities that were previously only in the hands of the government or nationals.

We conclude that even with all the not-so-encouraging outlook presented before, we are still convinced that Mexico is a country with great potential for any national or international investor. Economic activity is largely intertwined with global activities, mainly in the United States, which is Mexico's main trading partner in terms of the commercial exchange of goods and services. However, even though the United States is the main foreign investor, in recent years (historic in the country), investments from Belgium, China, Holland, Japan and Spain have increased significantly. For instance, the perception of Mexico abroad may contrast with the figures presented. For example, during 2014, more than 14 million tourists visited the country and spent more than $8 billion U.S. (Secretaria de Turismo). In addition, the country has not stopped attracting business; foreign direct investment continues to arrive. Just in the automotive industry, the same year companies like Audi ($1.3 billion U.S.), Hyundai ($130 million U.S.), KIA Motors ($1 billion U.S.), and BMW ($1 billion U.S.) have opened new production facilities in Mexico. Those interested in establishing or increasing ties with Mexico, should be aware that even when transaction cost may appear high at the beginning, a clear understanding of the socio economic and cultural aspects of the country will provide helpful. Not all Mexicans are corrupt, nor drug dealers, there are many hard working people, excellent universities, labor force, and in general business opportunities are open. As a recent campaign emphasizes: "We, the good people, are a majority."

Appendix 1: Worldwide Governance Indicators as Defined by the World Bank[23]

1. Voice and Accountability (VA)—capturing perceptions of the extent to which a country's citizens are able to participate in selecting their government, as well as freedom of expression, freedom of association, and a free media.

2. Political Stability and Absence of Violence/Terrorism (PV)—capturing perceptions of the likelihood that the government will be destabilized or overthrown by unconstitutional or violent means, including politically motivated violence and terrorism. (b) The capacity of the government to effectively formulate and implement sound policies:

3. Government Effectiveness (GE)—capturing perceptions of the quality of public services, the quality of the civil service and the degree of its independence from political pressures, the quality of policy formulation and implementation, and the credibility of the government's commitment to such policies.

4. Regulatory Quality (RQ)—capturing perceptions of the ability of the government to formulate and implement sound policies and regulations that permit and promote private sector development. (c) The respect of citizens and the state for the institutions that govern economic and social interactions among them.

5. Rule of Law (RL)—capturing perceptions of the extent to which agents have confidence in and abide by the rules of society, and in particular the quality of contract enforcement, property rights, the police, and the courts, as well as the likelihood of crime and violence.

6. Control of Corruption (CC)—capturing perceptions of the extent to which public power is exercised for private gain, including both petty and grand forms of corruption, as well as "capture" of the state by elites and private interests.

Appendix 2: Recent Changes in the Institutional Framework

The following are specific actions that legislators introduced in Mexican legislation in 2013 and 2014 which were intended to improve the business environment.

Competence and Telecommunications
- Strengthen the Federal Competence Commission (Comisión Federal de Competencia).
- Create special courts in competence issues.
- Provide the right of access to broadband and more effective resolutions from regulatory bodies.
- Strengthen the autonomy of the National Telecommunication Commission (COFETEL).
- Develop a robust telecommunication network in public buildings.
- Promote more competition in radio, television networks, telephony, and data services.

Energy
- State exclusivity over the property of resources.
- Reorganization of PEMEX: Exploration and Industrial Transformation.
- New fiscal and tax structure for Pemex: Lower payment of rights instead of taxes, gains (remains) to be used with more flexibility, e.g., more transparency and accountability.
- Utility contracts with private investors, domestic and international, to explore and extract oil and gas.
- Permits to private companies for refineries, petrochemicals, transportation, and storage of oil, gas, and derivatives.
- Private participation in the generation of electricity.

154 Mexican Business Culture

Political and Electoral
- Reelection for federal legislators, deputies, and senators (for 12 years).
- State congress to enter the reelection in State legislatures.
- Creation of a public prosecutor's office Fiscalía General by 2018 (replacing the current National Attorney or Procuraduría General); principal to be designated by Senate.
- Creation of the National Electoral Institute (replacing the current Federal Electoral Institute).
- NEI to designate state council.
- Rules regarding invalid elections for campaign spending above the limits.
- Parity in the number of males and females in both chambers.
- Possibility of coalition governments.
- Senate to validate the security strategy.

Fiscal
- Personal Income Tax (32%, 34% and 35%).
- General Value-Added Tax (VAT) (16%).
- Restructuring of Fiscal Regimes.
- Changes in the *Maquiladora* Regime.
- Restructuring of Corporate Tax.

Appendix 3: Socio-Economic Aspects of the Mexican Economy

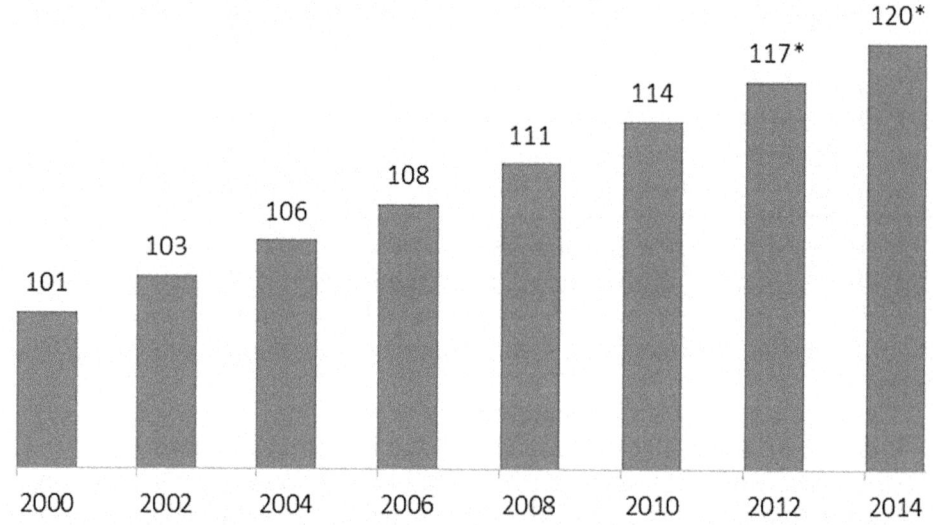

Figure 1. Mexico's Population (millions). Growing population: From 2000 to 2014, the country grew by almost 20 million people. Source: CONAPO.

Mexico has gradually become one of the world's major economies. According to the World Bank, in 2013 Mexico occupied 15th place in the value of the GDP (representing 7.5 percent of the value of the economy of the United States[24]).

GDP growth has suffered the ups and downs of the world economy, and Figure 6 shows this behavior from 2002 to 2012 with data from INEGI. Meanwhile, the International Monetary Fund estimates growth of 2.4 percent for 2014 and 3.5 percent for 2015.[25]

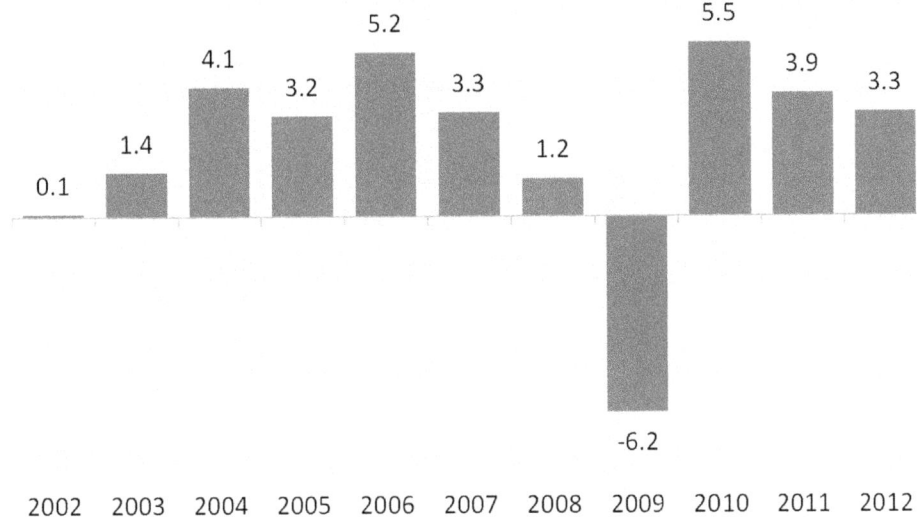

Figure 2. Mexico's GDP Annual Growth (percentage). Source: INEGI.

Figure 3 shows that Mexico's productive structure has actually changed little since 1993, with the tertiary sector representing more and more of the activities that make up the GDP. In 2013, the tertiary sector represented 60 percent of the total value of output, whereas the secondary sector about 34 percent and the primary sector slightly more than 3 percent.

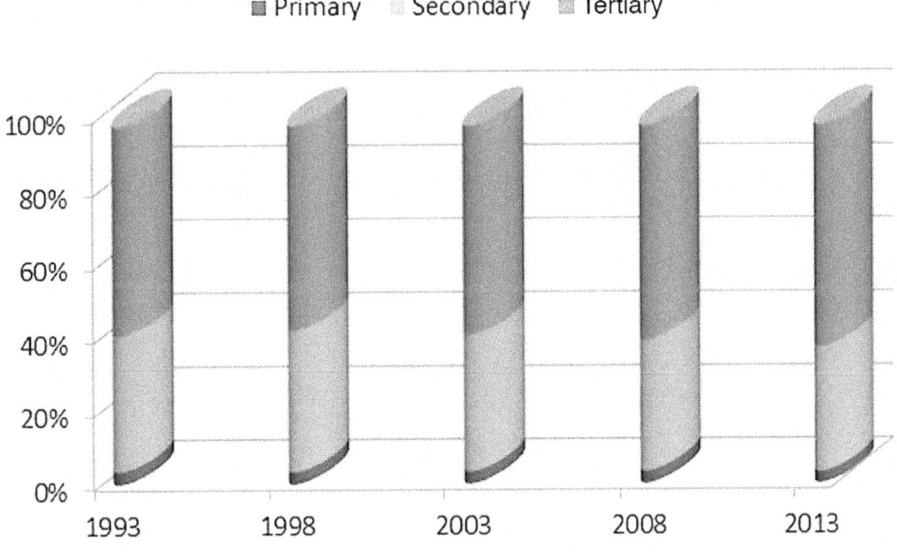

Figure 3. Mexico: Type of Productive Activities as a Percentage of GDP. Source: INEGI.

156 Mexican Business Culture

Figure 4 illustrates the volatile behavior of the labor productivity index. The recent INEGI figures show that this indicator increased slightly during 2014.[26] This index measures the relationship between production and employed personnel and its analysis and historical comparison shows us the way in which labor resources are used in production.

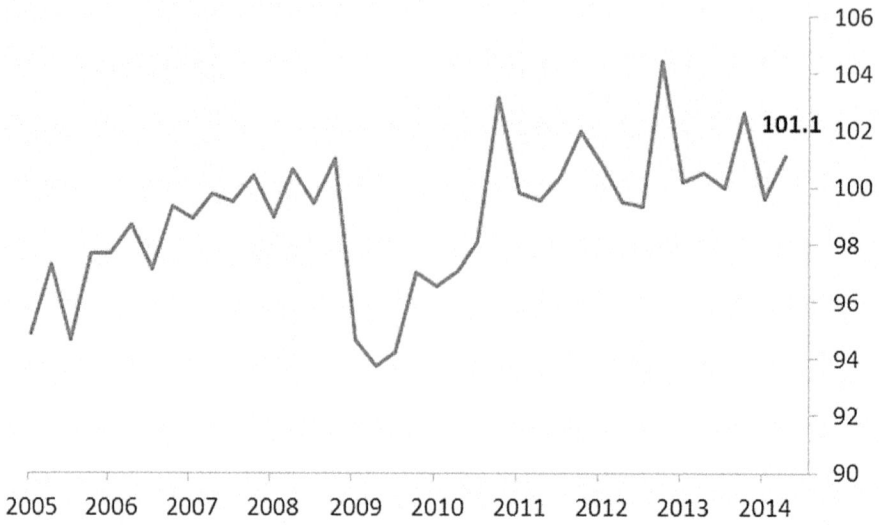

Figure 4. Mexico: Index of Labor Productivity Base = 100. Source: INEGI.

Another interesting relationship is the one that shows the behavior of the percentage of change in the sales indexes in retail and wholesale sales. In Figure 5, we can see that the recovery of sales after the fall in 2009 has been slow; even 2013 represented a setback in retail sales.

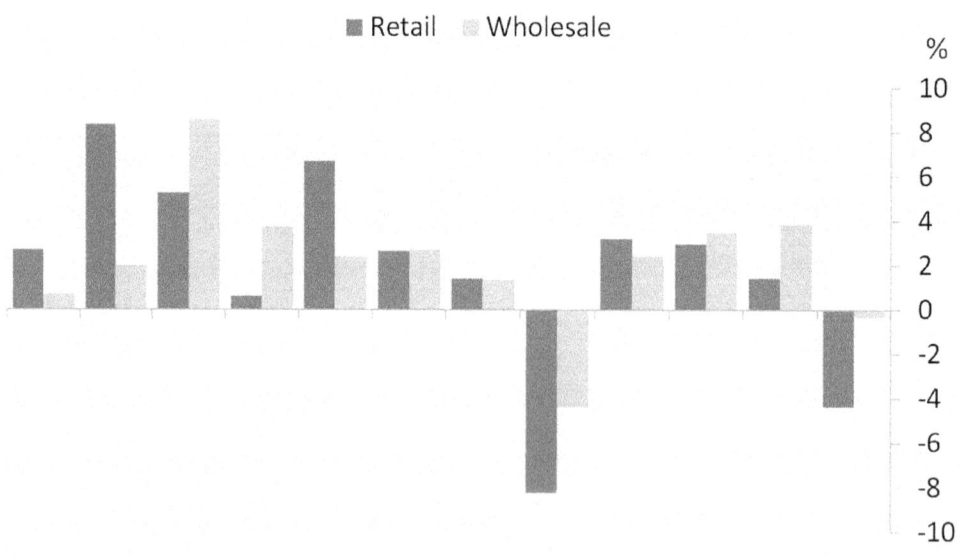

Figure 5. Mexico: Annual Changes in the Percentage of Sales Index Base = 100. Source: INEGI.

As for inflation, Figure 10 shows that the Mexican economy maintained levels less than 4 percent from 2010 until 2013; for 2014 (August), the cumulative inflation rate was 4.15 percent.

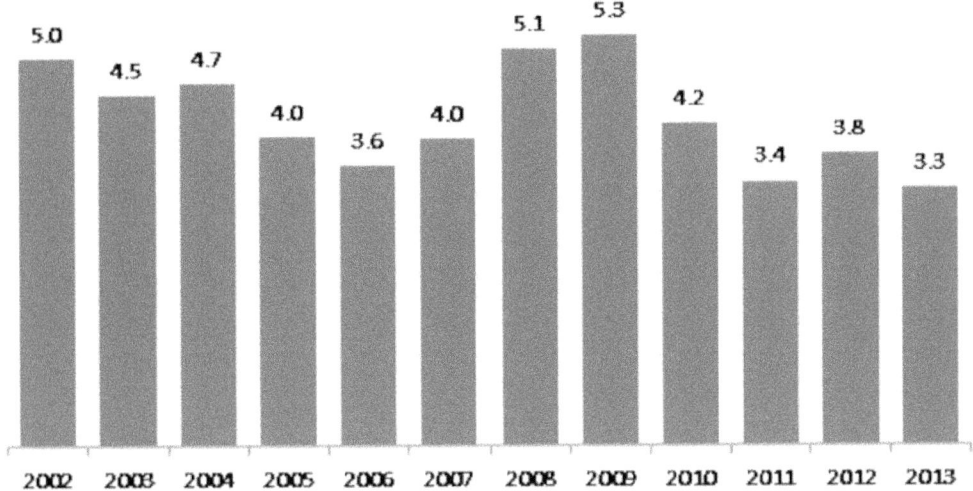

Figure 6. Mexico Annual Inflation Rate in Percentages. Source: INEGI.

On the other hand, the Mexican economy is one of the most open in the world. According to the Ministry of Economy[27]:

> Mexico has a network of 10 free trade agreements with 45 countries (FTAs), 30 Agreements on Trade Related Investment Measures (TRIMS) and 9 agreements of limited scope (Economic Complementation Agreements and Partial Scope Agreements) in the framework of the Latin American Integration Association (ALADI). In addition, Mexico participates actively in multilateral and regional organizations and forums such as the World Trade Organization (WTO), the mechanism of Asia-Pacific Economic Cooperation (APEC), the Organization for Economic Cooperation and Development (OECD) and ALADI.

Therefore, international trade plays an important role for Mexico. According to the World Trade Organization,[28] in 2012 Mexico ranked in 16th place in terms of imports of merchandise, while it ranked 14th in total merchandise imports and 34th in services. Mexico accounts for 2.02 percent of total world exports and 2.05 percent of total world imports. Mexico and the U.S. belong to the North Atlantic Free Trade Association (NAFTA); both also have FTAs in common with Chile, Colombia, Israel, and Peru, among other partners. Note that Mexico has a free trade agreement with the European Union (Economic Partnership, Political Coordination and Cooperation Agreement), and the U.S. and European Union have initiated talks to create the Transatlantic Trade and Investment Partnership (TTIP), which will be the largest trade agreement.

Figures 7 and 8 show the annual value of export and import volumes as well as annual variations. As can be seen, there has been steady growth since 2000, with the exception of the setback in 2009. The deficit in the trade balance is marginal compared with the total volume of trade.

158   Mexican Business Culture

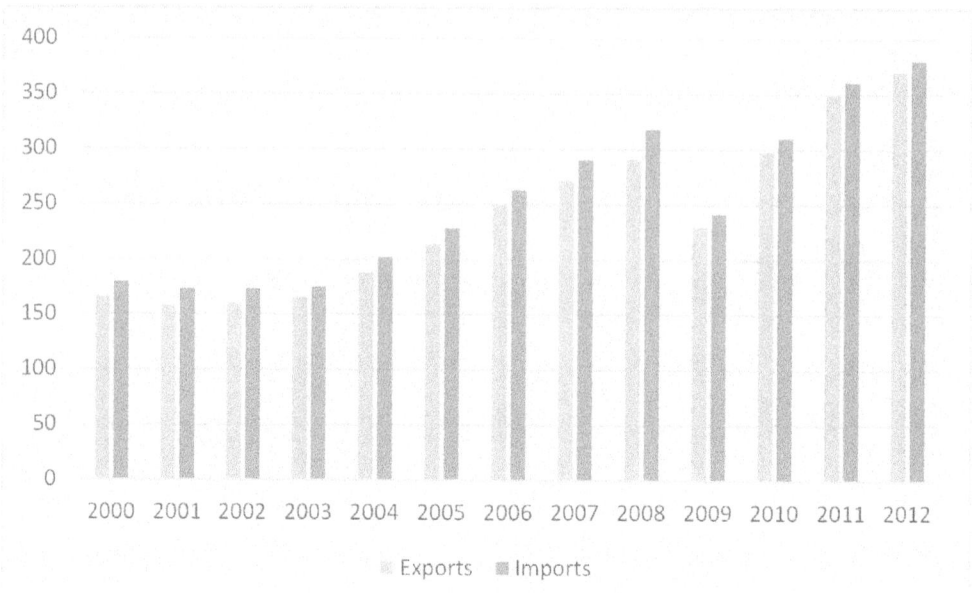

Figure 7. Mexico: Value of Total Exports and Imports in $ Billions. Source: World Bank Database.

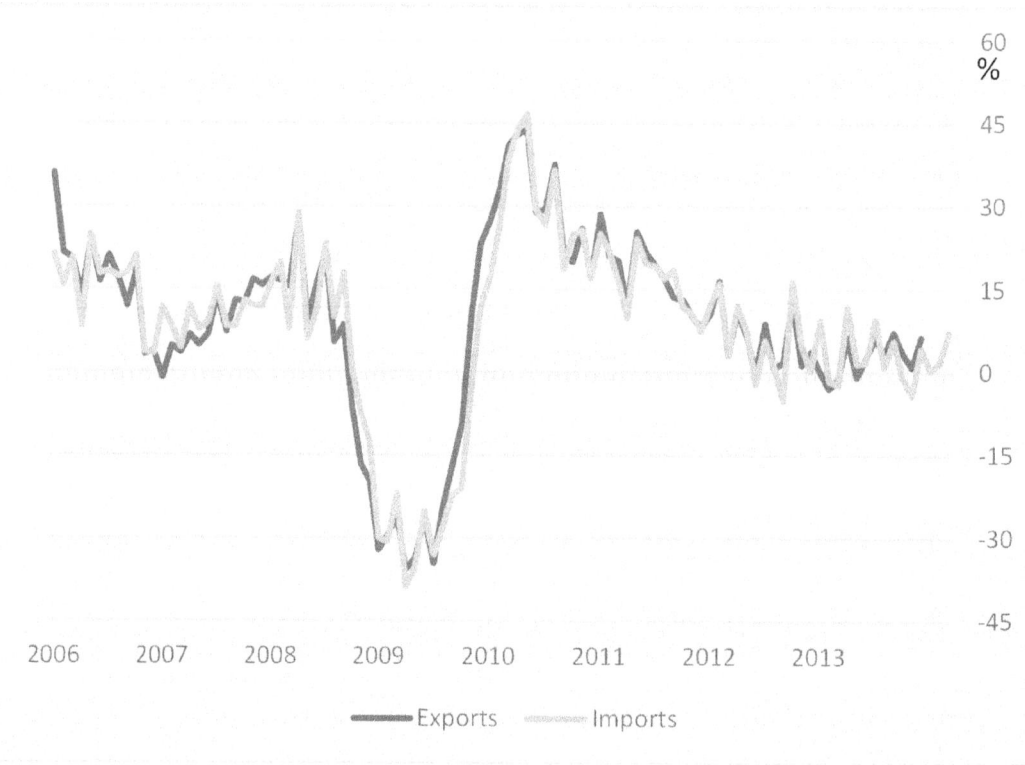

Figure 8. Mexico: Annual Variation of Trade Volumes in Percentages. Source: INEGI.

The following are the comparisons for 2010–2012 for trade per capita in USD and the trade-to-GDP ratio (2010–2012) for Mexico and the U.S. (WTO).

	Trade per capita	Trade to GDP
Mexico:	$5,525	61.3%
U.S.:	$14,701	30.5%

The comparison of export structures is:

	Agricultural Products	Fuels and Mining	Manufacturing
Mexico:	6.1%	20.8%	69.3%
U.S.:	11.1%	12.1%	71.3%

The comparison of import structures is:

	Agricultural Products	Fuels and Mining	Manufacturing
Mexico:	7.3%	11.6%	78.2%
U.S.:	6.1%	20.8%	69.3%

The principal destinations of Mexican exports and the origins of imports are:

Destination	%	Origin	%
U.S.	78.7%	U.S.	49.8%
EU	5.5%	China	14.9%
Canada	3.1%	EU	10.8%
China	1.7%	Japan	4.7%
Colombia	1.6%	Rep. Korea	3.9%

The principal destinations of U.S. exports and the origins of imports are:

Destination	%	Origin	%
Canada	18.8%	China	19.1%
EU	17.1%	EU	16.7%
Mexico	13.9%	Canada	14.0%
China	7.2%	Mexico	12.0%
Japan	4.5%	Japan	6.4%

On the other hand, foreign direct investment has maintained fluctuating flows over the past few years. Thus, for example, starting in 1999, there is cyclic behavior of inflows to Mexico. In 2013, they reached nearly $40 billion USD but, as will be seen later, these flows declined in 2014.

Note that historically foreign direct investment coming from the U.S. has represented a high percentage of the total flows that Mexico receives. However, as seen in Figure 10, this percentage has decreased.

By 2014 (through June), foreign investment saw less growth. As seen in Figure 11, the 2014 disaggregated flows declined considerably compared with the previous year; 2014 created very different expectations derived from the tax changes and other institutional changes that took place in the Mexican government. The expectation of the federal government, central bank, and various international organizations like the International Monetary Fund is that the Mexican economy will improve its performance starting from the last quarter of 2014, following the imminent recovery of the U.S. economy.

As for the sectorial distribution of foreign investment, the investment in manufacturing processes is pronounced, highlighting negative flows which were recorded in the first half of 2014 in terms of information services.

160   Mexican Business Culture

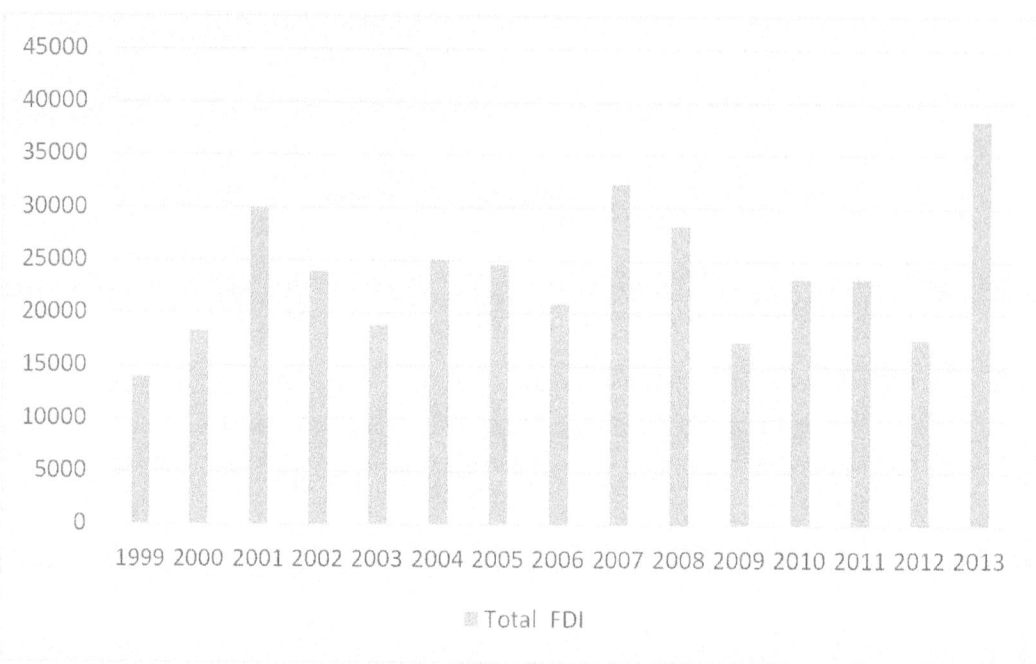

Figure 9. Mexico: Annual Foreign Direct Investment in USD Millions. Source: Ministry of the Economy.

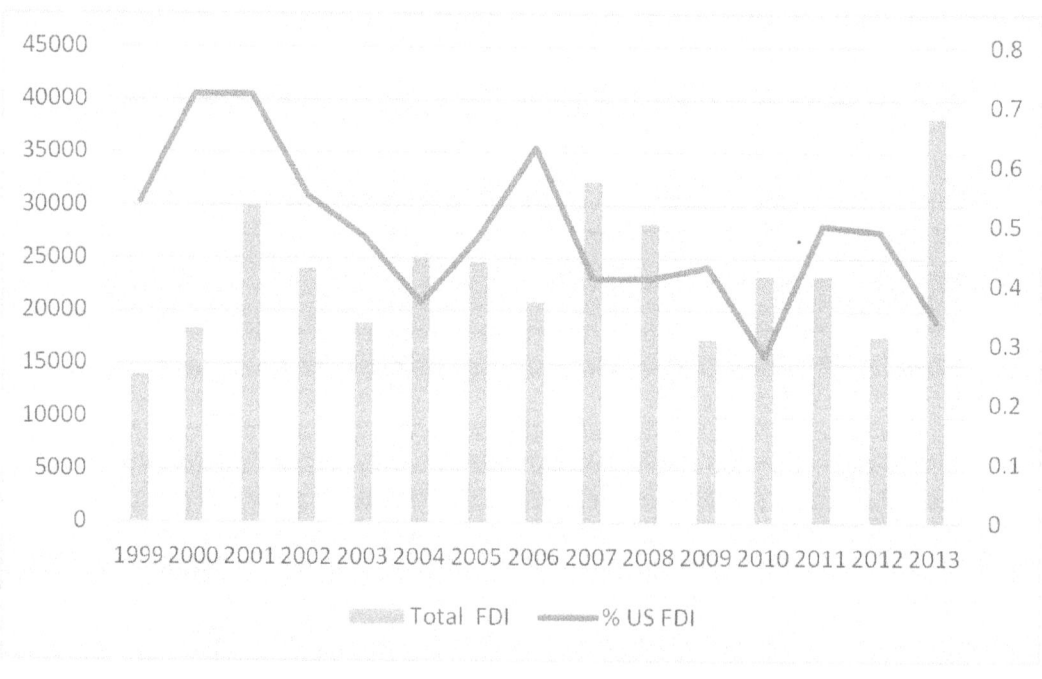

Figure 10. Mexico: Annual Foreign Direct Investment in USD Millions and the Percentage of U.S. Origin. Source: Ministry of the Economy.

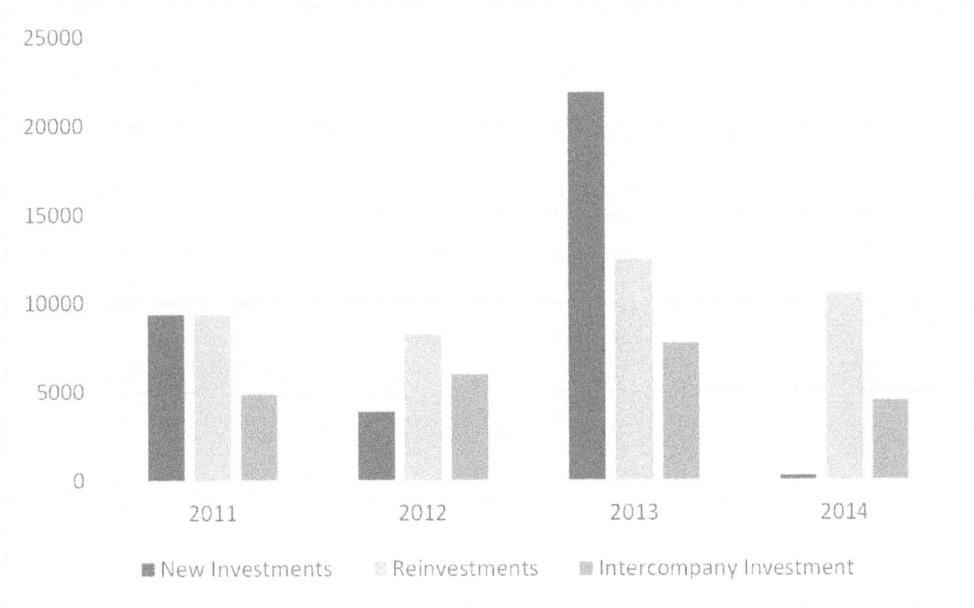

Figure 11. Mexico: Foreign Direct Investment Comparisons (January–June 2014) USD Millions. Source: Ministry of the Economy.

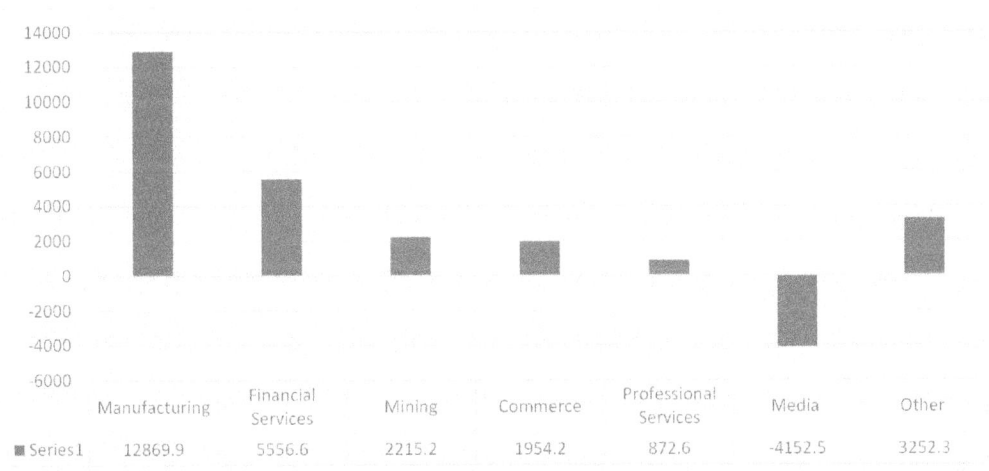

Figure 12. Mexico: Foreign Direct Investment Sectorial Distribution (January–June 2014) in USD Millions. Source: Ministry of the Economy.

In this analysis of various economic indicators, it is important to note that the Mexican economy has a high degree of dependence on and relationships with the United States. As seen in Figures 13 and 14, there is a close relationship both in the behavior of GDP and in the indexes of industrial production of the two countries. Therefore, any evaluation of a business strategy toward Mexico must be designed from the perspective of the economic behavior of the U.S. economy.

162   Mexican Business Culture

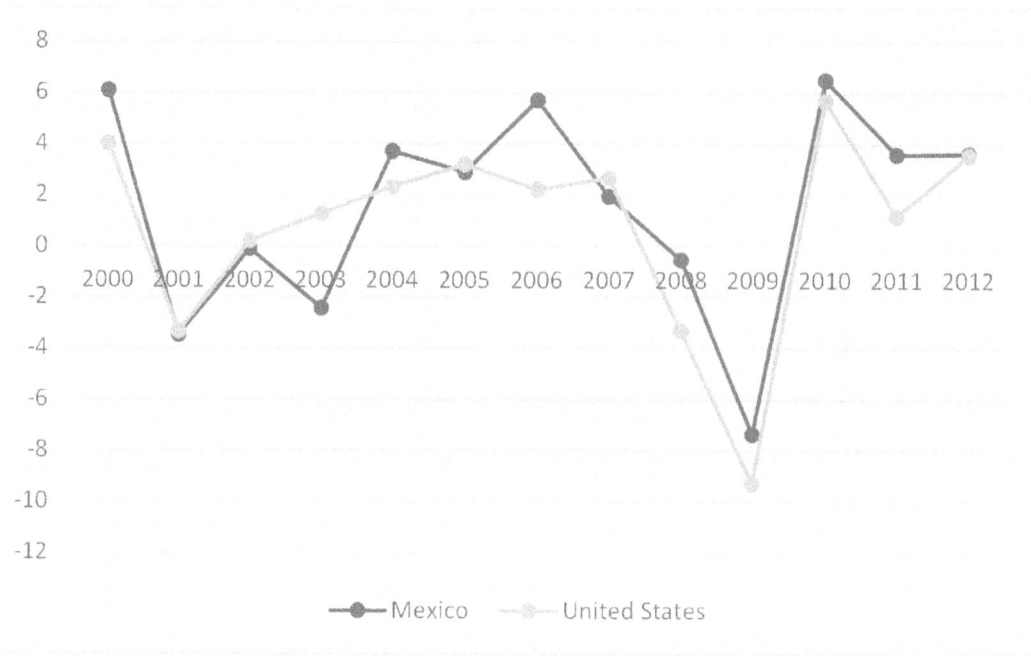

Figure 13. Mexico: U.S. Comparison of Industrial Production (Percentage of Change from Previous Year). Source: IMF Data Mapper.

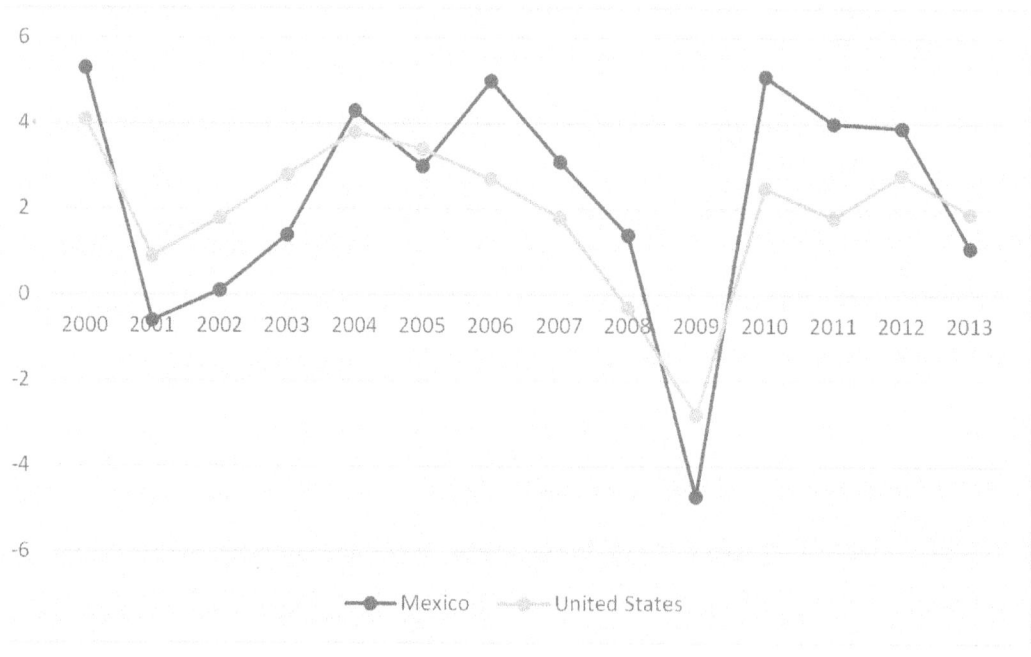

Figure 14. Mexico–U.S.: Real GDP Growth (Annual Percentage Change). Source: IMF Data Mapper.

Discussion Questions

1. Describe the economic and political relationship between Mexico and the world and especially Mexico and the United States as described in the essay.
2. What are the six indicators of institutional quality or Worldwide Governance indicators?
3. What is the worst institutional quality indicator in Mexico?
4. What does the essay say about tax policy and the business community? Also discuss the situation of tax collection strategy involving the informal sector.
5. List and describe the seven diverse actors involved in the relationship between the government and business in Mexico.
6. What are the time differences between Texas and Mexico when creating a company according to one of the interviewees?
7. In summarizing the series of interviews, what are the general feelings of those in the Mexican business community towards the government and its role in business? Is it positive or negative?
8. Describe the role of political parties in Mexico and how they specifically affect the relationship between business and government. Incorporate the thoughts of some of those who were interviewed and talk about the presidencies of the PAN and PRI in Mexico.

Key Learning Terms

Country of contrasts: The description of Mexico by Ensico in regards to the stark contrasts in the country such as wealth inequality and a modern society mixed with a traditional one.

Government-business relationship: The overall relationship between the government and business in regards to things such as taxation, regulation, security, rule of law, the promotion of business through incentives and programs as well as the promotion and passage of international trade agreements among other things.

Government-business relationship actors: A series of diverse individuals and institutions who all individually and collectively affect the complex relationship between the government and business.

Institutional quality indicators: Series of worldwide indicators which are indicative of the quality of a given government.

Quality of institutions: The overall quality, reliability and efficacy of government institutions to make and enforce laws among a myriad of other things in order to promote and regulate commerce in a country.

NOTES

1. http://www.wto.org/english/res_e/statis_e/trade_data_e.htm.
2. http://www.economia.gob.mx/comunidad-negocios/competitividad-normatividad/inversion-extranjera-directa/estadistica-oficial-de-ied-en-mexico.
3. For methodology, refer to http://info.worldbank.org/governance/wgi/index.aspx#doc-reading.
4. http://www.doingbusiness.org/~/media/GIAWB/Doing%20Business/Documents/Subnational-Reports/DB14-Mexico-Overview.pdf.

5. http://www.promexico.gob.mx/comercio/mexico-y-sus-tratados-de-libre-comercio-con-otros-paises.html.
6. http://www.inegi.org.mx/inegi/contenidos/espanol/prensa/Boletines/Boletin/Comunicados/Especiales/2014/julio/comunica4.pdf.
7. http://www.canacintra.org.mx/principal/.
8. http://www.concanaco.com.mx.
9. http://www.comce.org.mx/.
10. http://www.cce.org.mx/acerca-de/.
11. https://www.comprasdegobierno.gob.mx/.
12. http://www.shcp.gob.mx/EGRESOS/ppi/Paginas/Proyectos_APP.aspx.
13. For a detailed description, refer to http://www.inegi.org.mx/prod_serv/contenidos/espanol/bvinegi/productos/integracion/pais/mexvista/2012/Mex_ag12.pdf.
14. http://www.inegi.org.mx/est/contenidos/espanol/proyectos/censos/ce2009/pdf/Mono_Micro_peque_mediana.pdf.
15. http://www.anuies.mx/.
16. https://www.kpmg.com/MX/es/IssuesAndInsights/ArticlesPublications/Documents/Estudios/2014/Perspetivas-Alta-Direccion-Mexico-2014.pdf.
17. There is a very sad case in recent events in southern Mexico, in which the city mayor of Iguala Guerrero was directly responsible for the disappearance of 43 students.
18. Note that during recent years thousands of business owners have moved to the US, fearing the threat of the drug wars. Many of them were victims of kidnappings, bribes, assaults, or extortions.
19. Petróleos Mexicanos, the state owned company that has the monopoly for oil production in Mexico.
20. For a definition of the Maquiladora program refer to: http://www.economia.gob.mx/industry/foreign-trade-instruments/immex.
21. He was the only interviewee who allowed his name to be mentioned. He is the current director of COMCE, but his opinions are personal and not from the organization.
22. Appendix 3 presents additional economic figures for Mexico.
23. For reference consult: http://info.worldbank.org/governance/wgi/index.aspx#home.
24. http://data.worldbank.org/data-catalog/GDP-ranking-table.
25. https://www.imf.org/external/country/mex/index.htm?type=9998, http://www.imf.org/external/np/ms/2014/061614.htm.
26. http://www.inegi.org.mx/inegi/contenidos/espanol/prensa/comunicados/boplycumo.pdf.
27. http://www.economia.gob.mx/comunidad-negocios/comercio-exterior/tlc-acuerdos.
28. http://www.wto.org/english/res_e/statis_e/trade_data_e.htm.

References

Acemoglu, Daron, Simon Johnson, and James A. Robinson. "Reversal of Fortune: Geography and Institutions in the Making of the Modern World Income Distribution." *The Quarterly Journal of Economics* 117, no. 4 (2002): 1231–1294.

Aoki, Masahiko. *Toward a Comparative Institutional Analysis*. Cambridge: MIT Press, 2001. Print.

Ayala Espino, Jose. *Instituciones para mejorar el desarrollo. Un Nuevo pacto social para el crecimiento y el bienestar*. Mexico: Fondo de Cultura Económica, 2003. Print.

Dixit, Avinash K. *The Making of Economic Policy. A Transaction-Cost Politics Perspective*. Cambridge: MIT Press, 1998. Print.

Economic Freedom of the World Report. Fraser Institute.

Enciso Gonzalez, J. A. *Modelo de Análisis Institucional de Política Pública, El caso de la integración comercial entre México y la Unión Europea*. Germany: Editorial Académica Española, 2012. Print.

Furubotn, Eirik, and Richter Rudolf. *Institutions and economic theory. Contribution of the new institutional economics*. Ann Arbor: University of Michigan Press. 2000. Print.

Kaufmann, Daniel, Aart Kraay, and Zoido-Lobatón Pablo. *Governance Matters*. Policy Research Working Paper. The World Bank, Development Research Group Macroeconomics and Growth and Word Bank Institute Governance, Regulation and Finance, October 1999. Print.

Kaufmann, Daniel, Aart Kraay, and Massimo Mastruzzi. *Governance Matters VIII: Aggregate and Individual Governance Indicators, 1996–2008 (June 29, 2009)*. World Bank Policy Research Working Paper No. 4978, SSRN: 2009. Print.

_____. *Methodology and Analytical Issues.* Worldwide Governance Indicators. Policy Research Working Paper 5430. 2010. Print.

March, James G., and Johan P. and Olsen. *El Redescubrimiento de las Instituciones: La Base Organizativa de la Política.* Mexico: Colegio Nacional de Ciencias Políticas y Administración Pública A.C, Universidad Autónoma del Estado de México y Fondo de Cultura Económica, 1997. Print.

North, Douglass C. *Instituciones, Cambio Institucional y Desempeño Económico.*Mexico: Fondo de Cultura Económica, 1993. Print.

Ostrom, Elinor, and Margaret M. Polski. *An Institutional Framework for Policy Analysis and Design.* Workshop in Political Theory and Policy Analysis, Indiana University, 1999. Print.

Rodrik, Dani. *One Economics Many Recipes. Globalization, Institutions, and Economic Growth.* Princeton: Princeton University Press, 2007. Print.

Secretaría de Economía.

Servicio de Administración Tributaria. SAT. Secretaria de Hacienda y Crédito Público

Statistics database, World Trade Organization (WTO).

Trade Profiles. World Trade Organization. WTO Publications Geneva.

Voigt, Stefan. "How (Not) to Measure Institutions." *Journal of Institutional Economics* 9 (2013): 1–26. Print.

Williamson, Oliver E. *The Economic Institutions of Capitalism.* New York: Free Press, 1985. Print.

World Economic Outlook. IMF Data Mapper. International Monetary Fund.

Online Shopping in Mexico
Exploring the Promising and Challenging Panorama

Teresa Treviño *and* Flor Morton

There are approximately three billion Internet users around the world, nearly 40 percent of the world's population (ITU). Considering that it took 38 years for the telephone to reach 50 million users, the TV 13 years, and the Internet only four years, we are clearly experiencing a world phenomenon that is revolutionizing the way people communicate, make decisions, and make purchases (Ceballos 1). Additionally, online purchase intention rates throughout the world have doubled from 2011 to 2014 (Nielsen 2).

Electronic commerce or e-commerce can be described as the execution of buying and selling information, services or products through computerized networks. E-commerce involves making commercial transactions in an electronic manner. Specifically in Mexico, the use of electronic commerce is constantly growing. According to a study conducted by the Mexican Internet Association, there are 51.2 million Internet users in Mexico, and approximately 44 percent of them have purchased a product or service online (see Figure 1) (AMIPCI 6). As the Internet penetration rate increases throughout the country, the potential growth of electronic commerce also increases. Despite the particularity of the Mexican culture, characterized by lack of trust and confidence towards the unknown, each day, an increasing number of Mexican consumers have easy access to the Internet, which can translate in greater possibilities to make online purchases.

The present essay offers an overview of the overall Internet shopping cultural environment in Mexico, important trends in groups of consumers as well as their attitudes and behaviors toward buying online, new shopping channels such as social networking sites, and barriers that e-commerce has overcome. MercadoLibre is presented as a successful case of electronic commerce in Mexico. We provide information about the company and discuss the innovative strategies that it has implemented to attain success. Furthermore, specific insights on the positive experiences that Mexican consumers had had with online purchasing are also included, by presenting the results of a qualitative survey. Finally, this essay aims to provide important insights for international students, professors, managers and entrepreneurs interested in the Mexican culture with respect to online shopping.

The essay is structured as follows. First, the most important barriers that e-commerce has overcome throughout the years will be discussed. Then, a general overview of the

Mexican online shopping environment will be presented. Next, insights into consumer attitudes and behaviors with respect to online purchases are examined by addressing four consumer groups that are considered an important trend in Internet usage in Mexico. Subsequently, a new and rapidly growing shopping channel, social media, will be reviewed. Next, the methodology and results of the empirical research will be presented, which offer interesting insights on the Mexican consumers online purchases experiences. The final section will conclude by discussing the future of online purchases in Mexico.

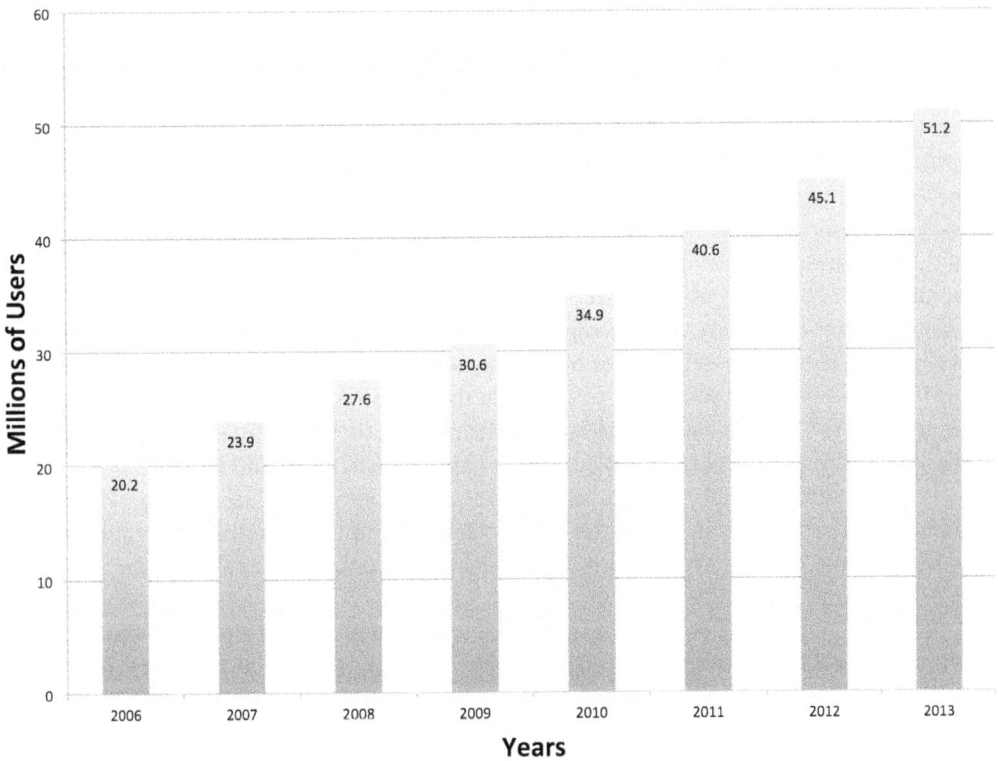

Figure 1. Internet Users in Mexico, 2006–2013. Adapted from AMIPCI: Estudio sobre los hábitos de los usuarios de Internet en México 2014.

The Birth of Electronic Commerce in Mexico and Its Entry Barriers

In Mexico, electronic commerce began in the early 1990s, and its steady growth has generated high optimism for business. The official birth of e-commerce in Mexico occurred in 1993, when the first ".com.mx" and ".gob.mx" subdomains were created and became available for Mexican users (NIC Mexico). However, the full launch of e-commerce in Mexico took some time, as it needed to overcome several barriers to its diffusion. One important barrier that has slowly being addressed in recent years is related to the Mexican culture of distrust, when engaging with credit card transactions, especially in the online context. This issue involved finding an appropriate form of payment convenient for Mexican consumers to enable electronic transactions, and other perceived risks by consumers also needed to be addressed. These days, Mexican consumers recognize the advantages of buying online, resulting in a more favorable perception towards online transactions with credit cards.

Over the years, the payment method has been identified as one of the factors that negatively affect online sales growth, as many Mexican consumers do not have access to credit cards (Palacios 8). Considering that both credit and debit cards may now be used to conduct electronic transactions, in this essay, the term "credit" will be used for both credit and debit cards interchangeably.

Since the late 19th century, the check has been the most frequently used alternative to cash in Mexico. Subsequently, technological advances allowed for the emergence of an infrastructure for new and more efficient payment methods, such as credit cards and electronic transfers (Garcia-Murillo 207). However, the use of credit cards was not widespread until 2004 when the LTOSF ("Ley para la Transparencia y Ordenamiento de los Servicios Financieros") law was created. This law promoted the substitution of checks with electronic payment methods by decreasing the costs and commissions that had been higher for these new payment methods (Castellanos, Garrido and Mendoza 231). Additionally, in 2004, the Fund for Media Electronic Payment Infrastructure (FIMPE) was created with the objective of fostering the use of electronic payment methods by extending access to an electronic network for both commercial establishments and consumers. The FIMPE has developed programs to promote the use of credit cards and to install point-of-sale (POS) terminals at no cost for establishments, these terminals are used to charge the amount of purchase to credit and debit cards (Castellanos and Garrido 95).

As a result, by 2008, the number of credit cards issued was 25.2 million, which is 3.2 times greater than that in 2002. Moreover, the total number of annual transactions with this payment method increased by 435 percent compared with 2002 sales of near $20 billion (Castellanos and Garrido 70).

In 2013, electronic commerce in Mexico was estimated to bring $9.2 billion in sales, representing 42 percent growth relative to 2012. The most popular payment method for these transactions is credit cards with 64 percent use, followed by cash deposits (12 percent), online transfers (11 percent), and cash payments in convenient stores (9 percent) (AMIPCI 10). Table 1 presents a comparison of the number of credit cards issued in Mexico and the United States in 2013 and 2014. Although Mexico's credit card use is still low compared with these countries, a considerable increase was observed as a result of the decrease in bank fees and technological infrastructure, and its use is expected to continue growing, according to Antonio Junco, CEO of MasterCard México and Central America (El Financiero). This situation will continue to influence electronic commerce in a positive way.

Table 1. Comparison of Number of Credit Cards Issued in Mexico and the U.S.

Year	Mexico		USA	
	2013	2014	2013	2014
Number of credit cards (millions)	23.40	22.77	405.89	410.54

Source: CNBV, 2015; Statists, 2015.

Another barrier to the growth of e-commerce in Mexico has been consumers' perceptions of the risks involved in this type of transaction. The most common concerns include privacy and security issues (Castañeda and Montoro). According to Ovilla, the

State, companies, and users/consumers should participate in the promotion of e-commerce by developing transparent protective mechanisms such as conduct codes, clear information, legislation, and precautions to generate trust and security in this medium. The author identifies several activities that consumers can do to overcome their insecurity when buying online, such as inquiring about the seriousness of the seller, considering return policies, having the option to pay upon delivery, using a virtual credit card whose sole purpose is for online purchases, and retaining all written information regarding transactions (e.g., emails, terms and conditions, transactions).

Additionally, it is known that there is a positive relationship between the socioeconomic class and education with the use of credit cards (Banamex and UNAM 18). In other words, people that belong to upper classes and have greater levels of education, tend to show higher credit card usage in comparison to those of lower socioeconomic class and lower educational levels. However, for the lower socioeconomic groups the main advantage of using credit cards is related to the possibility of buying even though they have no immediate cash available (Banamex and UNAM 18, Nielsen 8). Although payment method issues and security concerns of consumers still exist, implementing different strategies by both companies and government has mitigated these concerns. In the next sections, we provide a general overview of the shopping environment in the country and highlight some of these strategies for encouraging online purchases in Mexico.

Overview of the Current Internet Shopping Environment in Mexico

The growth of electronic commerce in Mexico has been boosted by several factors throughout the years, such as the increase in the number of personal computers in homes and the growth of Internet penetration in both companies and homes. Globally speaking, the U.S. and Canada are leading with respect to e-commerce spending, and this spending was projected to increase more than 90 percent by 2014. However, a major part of the world's online spending growth is expected to come from Latin America (Underwood 146). Data suggest that the Mexican online market is expected to grow at a rate of 20 percent rom 2012 to 2017. As it can be noted, the rate by which Mexican online purchases are expected to grow is still extremely low compared to those rates of U.S. and Canada. Specifically, this growth will be driven by a market primarily composed of the young and middle-class population (Research and Markets).

Although most online purchases are still being made through desktops or laptops, the rise of online shopping in recent years is also strongly related to the usage of mobile devices (The Cocktail Analysis 21). Mexico is expected to have 106.4 million mobile connections in 2015 (eMarketer). In 2013, 84 percent of Mexicans had at least one mobile device, and 67.7 percent of them were 25 to 70 years old (IAB Mexico and Millward Brown). These people qualify as potential owners of credit cards, which enable them to make purchasing decisions. According to a recent study of usage and consumption patterns of mobile devices in Mexico, 43 percent of users have made at least one purchase, payment or transaction through their mobile phones. Examples of these transactions include the purchase of telephone credits, apps, music, payments for public services, hotel reservations, online games and game credits, entertainment tickets, airline tickets, money transfers and clothing (IAB Mexico and Millward Brown). The travel category has been on top of the most frequent online purchase list; however, statistics have shown that mobile shoppers are focusing more on buying intangible goods, whereas shoppers using desktops or laptops tend to buy more diverse retail products (eMarketer). Additionally, Mexican consumers are beginning to use their mobile devices as a medium for payment instead of their physical credit cards, and although the rate of such use is still low (7 percent), consumers show a high disposition and willingness (46 percent) to adopt this new payment method (IAB). Based on a recent study by Paypal and Ipsos, the e-commerce through mobile phones and tablets is expected to show an annual growth of 42 percent from 2013 to 2016. Specifically, the millennial generation (18 to 34 years) is trending on mobile sales, as 88 percent of the mobile sales come from this segment (El Financiero).

Furthermore, the government and other institutions are willing to promote initiatives that enable important growth in online sales in Mexico. One example of these initiatives was launched in September 2014, with the first edition of the "HotSale" in Mexico. This event includes more than 60 companies, offers special discounts and attractive promotions on their online stores over a four-day period, aiming to attract new online consumers (Sánchez). Important retailers such as Dafiti, Walmart, MercadoLibre, Linio, BestBuy, Liverpool, Interjet, and others became involved in this initiative in favor of online commerce. The results were favorable, as companies registered a 450 percent increase in online sales, representing more than 1 million products and services sold to more than 100,000 people (Martínez). Considering this finding, experts are optimistic about the achievements that will be observed in 2015, expecting that the online industry will grow exponentially as new sales are boosted by government initiatives to bring small and medium companies into the digital world (Sánchez).

In general, we can see that this phenomenon is changing the overall shopping culture of Mexican consumers. In the past, people were more inclined to visit stores personally for all their shopping needs; however, this involved the investment of time and money. Today people recognize the advantages that the Internet can bring to their overall shopping process: looking for information, comparing products, prices and stores, buying and finally, receiving the product directly to their home. The convenience that the Internet offers to consumers is highly valuable for Mexicans, and therefore, this phenomenon is shaping new tendencies in people's preferences.

E-Commerce Models in Mexico

With regard to business models for e-commerce, there are four strategies that can be implemented. The first strategy involves starting an online business from scratch, buying a .com domain and selling retail products only through the Internet. The advantages of this business model are that the initial investment is relatively low, and it allows companies to have a new brand that might grow in the future. However, the cost and time to bring users to the new virtual store constitute the main disadvantage. Another popular business model in Mexico is the strategy of extending traditional business to the Internet. This model is a transition of the physical store that is already established and is incorporated with the same name and products on the web. Examples of this business model include large Mexican retailers that have also developed online sales such as liverpool.com.mx, elpalaciodehierro.com.mx, and sanborns.com.mx. The main advantage is that it represents an additional source of new sales and is relatively easier than launching a new store from scratch, as an established brand automatically brings higher sales. The third model consists of selling products through an existing portal by having a section that allows the company to commercialize its products. Portals such as Yahoo! enable users to build online stores and "rent" the online space. An important advantage of this strategy is that the portal ensures traffic to the new online store; however, the fixed costs of this model are sometimes high. Finally, the last online business model is selling through a virtual market. This strategy involves building an online business through specialized sites (such as Mercadolibre.com and Vivaanuncios.com) that are organized by category. The advantage of selling through this model is that there is access to a considerably large national market at a low rate of initial investment for implementation (Ceballos 5).

The presented models are all options that can help current and new businesses to adopt electronic commerce; however, choosing one model over another will depend on the characteristics of the industry, the product/service, the organization, and the available resources of the company. An increasing number of businesses in Mexico are certainly benefiting from the advantages of electronic commerce, especially those with small budgets. In the next section, a successful company is presented as a case study of how electronic commerce is changing the way people conduct commercial transactions, which has an impact on cultural behavior.

Case Study: MercadoLibre

MercadoLibre is a successful e-commerce website that has gained popularity in the Mexican context. In this website, users can buy and sell new or used products. In 2014, the number of users of MercadoLibre in Latin America increased to 100 million, and 83 million transactions were registered for more than $7,300 million (CNNExpansion). According to a Nielsen study for MercadoLibre in Mexico, in 2009, more than 3 million users in the country conducted commercial transactions through the website (Infochannel). The e-commerce sales of 54 percent of the respondents in Nielsen's study represents additional income and an opportunity to develop their own commercial venture without quitting their jobs (Infochannel).

According to the CEO of MercadoLibre in Mexico, 60 percent of Mexicans buy online from companies inside and outside of the country, and there are several factors that can help e-commerce to continue to grow in this context. Such factors include consideration of new generations of people who are growing up with the Internet and are entering the productive population, a greater penetration of technology and a generally better level of professionalism in the use of the Internet for commercial purposes (Netmedia).

MercadoLibre is a company that pays attention to market trends and takes action to promote the growth of the company. For example, the Federal Telecommunications Commission (COFETEL) indicated that 16 percent of the 94 million cell phones in Mexico are smartphones, and according to Google data, 26 percent of smartphone users in Mexico use their mobile devices to buy online (Violante). As a result, MercadoLibre responded to this opportunity and recently launched its company's app for iPhone, BlackBerry, and Android that allows sellers and buyers to interact more easily through their smartphones (Creativa Magazine Ad News).

Additionally, there are other activities that have driven the company's success, such as the creation of Mercado Clic, through which the company sells online advertising, and their payment method MercadoPago, a way to pay online in which basically anyone can buy a product using their credit card, even if the seller does not accept credit cards (Creativa Magazine Ad News). Furthermore, the company is betting on e-commerce growth and recently bought the Guiadinmuebles.com site that allows users to search for and publish information on the sale and rental of all types of real estate properties (CNNExpansión).

As we can see, MercadoLibre represents a good example of a successful e-commerce company, as it is one of the most rapidly growing sites for online sales in Mexico. The success of this company can motivate other companies that are deciding whether to venture into online business in the country.

In the next section, the attitudinal and behavioral aspects of Mexican consumers are addressed to provide a more complete analysis.

Mexican Consumers' Online Shopping Attitudes and Behaviors

Consumers' attitudes toward online shopping are constantly evolving in favor of online purchases. Studies have shown that online consumers identify some positive aspects of buying through the Internet, such as convenience—buying anytime, anywhere—and the possibility of finding the best possible price. Additionally, consumers also appreciate the stock availability usually found in online stores (The Cocktail Analysis 37).

However, several studies have agreed that shoppers are demanding more flexibility and control over their online purchasing experience. For example, consumers often search for retail stores that offer free and traceable shipping and on-time delivery (UPS 20; The Cocktail Analysis 40). With this consideration, companies interested in the online market should carefully analyze whether their delivery strategy meets the needs of consumers. Fast delivery is so important to Mexican consumers that 80 percent of them are even interested in applying for subscription programs to be able to order products automatically (Pulso). Additionally, Mexican consumers tend to be very loyal to their favorite retailers, as 8 out of 10 shoppers often return to the same retailer for a repurchase. However, these repurchases and the provision of positive recommendations to others are conditional upon having received fast delivery and safe and free shipping (UPS 20).

Another aspect that influences the purchase decisions of online shoppers in Mexico is the return policies established by companies. Although Mexico as a country has a low number of returned items that were purchased online and in retail stores, 62 percent of users have mentioned that they read the return policy of retailers before making any purchases. Additionally, reports have suggested that consumers would be willing to buy more often if return policies were less complicated (UPS 23). Based on previous studies, it can be argued that consumers develop specific needs in different stages of their decision buying process, and this argument also applies to the online context. Figure 2 presents the main concerns of online Mexican shoppers based on each stage of the buying decision process, first introduced by John Dewey in 1910.

The principal product categories bought by online users depends heavily on the demographic characteristics of shoppers. For example, fashion products are sought primarily by females who are under 35 years old, and such products usually include clothing and shoes. Popular sites in which users find such products include MercadoLibre.com, Privalia, and Dafiti. By contrast, males principally seek both culture and electronic categories, which considers both digital and physical products. For these products, consumers frequently rely on MercadoLibre.com, Gandhi, Amazon and iTunes to make their purchases. Additionally, more mature users ranging from 35 to 55 years old buy products and services from the travel industry, which are mostly plane tickets and hotel reservations. Popular websites used for these purposes include Despegar.com, AeroMéxico, Volaris, Interjet and VivaAerobus. Finally, the entertainment category, mainly preferred by younger generations, includes purchases of cinema tickets and concerts on Cinépolis and TicketMaster, respectively (The Cocktail Analysis 43).

Socioeconomic class can also influence the type of product categories purchased by Mexicans. Because middle and upper classes (ABC+) are the largest socioeconomic group among Mexican Internet users (17.4 million), and have access to a higher economic status, they are also who demand the majority of the "higher end" products mentioned above. Additionally, their culture, education and international exposure enable these groups to develop a more favorable opinion and trust towards Internet purchases. Lower socioeconomic classes such as D+ and D- are limited with respect to Internet access and economic resources, which automatically change the product categories they demand as well as the overall propensity to buy online. However, one mayor change in Mexico's Internet penetration has been seen specifically on the D+ class, as it has shown a 7 percent increase between 2012 and 2013. This statistic from a percentage perspective means that 36 percent of Mexican Internet users are now from this socioeconomic class (D+), and 17 percent of them belong to the D-class (Gimenez). These figures show an opportunity

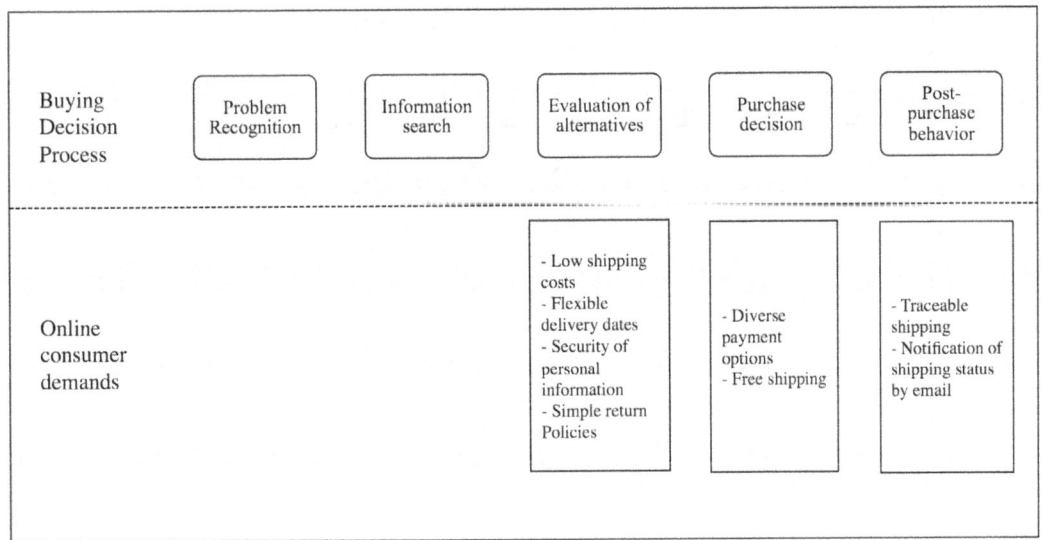

Figure 2. Mexican Consumers' Demands in the Online Buying Decision Process. Note: Adapted from Estudio UPS "Pulso del Comprador en Línea" Un Estudio de la Experiencia del Consumidor. Copyright 2013 by comScore and United Parcel Service of America, Inc.; and Dewey, John (1910). How We Think. Boston: D.C. Health and Research Company, 1910.

for companies and brands targeting these socioeconomic classes, which can implement strategies that can facilitate online purchases by lower classes with Internet access. For example, offering single serving products and physical payment in convenience stores might help this segment's propensity to make online purchases.

Internet User Groups Trending in Mexico

Knowing what drives behavior is essential to increase engagement, and marketers know that the desires of shoppers vary. For these reasons, researchers have identified several groups of Internet users in Mexico. Among the key segments are teens, executives, digital moms and silver surfers. The teen group is composed of young users between 13 and 18 years old; 84 percent of these individuals are students. On average, teens possess and use three devices to surf online. Typically, teens are online for a period of two to five hours daily, and their most common activities are sending and receiving mails, downloading music, and searching for information. Additionally, teens frequently visit movie download sites, online game sites, and blogs. With respect to social networking sites, most teens maintain at least one social networking account. For this segment, the number of online purchases and transactions has increased in the last year, as 45 percent of teens have made at least one transaction or payment on the Internet, with the most common purchases being online games, music and clothing (IAB Mexico and Millward Brown).

Another Internet user group in Mexico consists of executives, who are described as employees, staff, and middle managers with an average age of 35 years. This segment prefers mobile devices, such as smartphones and tablets, to connect to the Internet. For this reason, many executives are online for more than 12 hours, and their most common activities are information search in browsers, email, social networking sites, online courses, videos, and TV. With respect to online transactions, executives tend to make online bank payments, buy clothes, and purchase plane tickets (IAB Mexico and Millward Brown).

Digital moms are described as women who are 30 years old on average and who are married and have children younger than 12 years old. Nine out of ten digital moms have at least one mobile device and also use the Internet on a laptop or desktop, spending approximately 6.12 hours online daily. The most frequent activities of this group are social networking sites, information search, and instant messages. At least 49 percent of digital moms have made a purchase or payment online (IAB Mexico and Millward Brown). In fact, many digital moms engage in online transactions twice per week, with the most common purchases being clothing, perfumes, shoes, music, travel and entertainment services (Pérez).

Another interesting group of Internet users in Mexico is known as the silver surfers and includes users older than 50 years of age. These users access the Internet through their desktop computers or smartphones and enjoy informative websites, travel agency sites, dictionaries and specialized encyclopedias. The purchasing power of this segment is generally high, and for this reason, their online purchases include clothes, personal items, and luxury articles such as watches and jewelry (Dinámica Negocio).

The present classification may offer important insights for companies in general and for marketers in particular in developing interesting strategies that target these growing segments in Mexico. However, regardless of consumers' classification with respect to online shopping, three consumer needs are consistently found in every online consumer: a convenient experience, a cost-effective purchase and safety (Nielsen 16).

Social Media as a New Shopping Channel

Social media has revolutionized the ways in which people communicate and form relationships with others. In Mexico, nine out of ten Internet surfers maintain at least one active social network account, and following the use of browsers, social media networks occupy the second most frequently used place for users to obtain information (AMIPCI). Users are evolving to become more demanding and smarter consumers, and their purchase decisions are based on information obtained in social networks (Sánchez). For these reasons, Web 2.0 applications also play an important role in the e-commerce industry, and Mexico is no exception. These new web applications allow users to have a more active role than before by creating and sharing information. Today's companies can benefit from this new media, which can be considered a massive market research tool, a sales strategy, an advertising campaign and a customer support platform (Sánchez). As a consequence, modern e-commerce is becoming a tool both for customers to make online transactions and for Web sites to learn about customers and their buying cultural habits in order to suggest other related products or services (Andzulis, Panagopoulos, and Rapp 307).

As Mexicans are currently adopting social media as an essential element in their lives, companies are rushing to integrate various forms of such media into their marketing strategies. Evidence suggests that organizations are willing to expand their activities through this channel and are therefore expected to increase their social media spending (Constantinides, Romero, and Boria 3). Companies understand this need to evolve, as e-commerce itself is transforming into "social e-commerce," which can be considered the next logical step in the evolution of online and Internet business (Andzulis, Panagopoulos, and Rapp 307).

As people spend more time on social networking sites, they also share their feelings, interests and thoughts publicly. It is logical to assume that social networks influence what and how consumers make purchases. Therefore, the future of e-commerce is clear: the next large step is to make transactions from within social networks, such as selling products, adding products to shopping carts, and making payments. Today, there are several examples around the world in which retailers have embedded their e-commerce platform directly into their Facebook fan page, which allows consumers to make purchases quickly without leaving Facebook (Anderson, Sims, Price, and Brusa 3). In Mexico, social commerce is still in the early stages of development; however, there is no reason to believe that its development will differ from that observed in other countries. According to statistics of Internet and social network users, the outlook for implementing this new business model in Mexico in the near future is favorable. Data from several studies suggest that the industry is growing rapidly, and such tendencies should not be ignored in new marketing and sales strategies (Ceballos).

In the next section, we present an exploratory research conducted to better understand the attitudes and perceptions of Mexican consumers. Precisely, we intended to obtain additional and direct insights with respect to preferences of Mexican consumers towards online shopping. Specifically, the following research questions drive the present research: What are the consumer's perceptions towards credit card payments on online sites? What factors influence the positive experiences of consumers when buying online? What is the general perception and attitudes towards online buying in Mexico?

Methodology

A qualitative online survey was developed and distributed online, using Qualtrics software. Following a qualitative approach is useful to understand the reasons behind people's behaviors and the perceptions that drive it. In this case, the aim was to provide a more detailed understanding on the shopping experiences of Mexican consumers through the Internet, and the perceptions they have of these online transactions. In general, participants were asked about the things they have purchased online, a memorable experience that they have had when shopping through this medium, and to describe their thoughts on the things they enjoy when making an online purchase. Additionally, we included several close questions regarding payment methods, which provided interesting insights on how prone Mexican consumers are to use their credit card for this purpose.

In total, 120 people were invited to participate; having a response rate of 82 percent. From the 98 returned surveys, 91 surveys were fully complete and valid for the present analysis. Data was analyzed in both SPSS and Atlas.ti software, by following a iterative coding process that enable the researchers to find categories and patterns regarding positive aspects of online shopping. Based on the number of mentions, we obtained the most common and recurrent themes on the narratives of Mexican consumers that have purchased online.

Results

In order to be considered for this study, participants had to had experience with online purchases. In general, the survey distribution consisted of 39 percent females and 61 percent males (n=91), with an average age of 35 (SD=9.78) years old; 47 percent of them are single, and 51 percent are married with respect to their occupations, 81 percent of them are employees, 9 percent students, 7 percent housekeepers, and 3 percent other occupations. Forty-eight percent of participants live in Monterrey, a city located in the northern part of Mexico, with important influence of the United States culture. However, the rest of the participants are from different states of Mexico, such as Mexico City, Coahuila, Jalisco, Tamaulipas, Guanajuato, Aguascalientes, Baja California, Quintana Roo, Sinaloa and Sonora. Finally 10 percent of the participants are Mexicans currently living in other countries. Despite their location, it is important to take into consideration that the sample was obtained from a University's networking group composed of middle to upper class professionals.

Among the most popular things that have been bought through the Internet are transportation tickets (flights, bus, train), electronics, clothes, entertainment (concerts, parks, movies, theaters), and hotel reservations. As expected 87 percent of participants commented that credit or debit cards were used to pay for these purchases. Interestingly, the majority of participants expressed strong feelings in favor of using credit cards for online purchases (87 percent), as they perceive it as a convenient (90 percent) and secure (69 percent) payment method. Additionally, the majority also expressed confidence on e-commerce websites (70 percent) and 69 percent prefer not to use cash as a payment method for online purchases. Based on these results, we can confirm that the overall feelings of Mexican consumers towards online purchases, and more precisely, in the use of their credit cards as a payment method, are optimistic.

Several positive experiences when buying through the Internet emerged from the qualitative part of the survey. These positive experiences are derived from several motives that consumers find important when making online purchases. In the next section, examples will be provided from the five most common themes that emerged from the qualitative data. For a complete list of themes refer to Table 2.

Convenience

Convenience was the most popular reason why participants rate their purchase process as positive. For example, the following participants reflected on how the convenience factor enables them to enjoy this type of purchases:

> "It is SUPER SIMPLE! Once you log in in different portals they have your personal information saved, so you do not have to type all your information each time you make a purchase."
>
> "I think it is a very convenient form to buy, because you do not need to get out of your house. I enjoy buying clothes because without leaving my office or home I can buy the products I like."

In general, we found that convenience reasons are related to the fact that people do not need to be at a physical store, and the ease of use of the Internet websites where consumers make purchases.

Time Saving

Time is a valuable resource for consumers, and making online purchases is easy and fast. Participants in the study remembered how they enjoyed buying online because they do not need to invest a considerable amount of time in this act. The following quotes exemplify this idea:

> "It is fast and easy! In five minutes, I had already bought some plane tickets just as I wanted them."
>
> "Buying on the Internet prevents me to move from one place to another, and this saves me time that I can dedicate to my other activities, such as work or to my family."

Better Prices/Deals

Another popular reason why consumers enjoy buying online is finding competitive prices and attractive discounts. Participants in the study had a general perception that products that are available online have better prices than when buying them in a physical store. One participant commented about his positive experience finding better prices online:

"In general, I think the prices are much more competitive (than in the physical stores), I get very happy when I find the same product but 100 or 200 pesos ($7–15 USD) cheaper ... even on things that they don't sell in our country."

Timely Delivery

The fourth most mentioned reason why consumers enjoy buying online is related to the delivery times. Many participants agreed that online stores offer timely delivery, as they have received their products on time and in some other cases, even before the planned due date. In the following quotes, we can see how positive experiences of online shopping of these two participants, were due to a timely delivery:

"Recently, I was looking for an old TV series.... I ordered it through Amazon. They gave me a delivery date and surprisingly the product arrived a couple of days before the planned due date!"

"Amazon and Apple have the best delivery services and the tracking is very precise ... additionally the product always arrive MUCH earlier that promised."

Variety of Products and Options

Another common theme among the participant's narratives is related to the availability and variety of different products and brands that can be found on the Internet. Consumers reflect about their experiences in physical stores, where the availability of products is restricted to the inventory at that particular moment. However, buying through the Internet allows people to choose from a larger variety of products. For example, one participant commented about her experience with online shopping versus shopping in physical stores:

"[I enjoy shopping online] because it allows me to find items that will not be easy to find in physical stores.... We can see there are more options than in local stores."

Other Factors That Are Related to Positive Experiences with Online Shopping

Additional factors were mentioned by participants as determinants of their positive experiences when buying online. One interesting finding is that in general, consumers have a perception that their purchase is secured and that in case of a service failure, the company will respond to the encountered issue. There were interesting histories of participants that recalled not receiving their product, or reviving it in bad conditions. Regardless of this fact, consumers were happy and satisfied with the final outcome, as the company responded easily to these issues. Another theme recurrent in the narratives of participants is the possibility to compare options, of stores, brands, products and prices in the comfort of their home or office. This issue is related also to how consumers enjoy having the possibility to buy products from other countries, which enables them to have a broader product offering.

Receiving free products with their purchases was also mentioned as a factor they enjoyed, as they liked having these pleasant surprises of finding gift certificates or free samples of other products with their purchases, or by simply being member of a specific online store. Related to the delivery theme, purchase tracking and security on their purchases were also mentioned, as they feel secure to be able to track in a timely manner their package and be able to monitor it at any given time.

Surprisingly, one factor that was also mentioned by participants is the possibility to read online reviews of the products they are considering buying. This phenomenon is particularly interesting, as the impact that online reviews have on purchase intention must be considered by organizations and brands. Participants commented how reading other's experiences with the product enables them to make a more informed choice.

Finally, other themes mentioned included the high level of product personalization, which cannot be achieved in physical stores, rapidity of making purchases, and payment facilitation offered by online stores.

Table 2. Recurrent Themes in Positive Online Shopping Experience.

Themes	Mentions
Convenience	37
Time saving	19
Better Prices / Deals	15
Timely delivery	14
Variety of products and options	12
Secured by the company in case of service failures	8
Compare options	7
Possibility to buy in other countries	7
Receive free products	5
Purchase tracking	5
Security	4
Read Reviews of product	2
Product Personalization	2
Rapidity	2
Payment Facilitation	1

Conclusions

The future of e-commerce in the country appears to be promising: Mexico represents 12 percent of the total online consumption in Latin America, following in Brazil's steps, which represents 61 percent of sales. Statistics show opportunities for growth in the country; indeed, it is estimated that within five years, 50 percent of small and medium companies in Mexico will be online (Cruz; Netmedia; Sánchez and Soto). Additionally, several factors—such as the number of new Internet users, particularly those with mobile connections, government plans to increase connectivity, a dynamic economy, and new investments in talent for new technology development—provide important insights into the favorable future of e-commerce in Mexico.

Future growth comes with important challenges that must be considered, including the connectivity penetration in the country and the quality of Internet access. However, government representatives as well as members of the industry have acknowledged that it is an appropriate time to face these challenges. New telecommunication reforms will permit greater Internet penetration in the country, leading to considerable improvements in the infrastructure of e-commerce (Sánchez). Additionally, the online buying culture will be more accepted by Mexican consumers as younger generations are growing up with new technologies and are thus more likely to be e-commerce users.

As e-commerce becomes more popular, companies will also implement new marketing strategies. For example, companies may integrate social networking sites that enable consumers to search for and buy products from within their own social media accounts and share them with friends. Additionally, a more personalized and interactive experience—one that recognizes users' likes and needs—will mark a new tendency of online shopping.

In the present essay, we have provided a general overview of the overall Internet shopping environment in Mexico, important trends in groups of consumers as well as their attitudes and behaviors toward buying online, new shopping channels such as social networking sites, and the barriers that e-commerce has overcome. Additionally, the essay intended to include specific insights on the positive experiences that Mexican consumers had had with online purchasing. Recurrent themes on the participant's narratives provide interesting findings, as companies can consider these factors when establishing their online business model strategies. In general, results suggest that consumers look for a convenient, timesaving experience, which allows them to find a greater variety of products, and with a better price offering. Additionally, they expect to find in the company an appropriate backup in case of service failures, a timely tracking of their products, and a secure transaction.

Overall, this information provides important insights into the current panorama of e-commerce in the country; however, we specifically call for more empirical research studies to shed more light on the variables that may influence online purchases and consumer attitudes and behaviors, as only few academic studies in this area have been conducted in the Mexican context.

Discussion Questions

1. How has the cultural factor influenced the internet shopping trends among Mexican consumers? Discuss how this factor is changing in recent years.
2. Distinguish and describe the different Internet user groups in Mexico. How can organizations benefit from understanding these groups?
3. What are the different business models for e-commerce in Mexico? Think of an existing example for each of the models.
4. In your opinion, which of the different business models for e-commerce could be more attractive for new businesses?
5. Which factors have contributed to MercadoLibre's success in Mexico?
6. In your opinion, which is the strongest barrier for e-commerce in Mexico and how can this barrier be overcome?
7. Discuss how new digital technologies, such as social media, might change the future of e-commerce.
8. How can the recurrent themes mentioned by Mexican consumers towards their positive experiences when buying online help companies and brands to establish their online business models?

Key Learning Terms

Electronic commerce (e-commerce): The execution of buying and selling information, services or products through computerized networks. E-commerce involves making commercial transactions in an electronic manner.

Internet user groups: Groups of consumers that have similar interests, motivations, goals or concerns regarding the use of the Internet.

Online return policies: Rules that retail merchants establish to manage the process by which customers return or exchange unwanted or defective items that they have purchased previously.

Online transactions: Involves a password-protected payment method that authorizes a transfer of funds electronically.

POS terminals: Point-of-sale (POS) terminals used to charge the amount of purchase to credit and debit cards.

Social e-commerce: To make transactions from within social networks, such as selling products, adding products to shopping carts, and making payments.

Trackable shipping: Any method that allows the user to track and confirm the receipt of the package to the intended destination.

References

Anderson, Matt, Joe Sims, Jerell Price, and Jennifer Brusa. "Turning "Like" to "Buy" Social Media Emerges as a Commerce Channel." *Booz and Company*. 2011. Web. February 2015.

Andzulis, James, Nikolaos G. Panagopoulos, and Adam Rapp. "A Review of Social Media and Implications for the Sales Process." *Journal of Personal Selling & Sales Management* 32.3 (2012): 305–316. Business Source Premier. Web. 25 February 2015.

Banamex and UNAM. "Primera Encuesta Sobre Cultura Financiera En México." Compromiso Social Banamex, March 2008. Web. April 2015.

Castañeda García, José Alberto, and Francisco Javier Montoro Ríos. "La preocupación por la privacidad/seguridad como barrera al desarrollo del comercio electrónico. Evaluación, evolución y propuestas de futuro." *ICE* 14 February 2005. Web. February 2015.

Castellanos, Sara, and Daniel Garrido. "Tenencia y uso de tarjetas de crédito en México. (Spanish)." *Trimestre Económico* 305 (2010): 69–103. Business Source Premier. Web. February 2015.

Castellanos, Sara G., Daniel Garrido, and Alberto Mendoza. "La importancia de la ley para la transparencia y ordenamiento de los servicios financieros para propiciar el uso de sistemas y medios de pago eficientes en México." *El Trimestre Económico* (2008): 224. JSTOR Journals. Web. February 2015.

Ceballos, Francisco. "Mitos y realidades del comercio electrónico." *Razón Y Palabra*. Web. February 2015.

———. "3 tendencias en comercio electrónico para este año." *Altonivel*, 9 January 2014. Web. February 2015.

"Comercio Móvil Crecerá Hasta 42% Hacia 2016." *El Financiero*, 24 February 2015. Web. February 2015.

"La compra online en México." *The Cocktail Analysis*, 6 November 2013. Web. February 2015.

Constantinides, Efthymios, Carlota Lorenzo Romero, and Miguel A. Gómez Boria. "Social Media: A New Frontier for Retailers?" *European Retail Research*. Gabler Verlag, 2009. 1–28.

Cruz, Ariadna. "Comercio electrónico tiene futuro en México." *El Universal*, 15 November 2010. Web. February 2015.

Dewey, John. "How We Think." Courier Corporation, 1997.

"E-commerce: Evolution or Revolution in the Fast-moving Consumer Goods World?" *Nielsen*, 26 August 2014. Web. February 2015.

"Estudio de comercio electrónico en México 2013." *AMIPCI*, 2013. Web. February 2015.

"Estudio sobre los hábitos de los usiarios de internet en México 2014." *AMIPCI*, 2014. Web. February 2015.

Franco, Osbaldo. "México Móvil 2014: Consumidores Y Publicistas Conectan via Smartphones." *EMarketer*. 1 Feb. 2014. Web. Feb. 2015.

García-Murillo, Martha. "Institutions and the Adoption of Electronic Commerce in Mexico." *Electronic Commerce Research* 4.3 (2004): 201–19. *ProQuest*. Web. February 2015.

Gimenez, Fernando. "7 Surprising Facts about Mexican Internet Users." *Latin Link*, 11 April 2014. Web. February 2015.

IAB Mexico, and Millward Brown. "Estudio de consumo de medios entre internautas Mexicanos." *IAB México*, January 2013. Web. February 2015.

_____. "Estudio de consumo de medios entre internautas Mexicanos. Segmento digital moms." *IAB México*. May. 2014. Web. Feb. 2015.

_____. "Estudio de consumo de medios entre internautas Mexicanos. Segmento ejecutivos." *IAB México*, July 2014. Web. February 2015.

_____. "Estudio de consumo de medios entre internautas Mexicanos. Segmento teens." *IAB México*, August 2014. Web. February 2015.

Martínez, Everardo. "Ventas en internet crecen 450% durante hotsale." *El Universal*, 11 September 2014. Web. February 2015.

"MercadoLibre apuesta a crecimiento de comercio electrónico." *Netmedia*, 18 August 2010. Web. 1 February 2015.

"MercadoLibre compra inmobiliarias online." *CNNExpansión*, 10 April 2014. Web. February 2015.

"MercadoLibre generaría 9 mil nuevos empleos en México." *InfoChannel*, 25 August 2010. Web. February 2015.

"MercadoLibre y la estrategia de marketing que lo llevó al éxito." *Creativa Magazine Ad News*, 26 January 2012. Web. February 2015.

Nielsen. "Principales formas de pago en México." AMAP, November 2013. Web. April 2015.

"Number of Credit Card Accounts in the United States from 1st Quarter 2011 to 3rd Quarter 2014 (in Millions)." *Statista*, 2015. Web. February 2015.

"Número de tarjetas de crédito por institución." *Comisión Nacional Bancaria Y De Valores*, 2015.

Ovilla, Rocío. "¿Quién le teme al comercio electrónico? Protección del consumidor en el ámbito digital: El caso de México." *DEA Informatique et Droit, IRETIJ* (2003): 1–14.

Pérez Villegas, Oliverio. "Mamás digitales, las fans de las marcas." *Altonivel*, 13 February 2013. Web. February 2015.

Research and Markets. "Research and Markets: Consumer Attitudes and Online Retail Dynamics in Mexico, 2013." *Business Wire* (October 2012). Web. February 2015.

Sánchez, Marissa. "Gana con las redes sociales." *Entrepreneur Mexico* 19.9 (2011): 42–46. *Fuente Académica*. Web. Feb. 2015.

Sánchez Onofre, Julio. "Comercio electrónico en México, con los motores tibios." *El Economista*, 25 August 2014. Web. February 2015.

_____. "Fricciones limitan economía digital de México." *El Economista*, 1 October 2014. Web. February 2015.

Sánchez Onofre, Julio, and José Soto. "Google ve en línea a 50% de las pymes de México en cinco años." *El Economista*, 6 October 2014. Web. 1 February 2015.

"Tarjetas de crédito en México sustituyen el 1% de efectivo cada año." *El Financiero*, 21 January 2013. Web. February 2015.

"Tribus digitales que no debes perder de vista." *Dinámica Negocio*, 20 February 2013. Web. February 2015.

Underwood, Ryan. "Clicks from around the World." *Inc.* 32.10 (2010): 146–149. *Business Source Premier*. Web. 1 April 2015.

UPS. "Estudio UPS 'pulso del comprador en línea' un estudio de la experiencia del consumidor." *UPS*, September 2013. Web. February 2015.

"Ven potencial del mercado de compras en linea. Ciencia y tecnologia." *Pulso*, 17 August 2014. Web. February 2015.

Violante, Martha Elena. "Mercado libre apuesta al comercio móvil para el futuro." *Altonivel*, 2 October 2012. Web. February 2015.

"The World in 2014: ITC Facts and Figures." *ITU*, 2014. Web. February 2015.

Advancement of Mexican Women in the Workplace

CARLOS M. CORIA-SÁNCHEZ *and*
JOHN T. HYATT

Many American views of Mexican women in business as expressed by trade books, websites and self-help guides on doing business in Mexico portray the nation as a male dominated one in government, business and all aspects of society. The commonplace generalizations that Mexican women are submissive and relegated to subordinate tasks in a company are not always the case.

While machismo in Mexico is still alive in the business culture, the foreign businessperson who travels to Mexico under the assumption that all decision makers, managers and business owners will be male may be in for a series of surprises. In this essay we will argue that Mexico's history is one that has emphasized male dominant gender roles in society that persist today in most sects. Nevertheless, we have found in Mexico, as in many other Latin American nations, that traditional gender roles and ideas on gender are changing based upon a myriad of factors, especially among the nation's younger generations.

Writing about Mexican women in the 21st century requires providing the reader with a concise socio-historical context. The Mexican social structures that allow the oppression of Mexican women did not start with the Spanish conquest. Patriarchal societies such as the Aztec Empire had a social organization where women were in charge of "natural" chores for them; responsibilities were assigned based on gender. Pre-Hispanic women were not considered "as productive" as men.

The Spanish conquest didn't change women's situation and place in the new colonial society. During these times, the treatment that white and Indian women received was almost the same; both were victims of the same patriarchal system. On one hand white Spanish women were trapped in their homes all the time, giving birth to children, the future masters of the colonies, who would consolidate the system. On the other hand, Indian women kept giving birth to the future labor force that would keep the system working under their future masters.

Sor Juana Inés de la Cruz is well known for being the first Mexican woman to speak out on behalf of all women in the colonies. Sor Juana claimed that women had the same rights as men to be part of the social, cultural, and economic life of the New Spain. The patriarchal colonial system didn't allow Sor Juana, a woman and nun, to speak in such ways and to be part of the literary and cultural life of a society ruled by men. Sor Juana was told to remain silent and focus on her ecclesiastic duties, to save her soul, and refrain from learning sciences and being part of the men's world. After a life full of obstacles to achieve her literary dreams, Sor Juana decided to give away all her books which had made one of the richest libraries in the Americas.

The Independence movement in Mexico witnessed the massive and important participation of women such as Josefa Ortiz de Domínguez and Leona Vicario and many more. However, Mexican women's status in society didn't change in the next years. Despite gaining independence from Spain, Mexican women didn't notice any difference in the way society treated them; they continued to be under the influence of men and were not allowed to be part of the social and economic life of the new independent country. Women were not productive members of the new society. In the 19th century there were some women's movements to fight for their rights to be part of the public and social life of their country. Women's desires were to access the social, cultural, political, and business structures of Mexico. Their main goal was to torn apart the old patriarchal ideas of colonial times and allow them to take part in all the aforementioned areas of life.

During the Mexican Revolution, Mexican women fought alongside men throughout the conflict and the country. Mark Cramer makes an irrefutable comment about Mexican women during the Revolution: "While in contemporary United States they debate whether women are fit for combat duty, Mexican *soldaderas* fought in the front lines of the revolution between 1910 and 1920. And it was a Zapatista *soldadera,* comandante Ramona, and not subcomandante Marcos, who led the successful assault and occupation of San Cristobal in 1994" (78). Women were in search of finding a way out of poverty and their socio-economic status in the nation. Women from both the countryside and the cities were still not permitted to be part of the "men's world" and to participate in any important sectors of the country's society. Many Mexican women joined the revolutionary movement because they didn't have another choice; they didn't have a formal education to allow them more political, social and economic participation in society. The Mexican Revolution, as a social and political movement, promised a social transformation that would benefit the country. Increased social and political rights for women were one of the promises of the early 20th century Revolution. Although the Revolution brought up important social changes in the country; however, Mexican women didn't profit from them; the same patriarchal structures stayed in place. At the start of the Revolution in 1910, women made up 14 percent of the work force, by 2008 they were 38 percent. Almost half that increase occurred in the final 40 years.

During the final years of the Revolution the government named the first Mexican woman to be a Minister to Colombia in 1941, Palma Guillén. In 1954 Amalia de Castillo Ledón was named Minister Plenipotentiary to Sweden. And the first Mexican woman with the Ambassador title was Paula Alegria to Denmark. Mexican women obtained the right to vote in 1953, years after the end of the revolutionary movement; although, few drastic changes were made in their favor. Women were allowed to enter the political system but not the social and business structures of the country. Many women took part in Mexican cinema where they frequently were the main protagonists of many films. Nevertheless, other areas of society including business were still closed to their participation as important positions in both Mexican and international companies were restricted to men. Very few women dared to attend higher education and other technical institutions. Universities were still a man's domain where women didn't have a presence in areas like Engineering, Politics, Economics, and other disciplines created "for men."

Women's traditional areas of study in schools of higher education were nursing, education, some psychology, and others "fit" for them. One of these women, however, went as far as to become one of the most prestigious Mexican writers in the county and the world; Rosario Castellanos. Castellanos became a bastion for many Mexican and Latin American women to fight for their rights not only to access the arts, culture, and literary circles but to enter the political and business arenas as well. Castellanos became one more of the very few ambassadors for Mexico, serving as the ambassador to Israel from 1971 until her tragic death in 1974 in Tel Aviv. Castellanos' ambassadorship was largely seen as an anomaly as the patriarchal structures kept functioning in the same institutionalized manner as before.

The 1960s were a decade full of social conflicts between Mexican society and the government. In the late 1960s the students movement originated, says Carlos Fuentes, out of necessity and despair because thousands of students were opposed to the "corrupted Mexican political system; students wanted to be part of the making of a new country but they didn't have the democratic means to do it" (150). Throughout this movement women and men were equally active and participatory.

The 1970s witnessed a terrible economic instability in the country. There was such a crisis that, according to Landman R. Jerry, "price increases, with a fixed rate of 12.5 pesos to the dollar, resulted in a progressive overvaluation ... thereby leading to a ballooning accumulation of external debt" (15). In 1976, as a result of old economic policies, the peso was devaluated and the country found itself in a more severe crisis. The Mexican government initiated negotiations with the IMF to borrow $3 billion under rigid circumstances which included heavy cuts in social spending that adversely affected millions of Mexican women and their families.

The peso's devaluation increased unemployment, and women were the first to suffer this crisis. Women were laid off in the thousands around the country because they were "less educated than men," or "were weaker than men to perform certain jobs." Another reason for women to be fired is that they wouldn't be as productive as men in the long run as they might become pregnant; in this case the companies would lose money.

The 1980s brought another severe crisis to the country as Mexico followed the trend of the rest of the region in which the 1980s became known as "The Lost Decade in Latin America" due to the many economic crises that afflicted multiple nations from south of the Rio Grande all the way to Argentina. The sign of the times was the Mexican government's ineffectiveness to confront the economic crisis; the federal government kept dreaming of economic grandeur due to recent oil wells discovered in the south of Mexico. Mexican economic reality was one of despair, however. The splendorous dreams about becoming a first world country and to have free economic status from the IMF and other agencies disappeared. Again, there were masses of unemployed people with women being the most affected of all. According to INEGI, in 1988 the labor force in manufacturing, services, and commerce activities was comprised of 65.2 percent men and only 34.8 percent women.

Mexican families witnessed how their buying power diminished. Sara Sefchovich describes these times: "*Los ochenta llegaron al país cuando se encontraba en una situación crítica: desorden en la economía, fuga de capitales, alto crecimiento demográfico, concentración de la población y de los servicios en las zonas urbanas, la mitad de la gente viviendo en la pobreza, cuando no de plano en la miseria.* The eighties arrived in Mexico when the country was facing a critical situation: turmoil in the economy, capital flight, high demographic growth, highly concentrated population and services in the urban cities, half of the people living in scarcity if not in complete poverty" (375). This state of affairs did not change during the 1980s, 1990s and the first years of the 21st century; many Mexican women and their families still lived in poverty.

The aforementioned economic crisis demanded that women took a more active role in the country's workforce for their families' well-being. We should approach Mexican women's participation in the country's workforce as a human phenomenon, as a logical response, given the recent history of the nation and its economic crisis.

Despite the many setbacks for Mexican women though the years, there has been one primary victory that has allowed more women into the work force. One of the major successes of Mexico's federal, state and local governments over the past 30 years has been increased publicity toward and access to contraception for Mexican women. In the 1970s the average Mexican woman had nearly seven children to her name, all but sentencing her to a domesticated life with the duties of caring for a home and offspring. Today, that number has decreased to around two children per woman as a direct result of increased and aggressive family planning (*New York Times*, July 6, 2011). Despite the traditional dominance of the Roman Catholic Church and its rejection of contraception in Mexico and Latin America, the Mexican government chose decades ago to prioritize smaller families in place of traditional Catholic ideology, thus leading to higher living standards. One of the many government campaigns for reduced family size in the past decades simply marketed to Mexicans that "la familia pequeña vive major, the smaller family lives better." Today Mexico's public health institutes IMSS (for legally employed workers in the private sector) and ISSTE (for employees in Mexico's public sector) have several readily available birth control methods at women's disposal. Mexican women with public health coverage can obtain long-term contraceptives (known through studies to prevent pregnancy more effectively than condoms) such as the pill, the IUD device and the hormonal implant free of charge with no co-pays or deductibles for drugs or doctor's visits. It is worth noting that a woman in the United States who even has "good" insurance would likely face several hundred dollars a year in co-pays and deductibles in order to obtain such contraception. For an American woman paying out of pocket just the three-year hormonal implant will cost in the thousands of dollars. Additionally, the IMSS and the ISSTE offer condoms to women and their partners who are not ready for long-term contraception. For Mexican women who lack public health coverage from the IMSS or ISSTE, countless private options for contraception exist while the government's Seguro Popular (popular insurance) program exists for millions of vulnerable Mexicans who cannot afford private medical care.

This increased access to contraception for Mexican women has led to a revolution of sorts in the workplace while re-defining traditional gender roles in the country. While the family still remains one of the most important institutions in Mexican society, many Mexican women (especially from middle and upper class families) are choosing to eschew motherhood, albeit temporarily for most, for the classroom and subsequently a successful career. Following a global trend, Mexican universities today now boast approximately 55 percent of their student bodies as female (Kuper, Gina Zabludovsky, quoted in Pallares). Furthermore, Mexican women continue to represent increasing percentages of the nation's professional workforce as highlighted in the chart below. When visiting one of Mexico's major metropolitan areas, the involvement of women in business is conspicuous to the naked eye. And when speaking with young Mexican women in the nation's industrial cities, the desire to postpone motherhood and focus on a career is pervasive. A 28-year-old marketing manager in Mexico City spoke under anonymity about her future plans to marry and start a family while analyzing the path taken by her peers to marry young and have children:

> I want to get married and start a family one day, but not for some years down the road. If I had married and had children in my early 20s like some girls I know, I wouldn't have the opportunities that I have now. I'm so glad I didn't make that mistake. I instead was able to study my masters in marketing and now have many opportunities with my current company. I am traveling internationally with my company and am learning a great deal. My career is my primary focus in life now. Starting a family will come later when I have more financial and professional security.

This young Mexican woman's comments echo those of tens of millions of Mexican women in today's business world. Birth control along with globalization in Mexico is changing not only the mindset of today's youngest generation of Mexican women but of its men as well. A 32-year-old marketing assistant at an international firm in Mexico City spoke again under anonymity of the elevation of one of his female co-workers of a younger age to a management position, thus making her his boss: "Well she deserves her new position and I won't have a problem with her being my boss. She has studied a lot and has a lot of experience. That is why she received this promotion over the rest of us in the department. I look forward to us working together to grow the company."

The two aforementioned commentaries are reflective of a new, modern thinking in Mexican cities in which it is becoming growingly unacceptable for a young, educated, cosmopolitan Mexican professional to believe in traditional Latin American gender roles in a company that may sell products to the United States, Canada and Europe while sourcing raw material from Asia and South America. This new generation of Mexican professionals is working in a global arena with its suppliers and clients. Furthermore, this millennial generation is living in and out of the office in a globalized arena, which connects them to the world through the Internet and social media and only re-enforces the ubiquities of successful, educated women in the West and beyond. When Skyping with their European female friends who hold law and medical degrees and receiving tweets from the female export manager in Asia while just reading about the latest policies of female presidents in nations like Germany, Argentina and Chile, this new generation of Mexicans will continue to eschew traditional gender roles for Mexican women while watching them slowly but steadily climb up their nation's corporate and entrepreneurial ladders.

However it still must be noted that increased female involvement in education and in the business world is concentrated among women from Mexico's metropolitan areas as well as in the middle and upper classes of the socioeconomic realm. In many parts of rural Mexico traditional Latin American gender roles still apply as many girls are expected to be mothers by the age of 20. In such parts of rural Mexico and even in the cities, there are still strides to be made in gender equality in business. Nevertheless, even in rural Mexico, Mexican male migration to the United States is slowly chipping away at traditional gender roles. When men leave rural Mexico in search of work in the United States, it is often women who are left to take over the family farm or business. Jean Guerrero says that when Leonor Hernández's partner left Southern Mexico for work in the United States when coffee prices plunged in the early 2000s, Ms. Hernández was then forced to take over the family's 2.5-acre farm in rural Oaxaca. When coffee prices rose some years later Ms. Hernández shrewdly invested in more land to double the size of her farm while certifying her coffee as fair trade and organic only to subsequently be appointed the head supervisor of Oaxaca State's organic coffee council.

According to INEGI the following years (every five) showed a small increase in women's participation and a decrease in men's in the same areas.

Year	Men	Women
1993	62.2%	37.8%
1998	60.9%	39.2%
2003	58.8%	42.2%
2008	57.0%	43.0%

In spite of the increment of women's participation throughout the years on these sectors of the economy, there are still severe concerns when it comes to disparity in hiring and salaries. In terms of women in business some have become chief executives of both national corporations and international companies with offices in Mexico. *The Economist* says that according to Leticia Narvaez, president of the Mexican Association of Women Executives, "the acceptance of women in business has improved a lot over the last 15 years." Nonetheless, she continues, "equality with men in business is not happening organically."

Unfortunately, many men still believe that women's place is at home, taking care of the children and performing the wife's duties. Many companies still hold prejudices against women and they show them by hiring more men in spite of qualifications. *The Economist* says that Narvaez mentioned, "there is still a long way to go. Some companies, she points out, still specifically seek men rather than women to fill executive positions. In terms of salary discrepancy the same source says that 'official figures confirm a continuing gap in income between the sexes.' In ten out of elven main employment sectors, men earn more than women, a disparity that rises as much as 40% among shop-floor supervisors in factories." In a personal interview, an anonymous female director of an international company with heavy operations in Mexico revealed her paycheck stub to show that she was making around $72,000 per year after taxes. She went on to specify that she knew male directors with the same education, experience and responsibilities as her who were making approximately double her salary. In summing up her predicament she opined: "I know it's not fair but there's not a lot I can do about it if I want to keep this job. Despite it being unfair, I do recognize that my husband and I both have good jobs as directors at large companies and that we live far better than most Mexicans."

This director went on to explain that she and her husband were looking seriously into investing in some type of franchise store in Mexico to supplement their income in the short term with the hope of long term expansion.

It is safe to say that many Mexican women with the resources and know how may often choose entrepreneurship or other investments as an alternative to employment in what they may see as male dominated industries or job markets. A foreign businessperson who plans on doing business with a small or even medium sized Mexican firm should not at all be surprised when learning that the president or at least one of the partners that he or she will work with is indeed a Mexican woman who founded or co-founded the firm. In personal lived experiences in Mexico City, roughly 25 percent of the Mexican small business owners/partners have been women. It is also worth noting that in many small, family run businesses such as local accounting firms, export firms, convenience stores, restaurants, and even food stands from the informal economy among countless others, the husband, wife and even children split the responsibilities and decision making involved with running the business. It is not uncommon when doing business with the male owners of these businesses to hear, "Let me check with my wife as she is in charge of accounting" or "My wife takes care of all of our purchasing so I will have to talk to her when she gets here" or "My daughter takes care of shipping so please call her or let me talk to her first." According to national studies, as of 2013, of every five companies opened in Mexico three were run by women (Secretaria de Hacienda y Crédito Público, quoted in report by Centro de Investigación de Mujer en Alta Dirección). The official number of women who may not be the official owners of a business but are the chief decision makers is likely even higher than 20 percent. This is due to the fact that many Mexican companies list spouses, children, other relatives, friends or business contacts as the "official" owners of a companies for tax and legal purposes although such individuals have no real involvement in the business while a woman runs the company's operations. Furthermore, the aforementioned family businesses may not be considered to be "female owned" by many pollsters or analysts even though women may have equal influence in the company.

In his study on business culture Charles Mitchell says, "women have entered the Latin American business world in appreciable numbers" (115). However, with regard to the role of both men and women in business in Mexico, Karla Rojas says that according to INEGI the percentage of working women is 38 percent while that number is 62 percent for men. Women, says Rojas, "are a critical part of society because they are not only housewives, they also make decisions that have an impact on the way a corporation for which we work, private or public, functions; and not only that, but also on the progress and socio-economic development of the country" (1).

It is a fact that women's participation in the country's socio-economic life is vital; however, there are business owners who keep a patriarchal standpoint about them, Ricardo Salinas Pliego, one of the most important entrepreneurs in Mexico said, according to Arjan Shahani in *American Quarterly* that "women are not doing well because they want to do it all. They want to study, go out and get a job and be housewives as well. Well, that is really difficult to achieve" (1). This controversial statement came from the owner of one of the two TV conglomerates in Mexico, TV Azteca. Fortunately, for many women, there are many companies that don't agree with this point of view and are trying to change social beliefs about women to close the gap between them and men in the Mexican business arena.

Domestic and international corporations in Mexico have decided to take the "quotas" way. That is, fill positions depending on the gender of the applicant. This measure has had different opinions in favor and against. One of the points discussed on this issue is that it may create more discrimination against women "who may not have the education and experience" to perform certain jobs, creating a more hostile and "machista" environment" (1) says Arjan Shahani who continues and mentions, "Businesses should promote a cultural change that values talent regardless of gender.... Businesses must also understand that their decision to promote gender equality should not be viewed as a public relations campaign. It simply makes sense for business to attract, grow and retain the best talent available to them, regardless of gender."

Kenna and Lacy state: "Traditionally the male cultural role has included a strong sense of masculinity which stresses courage, virility and authority over women. Because of this cultural image, very few Mexican women have found their way into management yet, although an increasing number are found in the professions" (21). Perhaps Mexican women have suffered setbacks in their goals to reach CEO positions in the country or to become entrepreneurs compared to other industrialized countries. However, if not at the same rate as in the United States, for instance, Mexican women hold CEO or general director positions for some important domestic and international companies. Also, some of these women have reached prominent posts as entrepreneurs and founders of their enterprises. Mexican female entrepreneurs, says Karla Rojas are avid to break down barriers and get into the business world, which unfortunately, is still a man's domain. For that reason in Mexico there are associations that help women to learn all the necessary elements to create a business or to have a better organizational structure (1). Some examples of CEO and business founders are Blanca Trevino, CEO for Softteks; Pilar Aguilar Pariente, General Director Endeavor Mexico; Lydia Alpizar, CEO AWID; Lourdes Berho, CEO and Founder Alchemia; Sofia Bonnet, Country Human Resources Executive, IBM Mexico; Alejandra Calatayud, General Manager, American Express Mexico; and many more.

American businessmen and women must acknowledge that contrary to what some stereotypes continue to say, many Mexican women hold high positions in business and corporations; otherwise, they will have to make quick mental changes when in Mexico if negotiating with a woman who happens to be the CEO of a company. And that is never a good idea.

Conclusions

It is held by the authors that while gender roles for women in Mexican business have come a long ways in recent years, there is still much to be done in order for a more gender neutral society to exist, attitudes, company policies and perhaps laws will have to change. As explained, Mexico, even in pre–Columbian times was a society of strictly defined gender roles. It is only in the last half century that any substantial changes have occurred for Mexican women in social, political and business arenas. Nevertheless, it is conspicuous that the current trend toward upward mobility for women in the nation's business climate will only continue to grow as more Mexican women choose to educate themselves and step out of their centuries old gender roles. Finally, and as mentioned repeatedly throughout this text by several contributors in reference to changing trends in Mexico as applied to their essay topics, globalization, free trade, modernization and Mexico's ubiquitous and pervasive links to the outside world will continue to shape mindsets among Mexicans in business. Mexicans growing up today in Mexico City, Monterrey, Guadalajara and even smaller metropolitan areas are viewing their male and female peers with far more equal gender roles than did their parents and grandparents. This is a direct result of what they are witnessing within Mexico and through their lenses to the world outside of Mexico, be those lenses of televisions, smart phones, tablets or laptops. Furthermore, Mexican managers and business owners, faced with fierce international competition through globalization, will be forced to recruit and hire top talent, be it male or female, for their firms to remain competitive on a 21st century global stage.

Discussion Questions

1. How were pre–Hispanic women oppressed by their society?
2. Why were both Spanish and Indian women enclosed in their homes during colonial times?
3. Who was Sor Juana Inés de la Cruz? Why was she persecuted by her society?
4. Why is it important to remember Rosario Castellanos?
5. What can we say about the economic crisis that Mexico went through in the 1980s? What happened to women and their families?
6. How is Mexican women's participation in the work place changing since the 1990s?
7. Can we say that there is a real change in women's advancement in Mexico? Support your answer.
8. Describe the situation of Mexican women in the workplace in the present time.
9. What are some of the stereotypes about Mexican business women in the United States?
10. Would you be able to face a Mexican businesswoman who is the CEO or top manager or a company in Mexico?

Key Learning Terms

Globalization: The development of an increasing global economy marked by free trade and flow of capital between nations.

Machismo: A way of behaving that agrees with traditional ideas about men being strong and aggressive.

Patriarchy: An organization rule by the supremacy of the father; control by men of women, children, and society at large.

Stereotype: Characteristics given to groups of people in regards to race, nationality and sexual orientation.

References

Anonymous. Personal interview, November 8, 2012.
Anonymous. Personal interview, May 5, 2015.
Anonymous. Personal interview, March 22, 2015.
Cave, Damien. "Better Lives for Mexicans Cut Allure of Going North." *New York Times* 6 July 2011. Web.
Cramer, Mark. *Culture Shock! Mexico (Culture Shock! A Survival Guide to Customs & Etiquette)* Portland, OR: Graphic Arts Center Publishing Company, 1998. Print.
Encuesta Nacional de Ocupación y Empleo, ENOE. 2014
Fuentes, Carlos. *Tiempo mexicano*. México: Editorial Joaquín Ortiz, 1971. Print.
Guerrero, Jean. *Wall Street Journal*, June 6, 2012. Web.
Gomez, Ricardo. Personal interview, March 22, 2015.
Kenna, Peggy, and Sondra Lacy. *Business Mexico*. Lincolnwood, IL: Passport Books, 1994. Print.
Landman R. Jerry. "The Roots of the Crisis." *Mexico: A Country in Crisis*. Ed. Jerry R. Landman. El Paso: University of Texas Press, 1986. Print.
Mitchell, Charles. *A Short Course in International Business Culture*. California: World Trade Press, 2004. Print.
Pallares, Miguel A. "Mujeres directivas, en sólo 5% de empresas." *El Financiaro*, February 2, 2014. Web.

Rojas, C. Karla. "Mujeres emprendedoras rompen paradigmas." CNNExpansión, 2001. Web.
Sefchovich, Sara. *La suerte de la consorte*. Mexico: Editorial Océano, 1999. Print
Shahani, Arjan. "Women in Mexico's Workforce." *Américas Quarterly* (2013). Web.
"Rising expectations are still not much threat to the men." *The Economist* (2003). Print.
Torrez, Adriana. Personal interview, May 5, 2015.

About the Contributors

Carlos M. **Coria-Sánchez** is an associate professor at the University of North Carolina–Charlotte in the Languages and Cultures department and the Latin American studies program. He has co-edited, co-authored, and single-authored books published by Yale University Press, McGraw-Hill, and Plaza y Valdez.

Anabella **Dávila** is a tenured professor of organization theory and human resources management at Tecnológico de Monterrey, where she was formerly the research and Ph.D. program director of the EGADE Business School. She has co-edited several books on Latin American culture and human resources management.

Juan Antonio **Enciso-González** is the director of the master's in international business program at the EGADE Business School, Tecnologico de Monterrey. His research focuses on economic and political relationships.

Andreas M. **Hartmann** is an associate professor at Tecnológico de Monterrey, teaching in the fields of strategic management, cross-cultural management and international negotiation. His research focuses on multinational companies, knowledge-based firms and cross-cultural aspects of management.

Olivia **Hernández-Pozas** is an associate professor at the EGADE Business School of Tecnológico de Monterrey. She has been a visiting professor at universities around the world.

Marcela Adriana **Hernández-Romo** is a full-time research professor at the Universidad Autonoma Metropolitana-Iztapalapa. She has published several books on business culture in Mexico.

John T. **Hyatt** is involved in market development, product sourcing and consulting for companies in Mexico and the United States. He has lived in Mexico City and Guadalajara for more than eight years and has work experience in import/export, international sourcing/purchasing, international staffing and translation and interpretation within Mexico. He also has significant business and educational experience in over a dozen Caribbean and Latin American countries.

Sergio **Madero-Gómez** is a full-time professor of administration in the School of Business and Humanities at Tecnológico de Monterrey. He has been a visiting professor in schools in Central and South America.

Flor **Morton** is a Ph.D. candidate at the EGADE Business School, Tecnológico de Monterrey. She has worked as a marketing strategist for a marketing solutions agency working on diverse projects for national and international companies.

Miguel R. **Olivas-Luján** is the chairperson of the Management Education and Development division of the Academy of Management and a professor in the Management and Marketing department at Clarion University.

Jorge **Olmos-Arrayales** leads INNOVALIUS (www.innovalius.com), which aims to "facilitate learning environments and strategic change processes for both individuals and organizations." He is also a strategic partner of 7Mindsets (www.7mindsets.com) in Mexico and is also business developer for EPICENTER (www.theehalloffame.com).

Pramila **Rao** is an associate professor of human resource management at Marymount University. Her research has been published in *Employee Relations*, *Cross-Cultural Management*, *Strategic HR Review*, *The Learning Organization*, and *The Journal of Indian Business Research*, among others.

Teresa **Treviño** is a Ph.D. candidate at the EGADE Business School, Tecnológico de Monterrey. She has collaborated as an independent marketing consultant for several organizations, implementing strategies in the areas of market research, international marketing, and social media marketing.

Index

added value manufacturing 41
Alfa 30, 34, 55, 56, 58, 71, 72, 79
America Móvil 38, 63
Anglo-Saxon culture 45
Azcárraga Jean, Emilio 62, 63, 64, 65, 67, 68, 69, 71, 73

business ethics 6, 93, 95, 96, 102

Catholic Church 61, 64, 110, 186
CEMEX 21, 27, 29, 30, 31, 32, 33, 34, 35, 85, 86, 90, 91
Cervecería Cuauhtémoc Moctezuma 56
Chasteen, John 13, 23, 24
codes of ethics 6, 96, 100, 101, 102
collectivism 16, 81, 82, 83, 86, 89, 126, 127, 130
collectivist cultures 84
company patrimonialism 52
conflict aversion 109, 122
CONOCER 43, 51
contemporary management practices 36
contraception 186
corporate culture 4, 5, 26, 30, 32, 33
corporate philanthropy 6, 96, 98, 100, 101, 102
corporate social performance 103
corporate social responsibility (CSR) 29, 30, 34, 35, 36, 100
corruption 11, 17, 18, 19, 22, 23, 136, 137, 138, 141, 142, 144, 148, 149, 150, 151, 153
country of contrasts 163
CQ (cultural intelligence) 24, 130, 131, 132
credit card payments on online 176
cross-cultural 10, 15, 24, 81, 82, 83, 85, 92, 95, 102, 193; awareness 24; training 15
Crouch, Ned 12, 13, 24, 125, 128, 132
cultural awareness 22, 24
cultural differences 6, 7, 9, 10, 22, 83, 94, 124, 127, 129, 130
cultural perspectives 6, 143, 144
cyclical or event time 125

Directorio Estadístico Nacional de Unidades Económicas 39

e-commerce 7, 120, 166, 167, 168, 169, 170, 171, 172, 175, 177, 179, 180, 181
Esquezofrenia 43, 44, 51
ethical context 6, 95, 96, 105
ethical environment 95, 98, 101, 102, 103
ethical functions 98
Eurocentrism 12, 14, 21

family businesses 20, 21, 26, 189
fatalism 13, 14, 15, 112, 118, 122
Federal Labor Law 75
Federal Telecommunications Commission 171
FEMSA 35, 51, 57, 58
foreign direct investment (FDI) 3, 5, 17, 124, 135, 152, 159, 160, 161
formal businesses 42
formal economy 40, 41, 43, 135, 140
free trade 3, 4, 74, 75, 77, 78, 86, 110, 140, 157, 190, 191
Fuentes, Carlos 109, 112, 122, 185, 191
future-orientation 89

gender egalitarianism 81, 89
gender roles 8, 183, 186, 187, 190
globalization 165, 191
GLOBE (Global Leadership and Organizational Behavior Effectiveness) 81, 82, 83, 91
government-business relationship 163
government in business 135
Grupo Bimbo 34, 79, 85, 89

high context culture 119, 121
Hofstede, Geert 9, 10, 12, 16, 17, 19, 25, 81, 82, 90, 91, 101, 104, 126, 133
human capital 32
hybrid business cultures 36

Import Substitution Industrialization (ISI) 3

IMSS (Mexican Social Security Institute) 58, 186
indirect communication 112, 114
indirectness 122
INEGI (Mexican National Institute of Statistics and Geography) 39, 40, 43, 140, 141, 155, 156, 157, 158, 185, 188, 189
informality 51
institutional analysis 136, 151
institutional collectivism 81
institutional model 143, 144
institutional quality 7, 137, 138, 151, 152, 163
institutional quality indicators 163
Instituto Nacional del Emprendedor (INADEM) 43, 51
Inter-American Development Bank 33
International Monetary Fund (IMF) 3, 159, 162, 165, 185
international trade 5, 6, 109, 124, 131, 136, 150, 157, 163
internet access 173, 174, 179
internet shopping environment 180
internet user groups 181
ISSTE (Mexican Institute for Social Security and Services for State Workers) 186

Ley para la Transparencia y Ordenamiento de los Servicios Financieros 168
linear-active 132
linear time 125, 132
"The Lost Decade in Latin America" 3, 185
low contextual communication 132

Machismo 191
male-dominated 7
malinchismo 95, 102, 103
maquiladora 31, 78, 93
MercadoLibre 166, 170, 171, 172, 173, 180, 182
Mestizo 15
Mexican entrepreneurs 5, 39, 43, 45, 46

Mexican lens 131
Mexican Miracle 3
Mexican perspective 135
Mexican work ethic 92
Mexicanism 23
MIPYMES (tiny, small and medium sized businesses) 38, 39, 46, 51
monochronic 125, 128, 129, 132
Monterrey Group 55, 56, 59, 69
multi-active 132

NAFTA (North American Free Trade Agreement) 1, 3, 4, 9, 17, 19, 55, 77, 78, 88, 89, 91, 93, 110, 157
neoliberal model 5, 53
nepotism 11, 19, 20, 21, 22, 35

online shopping 176, 179, 181; attitudes 172; in Mexico 169; return policies 181
OXXO 57, 58

PAN (National Action Party) 53, 55, 60, 66, 68, 145, 151, 156, 163
parochialism 14, 23
paternalism 36, 37
paternalistic-benevolent leadership 26

patriarchy 191
patrimonialism 59
PEMEX (Mexican state owned oil monopoly) 2, 11, 69, 149, 153
Peña Nieto, Enrique 64, 65, 66, 67, 71, 145
polychronic 125, 127, 128, 130, 132
power distance 81, 89, 101, 132
pre-Columbian 127, 190
PRI (Institutional Revolutionary Party) 2, 3, 53, 60, 68, 71, 110, 111, 146, 163
profit-oriented society 126

quality of institutions 163

rational choice 70

shock therapy 3
short term appeasement 122
Slim, Carlos 29, 38, 51, 62, 63, 65, 66, 67, 68, 69, 70, 71, 72, 134
SME (small and medium enterprises) 5, 26, 33, 51, 87
social commerce 175
Spanish conquest 109, 112, 183
state corporatism 52
stereotypes 2, 4, 10, 13, 14, 15, 17, 23, 24, 93, 120, 121, 124, 131, 134, 190, 191

succession management 36

The Tale of Two Mexicos 79
Tecnológico de Monterrey (ITESM) 58, 80, 193, 194
Telcel 63, 65, 66, 72, 73
Televisa 62, 63, 64, 65, 66, 67, 68, 69, 71
Telmex 28, 65, 71, 80
time and business 7, 131
time horizon 126, 132
trade books 2, 4, 9, 10, 12, 13, 15, 17, 19, 21, 22, 23, 107, 108, 117, 118, 120, 121, 124, 183 traditional work culture 36
Trans-Pacific Partnership (TPP) 78

uncertainty-avoidance 81, 83, 89

Western perspective 22
Western superiority 12
women in business 7, 183, 186, 188, 189
World Bank 77, 124, 133, 137, 139, 140, 154, 158, 164
World Trade Organization (WTO) 135, 140, 150, 157, 159
Worldwide Governance Indicators (WGI) 137, 138, 139, 152, 165

www.ingramcontent.com/pod-product-compliance
Ingram Content Group UK Ltd.
Pitfield, Milton Keynes, MK11 3LW, UK
UKHW050525150426
5217IPUK00026B/1795